# WALK LIKE A GIRL

## A Search For Self

To Alexis,
 Lots of love,
  Claudia x

**Claudia Esnouf**

# WALK

## LIKE

## A

## GIRL

*A Search For Self*

To Alexi,
Lots of love,
Claudia x

Claudia Essouf

WALK LIKE A GIRL © 2025 Claudia Esnouf

Claudia Esnouf asserts the moral right to be identified as the author of this work in accordance with the Copyright, Designs and Patents Act 1988

This is a work of fiction. Names, characters, places and incidents are either the result of the author's imagination or are used fictitiously.

All rights reserved. No part of this publication may be reproduced, stored in or introduced into a retrieval system or transmitted in any form or by any means (electronic, mechanical, photocopying, recording or otherwise) without the prior written permission of the author.

Isbn: 978-1-914399-48-0

This book is sold subject to the condition that it shall not be resold, lent, hired out or otherwise circulated without the express prior consent of the author.

Printed and bound in Great Britain by Clays Ltd, Elcograf S.p.A

Cover Design © 2024 Mercat Design, images courtesy of Dreamstime. All Rights Reserved

SPARSILE
BOOKS

To my Dad, who inspired me to travel.
To my Mum, who asked me to write about it.
And to Peter, who encouraged me to share it.

## *Author's Note*

*Walk Like A Girl* is a work of fiction based on a true story. My true story. I travelled for almost a year in the Caucasus Mountains, Nepal, India and Europe. During this journey, I faced a rampant water buffalo, a freezing glacier crossing and spent a blissful night unaware that I was camping in a minefield—all of this while also experiencing the most painful heartbreak of my young life. When I flew back to Europe, I walked the Camino Frances. Upon reaching Santiago de Compostela, I realised I wanted to continue and flew to Portugal, where I walked the Camino Portugues.

In eight months, I walked approximately 1,800 kilometres.

It took me some time to fully understand the difference between memoir and fiction. When I first wrote this in memoir version by copying extracts from my diary, the writing was stagnant, dull and far too guarded.

I later recognised I was in denial about my fears for my future and my deteriorating relationship.

Changing my characters' identities – as well as using my middle name, Antonia – and compressing the route and timeline allowed me to coax the story into the light and see the truth of the glorious, gut-wrenching journey I'd taken.

# PART 1
# CAUCASUS

# 1

The taxi rattled through the dirt roads of Kutaisi. The city was encroaching upon us. Dogs roamed the dusty streets in gangs, owners of the roads. A kitten's corpse lay open in the middle of the street, its intestines spilling out. Cars blasted their horns through corners, narrowly missing pedestrians. Traffic lights were a thing of the future; this city was of the past.

Andy was trying to fight sleep, but my own mind was in overdrive. About fifty orthodox religious icons hung in front of the windscreen, and I wondered how the driver could see through it.

We sat squeezed next to a middle-aged couple with limited English. I wasn't sure if they were also passengers or part of the driver's family.

'We've come from Scotland. We booked one-way tickets to Georgia,' I explained to the smiling woman. 'Our plan is to go to the mountains and walk east, and eventually go to Armenia.'

'You stay in Armenia?' she asked, horrified. 'Georgia much nicer. Better food.'

I smiled. 'We don't know where we'll go after that.'

The unsteady driving made my red backpack bobble in my lap. I wrapped my arms around it like a hug. It was heavy and bulky, and right now it was my whole life. We'd rented out our flat in Edinburgh and had packed pictures, clothes and books into boxes and stored them in Andy's parents' cottage in Perthshire.

The driver dropped us outside a dilapidated church. Andy unfolded a piece of paper with a list of directions. I followed him closely as we navigated a maze of narrow alleyways. Dogs barked loudly and I could see their shadows flitting along the walls. We found a dark stairwell that seemed to have been built in the 1500s.

A man, dressed in long night robes and a cap, floated in from across the hall. He started talking to us in Georgian, with a couple of English words like 'hello' and 'no' peppered here and there. He motioned standard household instructions such as how to walk to our bedroom and switch on a light. As he talked, his hands gestured to every room. I imagined him saying things like 'and there's a hot tub on the roof which you can use before 10 p.m.' but his grim tone suggested 'if you don't bolt the windows shut, they'll toss a petrol bomb through'. Finally, content with his dense explanation, he floated back out to his own flat and left us to our own devices.

~~~

I could hear Andy's soft snores and saw a lump on the bed. I envied his ability to fall asleep so quickly. I wondered how he was feeling. I still couldn't quite believe he'd signed up for this. To his credit, he'd shown more enthusiasm than I'd expected. For the last few weeks, he'd been doing his research, printing out walks and hikes and downloading navigational apps onto his phone.

I crawled into bed next to him and lay with my eyes open for hours, watching the clock tick by. Each hour would make me more tired tomorrow. Tomorrow—the start of our whole adventure. The beginning of the rest of our journey. I had no idea what the Caucasus was even like, I just knew it had to be amazing. After all, he'd given up everything to do this with me.

I rolled over to my side and gently placed an arm on his.

'You all right?' he mumbled.

'Yeah I'm fine.'

Andy turned over, his arm draping heavily over my waist, his snoring resuming.

My words echoed in my head. *I'm fine.*

I squirmed out of his grip.

~~~

I wandered around the flat and stood outside on the balcony, feeling the mugginess set upon my skin. I stared out into the darkness, taking in the new smell of dirt, nature and humidity. I could hear a dog barking, someone's hacking cough, a car's spluttering engine in the distance.

I opened Google. I knew what I should be searching for.
*Distance between Mestia and Armenia*
*Kutaisi bus station location*
*Svaneti mountains weather forecast*
Instead, I toyed with my phone before finally punching the words into the search bar.
*How to know if you love your fiancé?*

## 2

Sunlight flooded the room, and the brightness of it and the noise outside indicated it must be mid-morning. I lay on a tangle of sheets.

Andy was carrying two mugs of coffee. I saw he was bare-chested, a nice change from his usual stiff white-collared shirt. He set a mug on my bedside table and sat down next to me, the bed creaking underneath his weight. 'Shall we make plans?' His forehead glistened with sweat. 'It's roasting outside and I think we should look at moving to the Svaneti mountains today.'

I sat up and sipped my coffee as Andy started using his phone to work out the routes out of the city. I listened absent-mindedly as he listed off ideas, sleepily enjoying the sensation of his rough hand stroking my calf. My eyes wandered from his fuzzy chest to the Saturn-shaped birthmark on his forearm.

'I think we should pack up our stuff and hitchhike north.' Andy's voice wafted through. 'Once we're there, we can figure out where the hiking route starts.'

I peered down at his phone. If I'd researched what I should have last night, I would have been able to contribute. Instead, I'd battled a rising dread as I'd scrolled endless forums of women desperately unhappy in their relationships. I'd finally fallen asleep knowing that for me it was different. Of course it was different. I was perfectly happy with Andy. He was my best friend. The trip, the planning, the fights leading to it…it was all just catching up with me.

I flicked through the dog-eared pages of the guidebook, wanting to centre my focus. I looked up the section on Mestia and at the map, tracing my finger from Kutaisi all the way up to the top of Georgia. The pictures of glaciers and snowy mountains seemed hard to take in when I was battling with the humidity of our room.

'How long do you think it'll take us to get to Mestia?' I looked up and saw Andy studying Google Maps on his phone.

'Depends on our luck with hitchhiking and the state of the roads. If we leave shortly, could take us a day.'

I read out choice bits about Svaneti from our guidebook. 'It's the remotest place in Georgia and the highest inhabited area in the Caucasus. It's literally in the middle of the mountains. It used to be inaccessible.'

'No one wants to go there because they have six months of brutal winter. Minus twenty degrees at night.'

I thought of the down jacket in my bag. It was the warmest thing I had. But winter didn't start for another few months, so hopefully it would suffice.

'There's an ethnic group that's been there since the Middle Ages. They're Georgians, I guess, but they call themselves Svans. I think you can stay in their homes during the hike.'

I watched Andy reorganising the two-man tent and wrestling with the heavy sleeping bags we'd brought, stuffing them into the smallest size possible. I wondered if we'd need them if we were staying in people's homes. We could always discard them en route.

I put the guidebook aside and joined in the packing, shoving my pyjamas into my bag. Everything was jumbled already, unlike Andy's items that were laid with military precision. I had a few T-shirts, shorts and trousers, underwear and socks. There were also waterproof layers for all the clothes. I had tossed in some novels, a few too many toiletries, a journal, hair straighteners and a pair of jeans. There were flip-flops for the evening, and trainers to switch into from the heavy hiking boots. I had a couple of jumpers, a waterproof jacket and the down one. I'd even managed to squeeze in an inflatable pillow, a thermos and some cutlery. I had a stove I didn't yet know how to use and a variety of pot noodles and coffee sachets. There was hand sanitiser, iodine pills, a first-aid kit and some foldable walking poles.

'Please tell me you fully understand that we'll be hiking up 5,000-metre mountains. Do you really need hair straighteners for that?' Andy had been giving me a hard time about my packing skills since the day we'd started planning.

I scowled at the black tongs curled up on top of my books. 'How high is that, anyway?'

'Trust me, it's a lot higher than the wee Scottish lumps when we walked the West Highland Way. And I carried your backpack for half of that.'

'Back in the day when you were trying to impress me, huh?'

'Seriously, though, do you really think you'll have time to read?'

I sighed and stared at my bag. I couldn't part from my books. That was non-negotiable. Instead, I pulled my tongs out, laying them on the bedside table. There'd probably be no sockets that high up anyway.

'Ready?' asked Andy, now standing by the front door. I could still smell the chemical scent from his new green Osprey backpack. 'Are we doing this?'

I zipped up my backpack, which didn't feel remotely lighter, straining to mute my winces and pains as I heaved all eighteen kilograms onto my back.

I forced a thumbs up, feeling my shoulders sag underneath the weight. 'Absolutely.'

# 3

I'd received an offer from the University of Edinburgh to work in the International Student department and had used most of my student savings to buy a one-way ticket to Scotland. On New Year's Eve, aged twenty-two and alone, I left my childhood home in Chile. My first days in Edinburgh were a literal haze. Thick fog swirled over the city, drizzle sticking to grey pavements and heavy clouds so low I felt as if I was walking through them. I spent a month in a hostel, going on flat viewings, each one further out of my budget. I finally found a room, miles out of town, with a group of international folk who were working as waitresses, tour guides and artists.

As beautiful as Scotland had looked on Google, the skies were black, the wind howled and I was constantly freezing and damp. My job was dull, unsocial and my evenings were long and lonely. I was used to being alone, but this was mixed with an enormous disappointment about a dream that wasn't panning out. Having never thought twice about leaving home, I wondered if I might be homesick. I hadn't left on the best of terms. My mum had been preoccupied with my nieces and had all but disappeared on the day of departure. Dad had dropped me off at the airport parking lot, closing the car door before I could say goodbye. I didn't like dwelling on it.

My favourite part of my day was the hour's trail from my flat to the office and back. It followed the Water of Leith, a picturesque river that went on for miles snaking through cobbled streets, forests and aqueducts. I'd take detours uphill, reaching a bench where I could look down at the river, about thirty metres below. To my left was the old, stone-built, Dean Bridge. Overgrown vines curled down the semi-circles, swaying in the wind. I could see the dark green outline of the Pentland Hills behind them and felt a familiar yearning to be in the countryside, walking through the footpaths. To my right, I could see across the Forth Bridge, over the hills of Fife. Behind those hills was the countryside of Perthshire, followed by the magnificent Highlands, spilling over to the Outer Hebrides, and even the Shetland Islands. The thought of all the unknown territories that I'd still not been to stirred something deep inside me.

With long, dark evenings to myself, I created a travel blog. Blog was an ambitious term for a website that only I had access to. It was my comfort zone, a sort of online journal, with lists of travel books to read, interactive maps I'd placed pins on and highlighted blogs of hikers' journeys.

For almost two years, I entertained myself populating the screen with bold images. There were pictures of Himalayan rice fields, Indian train rides, and Northern European mountain trails.

Instead of joining after-work drinks, I trailed to the bookshops that were open late to read about adventures. There was a girl who'd motor-biked from Cairo to Cape Town. Another who'd walked the Pacific Crest Trail. Then there was a man who'd hiked from Siberia to Europe. One was walking around the whole world. Another had left his job to live in a hut in Alaska.

I bought copies of Lonely Planet, Rough Guides and anything I could find in the charity bookshops. I watched trail documentaries, dated ones from Michael Palin going around the world in the nineties to Anthony Bourdain's food and travel expeditions. I dived into travel books: Paul Theroux, Dervla Murphy and Patrick Leigh Fermor. I became obsessed with Levison Wood's Channel 4 documentaries—a British explorer who walked the length of the Nile, then the Himalayas and the Caucasus. I fell in love with Nepal and the Georgian mountains on screen and felt them bounce off the pages in his book. I devoured Cheryl Strayed's book *Wild* in a day. This wasn't the stuff of mere dreams. This woman had really walked alone through a country and had written about it. I spent my lunch breaks turning pages, or discreetly researching long-distance walks on the computer screen.

~~~

I'd been living in Scotland for about a year when I decided to explore one of the country's most iconic routes—an eight-day walk that started on the outskirts of Glasgow and ended in Fort William, a town tucked in the Scottish Highlands. It was an awakening experience. I fell in love with the glens, corries and lochs, and relished the independence of walking at my own pace in my own time.

On the last day, a group of four young guys overtook me as I ate lunch on a rock overlooking Loch Lomond, turning the pages of my book. I'd grown familiar with the faces walking the same trail as me and had labelled these four men as the rowdy Scots who were probably on a stag do. I gave the smallest wave of acknowledgment and returned to my book.

One of them stayed behind to attend to his backpack. I noticed his friends laughing and glancing back at him as they walked on. He pulled out a bottle of water. His nose was sunburnt—probably due to the residue of badly smeared sunscreen on the tip—but the rest of his face was pale. He had dark red hair, which clashed with his nose.

'I think I saw you at the pub last night,' he said. 'I was going to ask you to join us, but you seemed pretty invested in that book.'

I felt myself blush. 'Oh yeah?'

'What are you reading?'

'Uh, *Full Tilt* by Dervla Murphy.'

I noticed a smattering of freckles across his nose and cheeks, the kind of freckles that would disappear in winter.

'What's it about?'

I studied his face. There was something about him and his mates that reminded me of the loud, boorish guys from high school. I couldn't tell if he was mocking me or not.

'It's a memoir by an Irish girl who travels from Ireland to India on her own, mostly on a bicycle.'

He looked at me as he sipped on some water. 'Are you walking solo too then?'

I nodded.

'I think that's pretty cool.' He smiled. 'Wish I could shake those loons off.' He glanced at the way his friends had gone. Drops of sweat slid onto his eyebrows, and he wiped them off. He wore socks up to his knees to keep the midges at bay. He looked a bit ridiculous, and I wondered if he was being genuine. I suddenly felt self-conscious about my own appearance. My curly hair was badly tamed into a bun which meant my big ears were exposed, and I had waterproof trousers that were two sizes too big for me.

He extended his hand. 'I'm Andy, by the way.'

I shook it. 'Antonia.'

The skies had turned a dark grey, and rain began to fall. Andy took his waterproofs from his bag and started to put them on.

'You should catch up with your friends,' I said, glancing at the skies. 'Don't think the rain's going to stop anytime soon.'

'Ach, they'll be fine.' He gave a dismissive wave. 'I can't place your accent. Where are you from?'

I felt my cheeks growing warm. My accent had always been a point of correction or laughter. I'd inherited the Scottish sing-song from my parents, combined with layers of Spanish intonations.

'Chile.'

'Wow, I wouldn't have guessed. Why the hell would you move from such a beautiful and exotic country to this?' He gestured at the rain around him.

I laughed. 'There's so much to explore here. The weather's part of its charm.'

He looked unconvinced. 'Tell me about Chile.'

'Your friends'll be waiting for you.'

He shook his head. 'Nah, they're good. To be honest, I've been meaning to speak to you. Made a bet with them that the next time I saw you on the trail, I'd go for it.' He shrugged. 'Can't have them taking all my money now, can I?'

'What if you're rubbish chat?' I asked.

He laughed. 'I probably am.' He looked behind him. 'Then I'll hide under these trees for a while and catch up with them later. Just promise me that if you run into them, you'll tell them how smitten you were.'

I tried to contain a smile and began to pack up my lunch.

'I'll give you a mile.'

'Challenge accepted.'

# 4

If we were going to hitchhike, we had to do it properly. We headed to the nearest petrol station with our backpacks to find scrap pieces of cardboard and felt-tip pens to write out our destination. As I set out to write *MESTIA*, Andy caught my wrist.

'Er, wait.' He hesitated. 'I think they write differently here.'

'What do you mean? They'll be able to read the same.'

'No, I mean they have a different script. Squiggly letters.'

It took asking several different people before finding a man who could vaguely understand English. I watched as Andy tried to pry him for directions for Mestia. The man looked incredulously at us when he realised we were trying to hitchhike there.

I imagined two foreigners in Edinburgh asking someone if they could hitchhike on Princes Street. They'd probably be escorted to a holding cell.

Handily, he wrote out our destinations in Georgian on a piece of discarded cardboard. The Cyrillic script looked like a Comic Sans font from Microsoft Word. A few people lingered around the petrol station and watched us as we gathered our positions.

'Great, now we have an audience,' muttered Andy.

I clutched the piece of cardboard. We stood millimetres from the deafening highway; our bodies pressed against the dented road barriers that did little to protect us from the steep drop to the gorge below. Cars beeped, trucks blared their horns, people gestured out of their windows.

'What do we do now?' I yelled at Andy.

We could barely hear each other amidst the traffic racket.

'Stick your thumb out.'

'I mean, that's pretty dodgy. It's quite forward and a bit embarrassing, really. I don't know, maybe we should just pay for a bus. We don't even really know where we're going.'

'Stick your thumb out!'

'Why don't you do it?'

'You're a girl; they'll pick us up faster.'

'You mean you want them to pick me up in the hopes they can have sex with me?'

'Antonia, just stick your fucking thumb out!'

~~~

An hour later, we were standing in the same spot, puzzled at the lack of Georgian hospitality we'd read such great things about.

Our small audience watched us lazily, amused. A man sitting in his car across the road was looking at us, shaking his head and fingers, and I shot him a defiant glare. He sighed and waved his hands and then parked his car on the side of the highway. He quickly ran across the two large lanes towards us.

He was yelling at us in Georgian, and I backed into Andy, terrified we were somehow insulting him or his country. When he realised we spoke English, he exasperatedly tried to find the words.

'No...No Mestia. Impossible!' he said.

We argued, pointing at our maps and phones. It was possible, surely.

He wouldn't even look at our maps. Andy realised that arguing in English was getting him nowhere and began gesticulating, pointing fingers and using some invented sign language.

Finally, the penny dropped.

'I think he's telling us we're hitchhiking the wrong way,' I said. I pointed to my right. 'Mestia that way. Yes?'

'Yes! Yes! Yes!' He sounded delighted, patting us both on the back.

Sheepishly, we grabbed our bags and crossed the road.

I heard laughter and looked back, watching the audience at the gas station cheering. On the other side of the road, I stuck my thumb out again. In moments we were in a van, rattling away at the back.

~~~

The hitchhike experience took us through the hills for hours on end. We sat in the back of a van where the men in the front sat drinking beer, then were squished in the back of a car where about eight family members were already sitting like sardines. A baby sat on my lap while another child held my hand without a word.

There was a father and son, where the son practised his English; and a lone lorry driver from Azerbaijan, who stopped at the side of the road and made us follow him up a hill so he could show us a holy cave.

Our last ride to Mestia was a car that seemed to date back to the sixteenth century. It looked like a patchwork quilt, made up of different parts and seemingly held together by string. It rattled up the hill, creaking around every precarious corner, cliffs plunging down for several kilometres into dark crevasses. We were driving up the Caucasus Mountains. I shut my eyes, but that made me more carsick, so I tried to focus on the broken road in front.

Andy wasn't doing much better. The car was meant to fit five people at most, but we were nine, squished in and moving around every corner together. It felt like we were very slowly rumbling around Everest, past base camp and up to the peak.

Suddenly there was a huge bang. The driver yelled. The car screeched to a stop. We all gasped, lurching into focus. Our driver climbed out and after much screaming, people climbing out on top of each other, we managed to slide out and saw a huge rock that had fallen from the mountain and dented the car roof.

'Lucky it wasn't the windscreen,' said Andy, who'd gone a further shade of white.

I gulped.

The driver, who seemed to have only just registered us all standing there, yelled at us to get back into the car, as he wiped his brow, issued a prayer and adjusted the wooden orthodox cross back onto the windscreen. Tension released and we heard nervous laughter. Some of the passengers clapped our backs, talking to us in fast, bubbly Georgian, and we nodded along in shock.

~~~

Five hours later, we reached the tiny town of Mestia.

As we got out of the car, I looked across at a green-coloured Andy.

'Where do you reckon we should stay tonight—'

Andy turned around and threw up spectacularly on the ground. He wiped his mouth and looked at me, wide-eyed.

'That bloody car. I swear, we're walking up that road next time.'

He grabbed his backpack, and I followed him out into the dirt road. There were huge mountains on every side of us. I could see steep green hills for miles, with stone towers dotted in the distance. A sheep bleated. The air was silent, still and cold. There was barely a soul around. I shakily breathed in the fresh air of the mountains. We'd gone from thirty-five degrees to minus five degrees in a day. I shivered into my thin raincoat, zipping it up to my neck.

We started walking towards what looked like a hamlet. There were two houses built out of stone with a large veranda, one of which had a cow sleeping on it.

I heard a growl.

'Watch out.' Andy yanked my arm. I glimpsed an enormous beast running towards us. Brown. Masses of fur. At least twice the size of me. I shut my eyes. I heard Andy scream.

And then a sharp whistle. A laugh and someone speaking Georgian. The beast backed off and trotted back to a man.

The man was large, well into his fifties. He walked towards us, the wild animal wagging its tail.

'You need place to eat? Sleep?' he asked.

'Yes,' responded Andy shakily. 'Is that…safe?' He pointed at the dog.

The man laughed and rubbed the beast's head. 'Nina. Happy dog.' The dog bounded back to us, now licking my hand. I stared in shock.

We learned later that these were Caucasian Shepherd Dogs, known informally as wolf killers, and were used to protect livestock from wolves and bears. They could weigh up to eighty kilograms. Some, like Nina, were domestic, but most were used for security, tied up in farms with thick metal chains, their howls echoing down the valleys.

Cautiously, we followed man and beast. He led us up a stream and into the back of one of the houses. He called out to someone, and a woman surrounded by a few kids tottered out and eyed us up. They welcomed us in.

There was a smell of damp and rot. To put us up would mean the whole family would sleep in the kitchen, where the cooker ran on a log fire. We dropped our bags in the room given to us, stepping over floorboards that hadn't been properly attached. The shower was a sink tap with cold water. Shivering, I pulled every layer of clothing—dirty and clean—on me to keep warm.

They'd set up a table in the kitchen, just for us, a large fire crackling away. Instantly, the wife set down a large basket of freshly made *kachapuri*—a traditional Georgian cheese-filled bread—large tomatoes, onion sauce and sausages. We didn't think or speak, just ate. Then the man came back through, holding a toddler in one arm and a large plastic water bottle in the other. I graciously reached for my cup and he filled it all the way to the brim. He toasted us, and I sipped, before spitting it back out.

'What's this?' I asked Andy.

The man chuckled. 'Vodka.'

# 5

Unlike the well-marked trails, gradients and distances in Europe, there was nothing remotely sign-posted or marked on the Caucus Trail. The trail was rocky and uneven. It snaked its way steeply upwards, often losing itself amongst rocks.

There were many things I'd researched and prepared for. I had downloaded offline maps, had the right shoes and the right backpack. My clothes were comfortable. I had waterproof bags, sleeping-bag liners, sunscreen and bug spray.

What I hadn't taken into account was my lack of fitness. I'd figured that after walking every day to work and back, and spending the weekends roaming around Edinburgh, I'd be able to conquer a few mountains.

I heaved my way up the steepest bit of hill I'd ever encountered. I panted, puffed, swallowed down bile, and adjusted my backpack belt so tight, I cramped up. Giving up, I took my backpack off and let it fall to the ground, landing on top of it, as I looked up at the miles left to go.

'I'm already exhausted,' I said, now fully regretting last night's digestif. I'd woken up with a headache and a dry mouth. Not the best start to a long-distance hike. The vodka had made us light-headed and frisky. We'd tried to have sex as quietly as possible, but the combination of creaky floorboards and a broken bed frame had led us to fits of giggles.

Andy sighed and joined me.

'My bag is killing me.'

'Come on, just don't think about it too much. I'm the one carrying the tent,' he pointed out.

'Shall we take a quick break?'

'Antonia, it's been five minutes.'

~~~

Loose rubble and pebbles glared at me underneath an unexpected scorching sun. There must have been a thirty-degree contrast between the freezing cold last night and today's late September heat. I could feel my cheeks starting to burn underneath my hat.

I took a break after a few metres to put sunblock on. As I got my breath back, I scanned our surroundings. Beneath us were slopes leading into tousled meadows, wildflowers of purple, pink and yellow glittering in the sun. There were mountains everywhere I looked, gigantic ones, with snow that gleamed against deep blue skies. A haze of hills encircled us, with no sign of a city for hundreds and hundreds of miles. It felt like we were high above any kind of civilisation, totally alone. I'd only stood for a couple of minutes, and I could feel flies and bugs landing on any patch of skin it could find. I patted them away, wiping the sweat off my forehead.

The sounds of twigs crackling startled me.

I turned to see two men walking towards us. They looked like experienced hikers. One had a buzz cut, the other a tight ponytail. Both had trimmed beards, impressive hiking boots and small backpacks. They stopped when they reached us and introduced themselves.

They were from Israel, just out of the army, taking some time off before work. They were only hiking for a few days before flying back to Tel Aviv.

'Wow. Are those your backpacks?' asked the one with a buzz cut.

I glowered at him.

Andy seemed to be in the same mindset as he also stayed silent.

'Are you carrying those backpacks around you for the entire hike?' he asked again. 'They look very heavy. What do you have, ten, twelve kilos?'

I nodded. Eighteen, actually.

'We only used to carry that amount in the army. Not ideal carrying that through this trail. Did you know tomorrow is a nine-hundred-metre climb?'

I didn't. I couldn't imagine walking to the top of this hill, let alone that, so I opted not to answer.

'Yeah, well, we're carrying a tent and sleeping bags,' said Andy.

'Wow. You're camping the whole way?'

This guy was annoying me now.

'It can get to minus fifteen degrees at night. It's dangerous if you don't have the right equipment. Your tent is a four-season one, right?'

'Yes,' we lied in unison. The only perk our tent had was that it was thirty per cent off at Mountain Warehouse.

The one with the ponytail gave a low whistle. 'Respect, man. Your camping spots will be awesome. I don't think I could be bothered carrying all that stuff when you can just stay with the locals every night.'

'But the next village is still fifteen kilometres away,' I said.

'Yeah. We'll get there tonight if we keep the pace up.'

I didn't dare look at Andy. There was no way we'd make it there tonight. The tent didn't seem like such a bad idea after all.

'One thing is to carry a lot of weight, that's your choice. But you need to pack it right. The heavy bits go on top, the lighter ones at the bottom. You need to redistribute it so that it lessens the load on your back.'

Before either of us could think of anything to say, he spoke again.

'We heard that the trail is broken about twenty kilometres from here. We'll probably get to that section tomorrow. You have to cross a river instead, but it's dangerous because of the powerful current, and the water is freezing. It comes directly from the glacier. You have to watch out for chunks of ice. You guys should think about that with your heavy bags.'

'Thanks for the heads up,' said Andy. I could see a muscle twitching in his jaw.

'We'll see you tonight then,' said the man with the ponytail.

I gave them a forced wave as they charged past us, watching the bobbing ponytail grow smaller.

'Do you think we should turn back?' I asked.

There was silence. I looked around and saw Andy starting to charge up the hill on my left.

'Andy, wait.' I pulled my backpack up and trotted to catch up with him.

He seemed to be forcing himself to go as fast as he could. I couldn't catch up, so I stopped.

'Andy,' I yelled. 'Do you think they have a point? We're so unprepared!'

~~~

I continued to shuffle my way up the trail, a few metres behind Andy. There were gorges on either side and the distant sound of a gurgling river. I felt an urge to dip my hot feet into the waters. As I got higher, the emerald valleys undulated beneath us until the town appeared to be a scattering of rocks in the distance. The trees and bushes were alive with insects and birds. I wanted to take photographs and soak it all in, but unpacking and repacking my bag required energy I didn't have. Plus, I was scared I'd lose a determined Andy, who was panting up the trail ahead.

~~~

I was wondering how we'd know when we reached the summit, when trees started to give way to a clearing and a large meadow opened up with a thin, plain wooden cross that overlooked the valleys below.

I smiled, wiping the sweat off my forehead, and collapsed into a heap.

'There's a good viewing point, a couple of hundred metres ahead—' said Andy. He took one look at my face and decided to join me instead.

The Israelis were at the top too. They were packing up their lunches and coffees which they had made on a gas stove. How they managed to fit that all in their tiny backpack was beyond me. Their calf muscles gleamed in the sun, as they glided back onto the trail and waved at our red faces. It was still another ten kilometres to go until we reached the hamlet, but, myth had it, it was now downhill.

'Are you sure this is it?' I asked Andy.

He was surveying the desolate lands as glumly as I was. 'It's getting too dark to go further, and this is the closest we'll get to… civilisation?'

The map had indicated a hamlet halfway between villages. We must have gone wildly off-piste. I had envisaged a small town, possibly a shop or a cafe, even people as a minimum expectation. This was barren land, with two derelict stone structures resembling abandoned houses, no roads or sign of anything dated post-1500s. A couple of cows stared at us from a field.

I was exhausted. We must have walked for over ten hours. My legs were stiff and cramping up. We'd walked uphill the last two kilometres only to discover we'd been going the wrong way. We'd had to backtrack ourselves and go steeply downhill.

Andy began sussing out a camping spot. There wasn't much of a choice. We pitched the tent on rocky terrain. Finding the pegs and the poles with the vast dark sky above us and our phone torches was near impossible.

Afterwards, we crawled into our sleeping bags. I wrapped mine tightly around myself for warmth. It was freezing cold, and there was no chance of making a fire with only rocks and no kindling. I noticed we were on a slight slope, but kept my mouth shut. I craved a hot meal but we were far too exhausted to get the stove out and learn how to use it. We'd eaten some cereal bars instead. I tried my hardest not to imagine the meat stew the Israelis were probably tucking into right now.

Andy breathed heavily. How on earth could he sleep? My legs throbbed from the hike. I longed for a hot shower and clean clothes. I lay there, looking up at the dark canvas, feeling the rocks and twigs digging into my back.

With no usual car and city distractions, I could only hear the occasional wind ruffling the tent. What else was out there? What if there were bears or wolves? Our thin piece of plastic would do little to protect us. Was this really how we were going to sleep from now on?

# 6

The first time I went on a real date with Andy, it was in a George Street bar in Edinburgh with high ceilings and chandeliers. I hardly recognised him sitting down on a barstool in his dark blue suit and freshly shaved face. I'd last seen him in an exhausted and elated state in a pub in Fort William on the last day of the West Highland Way where he'd bought me a glass of whisky (ten-year-old Talisker) to celebrate. The smokiness of the liquid gold had made my eyes water, but it tasted of the heather, corries and ancient Scot pine we'd just conquered.

I preferred him in hiking gear, and I wondered if he thought the same about me. I'd put on some mascara, straightened my tangled hair and had slipped on some high heeled boots to appear taller.

When I walked over to him, he pretended to look around. 'Sorry, I think I'm waiting for another girl. She's small, with messy hair, mud on her face and wears enormous hiking boots.'

I laughed as I joined him, and we resumed our chat as we'd last left it in Fort William.

Andy was three years older than me, originally from Edinburgh, and had been to university in St Andrews. He was about to start a job as an associate for a worldwide consultancy company.

I listened to him talk about his job and career enviously. I wished I could find a job that made me feel as passionate. He knew exactly what he wanted from life and was on track to achieving it. He'd studied Economics and Finance and had been an intern at his current company before joining as a graduate associate.

'I'm hoping to work hard enough and take up any extra hours so that I can become a consultant in two years.'

'What happens when you become a consultant?'

'You graduate from the programme. It's a big jump in responsibilities. You go from being an intern to a manager and you get to choose where you want to relocate and run your own projects.'

'Where would you want to go?'

'There are offices in pretty much every major city in the world, but London makes the most sense for me, and it's also the company's headquarters. It's also the best place for networking.' He paused to thank the waitress who had brought over a bottle of wine and two high-stemmed glasses. 'My goal is to become a company director there.'

I'd been to visit London a few months after arriving in Edinburgh. I loved the enormous bookshops, the pulsing river that broke through the labyrinth city and all the different accents I could hear on the tube. But the crowds and skyscrapers had made me feel claustrophobic.

He poured me some red wine. 'Anyway, I won't bore you with crap chat. I want to know more about you.'

I smiled as I held up my wine glass. I wasn't used to having wine with a cork, so I figured it must be good.

I thought back to what we'd spoken about on the West Highland Way. I'd told him a little about Chile and then we'd mainly commented on the route, the lochs, the midges and our blisters. We hadn't really provided much of a CV to each other, neither had it seemed necessary.

'Did you finish reading your book?'

'I did.'

'Inspired?'

'Always,' I laughed. 'That's the reason I moved here. The plan is to save enough money and then go travelling.'

Andy put his wine glass down. 'I thought you were half joking when you said that on the walk. What do you mean by travelling, then? Are we talking Eurotrip or Phuket?'

'The Caucasus.'

Andy frowned. 'Where's that?'

'It's the mountain range around Georgia, Armenia and Azerbaijan. It's uncharted, relatively safe and has the most dramatic landscapes.'

Andy was looking down at Google Maps on his phone. 'It's right next to Russia. There are a few war zones around it. You sure that's safe?'

'The books and blogs I've researched all say it is.'

'It does look pretty awesome,' he said, scrolling through pictures of the mountains, glaciers and valleys. 'So why there? I mean, if you could climb mountains, why not Scotland or Switzerland? Why go east of…Turkey?' he said, double glancing at his map.

'I know it's random, but I seemed to have ruled every other country out. I don't want to go anywhere too crowded, hot or touristy. I'm looking for a place that's relatively untrodden, with no preconceptions, that's still fairly connected to other countries. And somewhere I can—hopefully—be safe enough to walk and hitchhike.'

'But why not just go on a bus or train? Surely that's also a local way of travelling.'

'I'm not ruling anything out, but walking obviously gives you the rawest medium of experiencing a country. You can experience each change of surface, smell what someone's cooking, speak to people on the way. I'm not totally delusional. I'm not planning on walking throughout a whole country or anything. I guess I just want to walk and see how far I go, and when I get tired, I'll catch a ride, or go to a new country.'

'So are you a professional hiker?'

I laughed. 'No. The West Highland Way was the first long walk I've ever done. But I figured if I could do that…'

'You could climb Everest…?' asked Andy, his eyebrows high.

I looked down into my almost empty glass. 'I know what it sounds like.'

'No,' said Andy quickly, 'it sounds amazing. Really. I just love your confidence about it. I could barely walk for a week after the West Highland Way and just the thought of living in tents and hostels and not showering for months…' He laughed, 'I just think eight days was my limit.'

Andy topped up my glass. 'So. You've conquered the Caucasus. Where do you go to next?'

'I've always fancied Nepal.'

Andy pretended to shudder. 'Earthquakes, rats, squat toilets.'

I rolled my eyes. 'Mountains, pagodas, yaks, temples,' I said, stretching out my hands.

He smiled at me, his eyes searching my face. 'So I guess a weekend in Paris wouldn't do it for you?'

'I'm after more of an adventure. A bit more of a long-term journey. Taking a backpack and seeing where I end up. A one-way ticket with no return.'

'So where does the inspiration come from? You know, what made you start reading about all these adventures?'

I swallowed more wine. Was it my second or third glass? It was enough to make his face look fuzzier. His smile made me feel confident. 'I grew up in an expat family. My parents are Scottish but I was born and raised in Chile. My dad's retired now, but he used to travel for work all the time. I missed him of course, but I used to love that first night when he'd come back. We'd sit outside and have dinner, and after a few whiskies he'd tell me stories. They always started the same way.' I dropped my voice in an attempt to imitate him. 'Many, many years ago, long before the notion of you even existed, your great-great grandfather left Scotland to go on a big adventure...'

Andy grinned. 'Go on then.'

'He'd invent all these stories about ships, lions, hidden treasures in Mauritius, or plane wreckages off the coast of France, desert oasis in Africa. I'd lap them all up. And then he'd end them in the same way, too.' I cleared my throat and dropped a decibel. 'He held onto the raft with all his might as enormous waves crashed onto him. Then a wave—bigger than any wave he'd ever seen—started to form. He knew this was it. There was no way he'd survive this. The wave started to curl downward. He closed his eyes, clinging on to his raft by his fingertips.' My voice dropped to a whisper. 'And then a very strange thing happened...'

'What?' Andy's eyes widened.

I laughed. 'You'll have to wait until his next trip.' I winked. 'Or at least that's what he'd tell me.'

'That's awesome. I love that,' said Andy. 'Fuck, all my dad talks about is his shares.'

I snorted into my glass. Andy's eyes were flickering in the candlelight, his smile returning to a straight line. 'So when would you leave?'

'Sorry?'

'When will you go, you know, on your grand world tour?'

'Not anytime soon.' I leaned back into my chair. 'Things haven't really gone as planned,' I admitted. 'I'm not saving much—well, anything—to be honest. I think it's going to be a long time until I actually save up and become brave enough to go.'

I wanted to project good energy, a sense of humour, prove I could be interesting. But as the wine disappeared and turned into another bottle, the words blurted out without filter. I told him how I was miserable in a city I desperately wanted to be happy in.

'I think it means I have to rethink what I set out to do. If nothing changes after a year, maybe I should get a better job back home, and try again a few years later.'

Andy tilted his head to the side as he looked at me. 'Or maybe you just need a reason to stay.'

~~~

I pulled away from our snogging session. The cobbled stones were speckled with frost, which I only realised when I took a step forward and fell on my backside, grabbing Andy's coat with me. He laughed off the tear as he hauled me back up, offering to drop me back home in a cab.

The wine fogged up facts, but we somehow ended up in his sleek flat in the New Town instead. There were bar stools, brown leather couches and an oak round table with Impressionist Art books. A throw cushion with his initials on, presumably a present from his mum or granny. Two framed photographs on the mantelpiece. One of a black Labrador, the other of him standing next to what looked to be his brother and his parents with the Sydney Opera House in the background. A 'Good Luck' card lay discarded on a thin black television stand. Fitted under the sleek kitchen island was a rack of red wines and a dusty bottle of champagne. A Nespresso machine was on top, with only purple capsules lining up a slender rack. An oven so polished on the outside I wondered if it had ever been used.

'It's my parents' flat,' he explained. 'But they've moved to a cottage in Aberfeldy now, and my brother lives in Sydney, so it's only me ...'

~~~

Before long, we were spending most nights together, sometimes with wine, other times with coffee, mostly sitting on the floor and chatting.

We were opposites. He was a grafter; I was a free spirit. He loved routine and order, both in his schedule and in his emotions. I was a firework, unpredictable and passionate. He could keep half a chocolate bar in the fridge for months and forget about it. Mine didn't even last the walk home from the shop. He loved cooking, and would handle a recipe like a maths problem, ticking each step off. He would save portions for lunch, and even some in the freezer for another day. If I offered to cook, it always ended up being an improvised, too salty concoction of pasta which Andy would politely chew. There would never be enough for the next day, as I'd probably eat it during a second sitting a few hours later.

Andy grounded me. He helped me manage my spiralling emotions with logic and optimism. He gave me a reason to settle down in Edinburgh while encouraging my desire for hiking and travelling. I helped him loosen up and brought change to his rigid schedule. We climbed through the fire escape of his building onto the roof to look down over the New Town, watching the city go by. We'd spend weekends walking up Scottish Munros or around lochs. On holidays, we'd fly to Europe and visit Paris, Stockholm or Lisbon. I introduced him to wild swimming, taught him how to make Chilean *sopaipillas* and *pisco sours*, and convinced him to accompany me to Catholic mass.

Our differences were like clouds moving parallel and calmly, occasionally colliding to form a compromise. His career was his calling, and he didn't resent having to work late hours (most nights) or on weekends (most Sundays).

It might have been a year after we'd met that Andy asked if I wanted to move in with him. I panicked. What if moving in together meant that we'd forever be tied to Edinburgh? What if things didn't work out? What if I couldn't afford to live with him? When I presented this to Andy, he laughed.

'It was just an idea, not a prison sentence.' He'd wanted me to move in so we could see each other more often. His work hours were increasing and most of the time dedicated to our relationship was spent travelling to each other's flats.

I took my time to think about it. Yes, my flat was mice-infested, slightly out of town and overcrowded with baristas and buskers trying to make it big at the Edinburgh Fringe festival, but it was my own space.

A few months later, the mice population had multiplied and so, it seemed, had the tenants. I agreed to the move. We divided the rent and bills and redecorated his sleek leather sofas with my charity shop throws and fairy lights. He didn't seem to mind.

I had a boyfriend who had become my soulmate. A best friend. He was my home. My dreams of travelling the world had paused. Instead of pursuing my journey, I started prioritising our relationship. I had come looking for an adventure, and maybe Andy was it.

# 7

My worries must have put me to sleep. I woke up to sunshine and cows mooing. We'd slept for twelve hours straight.

We packed up our tent and bags, and by the time we soldiered on, the sun was out at full throttle. I could feel it burning the back of my neck. I could hear the distant sound of a river running, like thunder in the distance. As we grew closer, the roar grew louder. Andy, who was walking ahead, suddenly stopped in his tracks. He was looking intently around the corner and then back at me.

I caught up with him, only to see the trail had been eaten up by shrubs, rocks and mud. The tearing current smashed into jagged rocks, hurtling pebbles sideways and dowsed us with waves of water. We were at the foot of a glacier. The only way forward was fording the river.

I stared at the fast-flowing water. Crossing it seemed like a death sentence. There was no way. Had the Israelis done it already? Dread settled in my stomach. Were we going to have to walk the entire track back to the start? Was it over?

Andy seemed to be in a different mindset.

He was on the banks of the river, walking alongside it.

I raised my voice over the noisy current. 'What are you doing?'

'Seeing where the best place is to cross.'

I watched him scrutinise the river, crouching down and eyeing up every option. My heart raced. Was he actually serious?

He trotted back to me. 'We need to hurry. The current is only getting worse.'

'Andy, there's no way.'

'Look, come see. There's a section with quite a few rocks we can use as foot holders. I think someone might have put them there for getting across.'

'Who? There's not a single soul out here.'

'Antonia, trust me.' He turned back and reached out for my hand, squeezing it. 'We can do this. We haven't come this far for nothing.'

With the pulsing river in front of us, I watched him pack our phones, passports and wallets into the waterproof bag and take off his shoes and socks. He rolled his trousers above his knees, hauling his backpack over his shoulders. As his foot sunk in, his eyes grew big. 'It's fucking freezing.'

He took a step forward, but the current threatened to knock him aside. He hobbled but managed to stay upright, forcing his legs to move.

'Crap! Fuck! Ahhhhh!'

I watched his body submerge deeper until it was waist-high, his shouting fading in the noise of the current. He went in deeper, his backpack thrashing from side to side. The bottom of the pack submerged fully into the water. I held my breath—how deep would he go? I didn't want to look.

Then, the backpack seemed to lift from the water. I could see his backside. Then the back of his knees. Then his calves. My heart resumed a normal pace.

He clambered over to the riverside and threw his bag down, collapsing on the ground, where he scrunched his face in pain and grabbed his feet. I could faintly hear him screaming and swearing. He got up and started doing star jumps to get warm.

He signalled for me to start.

There was no way…

He beckoned again.

Terrified, I dipped a foot in before yanking it back out. The icy water shocked my foot instantly. I'd never felt water that cold before.

'I can't, I can't,' I shrieked.

Andy couldn't hear me over the sound of the water. He jumped and waved at me. His hands signalled me over.

I tried slipping into the water again. It was agony.

I knew he couldn't come back my way, but I knew I wouldn't be able to do it either. How on earth would we meet up? I retraced my steps and crouched down on the rocks, shaking my head. I felt tears setting in. 'I don't know what to do.'

To my horror, I saw Andy get back in the water, grimacing in pain as he did. Cursing and yelling, he made his way back over.

'Oh my God, Andy.' I tried to take his hand as he made it over. His cheeks were flushed and his jaw tightly clenched.

He jumped on the spot and turned to me. 'Come on Antonia, you can do this.'

'I'm too scared,' I said, as he reached my side of the river. 'Can't you take me on piggyback?'

He shook his head. 'That's far too dangerous. The undercurrent is too strong. Look, I'll go first. I'll take your bag. Follow my steps. Don't think about it. Do it as quickly as possible,' he insisted, getting ready to go. 'Promise you'll follow me because I'm not coming back again.'

He waited until I nodded and then stepped back into the water.

I watched the rapid water with visions of being taken by the icy current. I wiped my face and tried again. I had no choice if I wanted to continue this hike.

The shock of the icy water revitalised my movements. Adrenaline pumped through my veins. Instinct overtook any feeling. I needed to get to the other side. I waded from side to side, pushing through rocks, too focused to panic. I looked only at Andy's back, trying to follow his exact footing. It was difficult to hear his instructions through the noise.

'Now what?' I cried.

'OK, just move your foot to the next one along—no, the other foot!'

'I'm going to die!'

'No you're not.'

Sharp rocks stabbed the soles of my feet. The current threatened to push me over, but I fought back to stay upright. I could feel my backside, stomach and elbows getting soaked. My legs were painfully numb. The cold breeze froze my wet body, but it meant I was reaching the shallow bit. I watched Andy getting out. He threw my bag down and turned to grab me.

Before he could get back in, I was at the riverbank, grabbing his arms as he yanked me out.

I yelled out in relief and pain, collapsing onto dry ground. My feet felt like they were burning.

'Move, jump, keep moving,' said Andy. 'It's worse if you stay still.'

I tried hobbling. 'Ow, ow, ow!'

'Tell me about it,' said Andy, 'I did it three times.'

## 8

The hike went on. Long climbs up what felt like eighty-degree angles, with not a soul in sight until we reached the tiny mountain hamlets; Zhabeshi, Adishi, Iprali. We would stay in homes of Svans who spoke no English, most who'd never left their own hamlet, some who'd only ever been as far as Kutaisi. Their homes were built and decorated with stone ovens, hard beds, log-fires and no electricity. Water was taken from wells, vegetables from their gardens and meat from their cattle.

We trudged onwards. I gritted my teeth as my bag creaked and snagged against my T-shirt. The tight straps caused blisters on my collar bones, which would form overnight and burst during the day. I had a patch of rashes there with pus, dried blood and dirt. The straps made it painful and itchy, but undoing them would make the bag a lot heavier.

I preferred it when Andy walked ahead of me. That way, he didn't have to hear how out of breath I was or how many times I stopped in one place. He didn't have to see me sweating from my armpits and upper lip and guzzling down water. I felt self-conscious of the frizz cloud no longer tamed by sweat, that used to resemble my hair.

Andy looked back often, and I gave him a forced grin. I envied his strength and self-sufficiency. He could survive without much water. Lack of food didn't seem to make him cranky. He never complained about wearing drenched, sweaty clothes and not knowing where the next shower would be.

I did. I didn't think I would, but I did. For starters, I was far less fit than I had imagined myself to be. The upward climbs were a painful, physical struggle. My calves were always burning or cramping, and the tightness in my back and shoulders from carrying all the weight was like a persistent migraine. And the headaches! They would form behind my eyebrows and throb underneath the sun. We weren't drinking enough water, only relying on rivers when we came across them and then waiting for an hour until the iodine tablets had fully dissolved. I hated the taste and could only drink the bare minimum. We were surviving on a diet of noodles, cereal bars and crackers, in the continual hope that we'd reach a town soon to stock up on supplies. I was running out of stamina and we had barely begun our trip.

After each day of hiking, there was no recovery time. We'd have to set up our tent, roll the sleeping bags and mats out, and sleep on solid ground. There was nothing more like adding salt to the wound than having a thick root sticking through my sore back all night. The thought of Andy knowing any of this would be admitting defeat. I'd dragged him all this way, painted him my dream, convinced him to give up practically everything for this. This had to be amazing. Even if I had to fake every minute of it.

In the moments that I didn't think about my exhaustion—mostly during the time between setting up the tent and lying down inside it—I felt angry. I was mostly furious at myself for letting myself down, for not being fit enough, for not being able to enjoy this. How had I not prepared for this? No part of me was enjoying the views down Georgian valleys or marvelling at the snow-capped mountains and the sound of pure, untouched, untamed nature. I was too fatigued to appreciate anything.

In the late afternoons, when my noisy mind would be so exhausted, my survival mode would kick in. The silence became sounds and I had no option but to tune in to listen. It was boots on sand, the snapping of twigs, the ruffle of leaves. It was the heavy breaths and the unzipping of a bag, the gulp of water and the chink of a metal clip on a bottle.

Towards the end of one of these afternoons, Andy's map indicated that tonight we would reach a bothy at the highest point of our trek; 3,000 metres. The sun had just set, leaving us with a grey misty light to follow the last bit of the trail. Neither of us had ever stayed in one. We'd walked past them during the West Highland Way but hadn't been inside. I wondered if there'd be some facilities—like showers—or, even more exciting, other hikers there. We hadn't seen a soul in over a week. Maybe we'd meet the Israelis. They probably thought we'd quit by now.

I could feel my period coming. At first, I could walk through the cramps, but they had intensified in the afternoon, causing a dull, heavy pain that made me limp slowly uphill. Surely it was just premenstrual symptoms. My actual period wasn't due for a week or so, and I was hoping by then we'd reach a town where I could buy sanitary pads.

I walked in silence. I was just focusing on getting through each step and not on the cramps. I broke the hike up into moving my feet forward. Left, right, left, right, left. To think beyond the corner, the crossroad or, worse, a false summit, was far too agonising. I looked down at my feet the entire time, studying the mud-encrusted laces, listening to the crunching of the gravel, imagining that each tiny step was a step less for the day to finish.

I felt a warm sensation between my legs. I eased forward. Maybe it was just sweat. I moved again and felt a trickle down my leg. I looked down and saw my leggings caked in blood.

'Shit,' I mumbled, stopping in the tracks. I removed my backpack. I couldn't see Andy but knew he wouldn't be too far away. 'Andy!' I called for him. I started to look through the contents of my backpack. Nothing seemed useful. Books, a toothbrush, dirty clothes, a cap...

'You all right?' asked Andy, catching his breath as he came back down the hill. He glanced at the strewn clothes. 'Did your backpack break?'

'No,' I muttered. I fumbled through more useless items: a hairbrush, flip-flops, sun lotion. 'I've just got my period and I didn't bring anything to...' I felt stupid and embarrassed as tears of frustration pricked my eyes.

I heard Andy unclip his bag and open it. He started looking through his things, and I shook my head. It was useless. I had no idea when we'd next come across a bathroom but, considering we were in the middle of a remote mountain trail, I wasn't holding my breath.

'Hold this,' said Andy. I looked down at what he had handed over and saw a pair of damp socks.

'What are you...' I looked as he unclipped a penknife off his backpack and with the knife's sharp edge grabbed his socks back. He laid one flat against a rock, put the knife inside and started tearing them apart at the seams. He tugged at the torn edges and then ripped the remainder with his hands. Soon, a pair of socks had become four cotton rags.

He passed them over. 'I know it's revolting. But it's better than nothing. I've got another pair you can use tomorrow.'

I started to laugh through my tears as I gripped them in my hand. 'Don't ever bring this up again.'

~~~

With socks now stuffed down my underwear, I continued to walk until the trail gradually gave way to a wooden shack, perched on top of a summit and exposed to the winds. From where we were standing it looked tiny, we'd be lucky to both fit in there. We could hear a broken shutter being battered by the wind, banging and creaking against the wall. Scrawny trees, thorny shrubs and stone boulders encroached closer on us. All around were unforgiving slopes, dropping down into rocky gorges.

Andy reached for the door handle. The door creaked open, and I swallowed dust. I wondered when it had last been inhabited. There was no electricity; the room was lit by an ashen light from the evening outside. It was all one derelict room with two separate wooden bed frames complete with a thick layer of dust on the floor. A thin window frame rattled in the wind.

'I guess we just roll our mats out on these,' said Andy, gesturing at the old frames. It felt like the first time I'd heard his voice all day. The words came out crackling.

I swallowed down my unease. I didn't fancy this at all.

'What if we camped?' I asked, my voice small. Somehow the idea of a thin canvas around us seemed cosier than this. At least in a tent we could cuddle.

'It's going to rain any minute. This'll do.'

'This looks like a horror film.'

Andy forced an empty laugh which bounced off the gorges.

~~~

We heated up some packets of pot noodles. We only had a few more bags of those, a packet of oatcakes and some cereal bars. They were all starting to taste the same and the thought of eating them again was starting to make me nauseous. Still, I was so tired and hungry that we polished off the whole lot in the dark with only our phone torches for light.

I could feel dread approaching as the last of the evening light disappeared—forcing us to go to sleep. At least camping meant there was more to do. It normally took a good hour to find the flattest spot for the tent, set up the poles and the canvas and stab the ground with the nails and wind fasteners. We'd then roll out our sleeping bags and take out the food, stove and water out of our bags. One of us would go down to the nearest river, if there was one, to fill up our bottles, while the other would start building a small campfire, finding rocks and kindling. We'd both have a quick wash of our faces and teeth using the water from one bottle, and we'd use the other for cooking and drinking.

By the time we'd set up, eaten, washed and watched the fire dwindle, we'd fall into our sleeping bags.

Tonight, though, with nothing to keep me busy, there was too much time for me to stew alone with my thoughts. Andy was exhausted. He soon got into his sleeping bag, and I could hear him snoring. I lay there on my mat wide awake. Wind battered the windows. It was pitch dark, the kind of darkness where I couldn't even see my hands in front of me. I was filthy, too—desperate for soap and a sponge to wipe myself down. My clothes were damp and stank with accumulated sweat and menstrual blood, and my mouth felt dry and gritty. I had a tiny bit of water left, and I wasn't going to waste it brushing my teeth.

A noise startled me. A knock against something hard. It was in my head. It was all in my head. The wind was making this whole bothy creak. Was someone trying to come in? What if it was an animal? What if it was a wolf? I tried to make out where the door was in the dark.

I sank deeper into my sleeping bag. Another noise. A similar knock. Then another one. Maybe it was the floorboards. Wasn't there something about wood expanding in the heat and—

A rustle. It sounded like bags. Where were our bags? Weren't they in the space between our beds? It sounded close. My heart thumped. Oh please, Andy, wake up, wake up, wake up.

I grabbed my phone and switched on the torch. I flashed it on to the floor beside me.

Rats.

Three enormous brown rats were scuttling over our bags. They were the size of small cats. I screamed, and my phone fell to the floor. I heard the rats scurrying.

'What's going on?' mumbled Andy.

'Rats!' I managed between breaths. 'There're rats in the room!'

I could hear Andy shuffling in his sleeping bag, probably still half-asleep. 'It's a bothy, what do you expect?'

'We can't sleep here!' I gasped, near tears. 'They're enormous.'

'Antonia, calm down. They're field rats. They're just looking for food.'

I could feel my hands shaking. There was no way I was picking up my phone off the floor. I said nothing, my heart hammering.

I heard Andy's bed creak, then footsteps. He tried to feel me through the dark. 'Move over then.'

The bed frames were tiny, but I shuffled against the wall. Andy lay down next to me, wrapping his arms around me, letting me cuddle into the millimetre of space we had. I grabbed onto his arms, trying to pull him as close to me as I could. His heavy breathing tickled my face. The room fell silent.

I took some deep breaths, wanting my heart to slow down. I followed my breathing for some time, then heard Andy snoring again. I didn't mind his sweaty odour or the noise. I wanted him as close as possible.

'Andy,' I whispered. 'Andy, are you awake?'

'What?' he muttered.

'I can't sleep.'

I waited some more. No movement. Not even from the rats.

# 9

I could see Andy's jacket hanging on the coat rail, his shoes tucked neatly beneath it on the floor. I tossed my things on top of the shoe rack. He'd come home early, threatened by a text I'd sent him at work, that universal line that shook the foundations of relationships. *'We need to talk.'*

I pushed the bedroom door open without knocking, to see Andy getting out of his suit. He still had his shirt on but was wearing grey boxers, an old pair with holes in them. I glanced at his white, almost translucent Scottish legs that seriously lacked vitamin D, with dark golden hairs that grew lighter up his thighs. He held his suit trousers in front of his body, partially blocking the view, as he rummaged for his rugby tracksuit.

Five years ago, when I'd first met him, he used to play rugby a few times a week with a local club. This was more social than competitive. It usually involved the other girlfriends and me joining them for pints on a Saturday after the game. It was the one time I'd see him completely relaxed, where he chatted easily and had a few too many pints. We'd walk back the dark streets, singing and dancing. We'd be unfazed about tomorrow's headache, knowing we'd spend Sunday eating pizza, watching *Game of Thrones* and falling asleep on the couch. I couldn't remember the last time we'd done that, or when he'd last played a game. Work had taken up all of his free time.

I sat down on the bed. The window was open and, despite it being July, there was a cool draught coming through.

He pulled the tracksuit on, relieved to be clothed. Less vulnerable that way. His eyes were searching my face for any sign of dialogue.

'So you want to talk?' he asked.

He'd half unbuttoned his shirt but had second thoughts. I could see part of his chest, a scattering of freckles and moles. He slowly sat down near me, enough space between us to fit a desk, his emerald tie in his hands.

Andy looked up. 'Is it about the wedding?'

'Sort of.'

'Look, I've told you, please don't worry about spending your savings on this. I'm happy to pay for it all, and my parents also want to contribute.'

'I don't feel comfortable with that.'

'Okay, well, what if we downscale it? Have an intimate ceremony, and then a party at my parent's place? We could fly your parents over, and I'm sure your siblings would want to come too. It would be way cheaper than paying for a venue. Unless you've changed your mind and want to have it in Chile? We can also arrange that.'

'It's not that. I just…I hadn't planned on holding on to my savings for a rainy day. I'd planned to use them to travel.'

Andy frowned and squeezed the skin between his eyebrows. His eyes were red and I could see he was struggling to stay focused. He'd hardly slept the night before with the mountain of work his boss had sent home. 'Well then, save them for travelling.'

I tilted my head at him. 'That's the point,' I sighed. 'If we put down the money for a wedding in September, it doesn't make sense. I won't have the money—or the time.'

'So you want to postpone the wedding?'

'Yes.' I nodded slowly.

Andy bowed his head. I looked at his coppery coloured hair and could see some white hairs down his temple. He sighed loudly and then looked up, lifting his head back at the ceiling. 'Hang on.' He sat back, blinking hard to keep his eyes open. 'You want to go travelling now?'

'When else will I go? After we're married? Once we start having kids?'

'Antonia, I'm working towards the promotion now, you know that. It's not a good time.'

'It's never going to be a good time.'

Andy scratched the inside of his arm, a habit he resorted to when stressed.

'Andy,' I continued, 'you know I've always wanted to do this. I told you this the day we met. I want to book a one-way ticket to Georgia and go from there.'

'I know, I know. I just thought…I don't know, I thought maybe you'd change your mind a bit, what with your job, us getting married…'

'I want to do this.'

'How long would you go for?'

'I don't know. I don't want to make fixed plans. Maybe a year?'

'A year?' His voice rose. 'Wow.' He gripped the side of the bed with his hand. 'You're okay leaving me…for a whole year?'

'I don't want to, but—'

'Then don't go.'

'So what? I'm meant to give up my dream?'

'You have many dreams. It's not like this is your only one. You said you can't wait to be married. To be a mum. Write a book. Run a marathon. Aren't those all good dreams too?'

'And I want all of that too, but after I do this.'

'A year's a long time.'

'I know.'

'It would be too hard.'

'What does that mean?' I scoffed. 'That you won't wait for me?'

'No, it just means I'll fucking miss you,' he snapped. Something in his voice cracked, a small moan at the back of his throat. Exhaustion. He swallowed hard.

'What do your parents think about you going? I'm guessing you've told them?'

'They're happy for me,' I lied.

Andy said nothing, but he sat back up and braided the tie through his fingers. I could see flashes of green silk as he moved his fist.

I looked at my nail-bitten hands and covered my engagement ring with my thumb. I pressed the skin into the diamond so that it hurt and then slowly released it, looking at the imprint.

'I...' He inhaled deeply and then set the tie aside. 'I don't know what to say. I can't stop you, but I obviously don't want you to go.'

I grimaced. I glanced at Andy's clenched fist, his green veins protruding, his Fitbit pressing into his wrist. I felt an urge to hold it. I knew that touching it would melt so much tension. But I couldn't bring myself to feel his skin. There was too much pride in the way. I started to get up.

Andy stood up with me. 'Wait.'

I looked at him.

'Fine...what if I came with you?'

I forced a laugh. 'That's not going to happen. We've tried, and you always come up with a million reasons not to. Plus, it doesn't make sense. You're flat out with work, and you might risk the promotion—'

'No. You're right.' He clenched his jaw. 'I think they might delay the promotion again.'

I looked at him, but he avoided my eye.

'I'm sorry,' I said.

'Fuck it. I've worked my ass off for years, and it's not coming to anything anytime soon. I can apply for a sabbatical. It's two months' notice. It's not an ideal scenario for me, but it's better than seeing you unhappy.'

I searched his face. 'Andy, I'm serious about this. I'm not going to change my mind next week. I want to travel in the way I've always spoken about. You know, long-term trekking, heavy backpacks, meeting the locals...'

'I know. You've not shut up about it for years.'

'I want to do this properly.'

He was looking at me in earnest. 'Okay.'

I thought back to the countless discussions we'd had over the years about taking a year out to travel, where Andy always found reasons why it sounded whimsical and unrealistic.

He continued. 'Look, it's not exactly what I want. I have a good job, and I'll need to rent out this flat. But you've compromised your dream for me for the last few years, so I guess it's my turn now.'

My stomach was fluttering with excitement. 'You'd really do this?'

I slowly reached over and touched his hand. It was warm and familiar. He intertwined his fingers in mine.

He sighed and smiled tightly. 'I've got a meeting with my boss tomorrow. I'll speak to him then.'

# 10

'Welcome to Armenia.' A man with a toothless smile stamped our passport in an empty office, waving his hand when we tried to put our bags through a stationary conveyor belt. 'Not working. Go.'

We'd been hiking and camping for almost a month now. We'd hitchhiked to central Georgia, to Borjomi National Park (where the Romanov family spent their summer holidays), paused briefly in Tbilisi and continued to the vineyard region of Sighnaghi. We joined the Trans-Caucasian Trail. This was a new path being developed across the Caucasus with the aim of establishing a hiking trajectory that united Georgia, Armenia and Azerbaijan. Because of its novelty, the trail had little signage and reputation, with no information available online.

We made our way through forests, climbed over rocks and waded across streams. We mostly headed east and hoped for the best.

With not a single soul out there besides us, the nature surrounding us felt even more peaceful and soul-filling. As most of the trails we had discovered in the Caucasus, it was steep uphill. There was an advantage now; it was a lot cooler. But with the autumn came the rain. For days it drenched our gear and moods. Through the mud and wind, I wiped the rain off my brow and dragged my feet onwards.

A lone driver with no English had driven us to the Armenian border, which was distinguished by nothing more than a small concrete office in between highways.

After getting our visas, I followed Andy's footsteps out of the office back to the highway. The skies were dark grey, and rain had begun to fall. The highway was empty. From where we stood, we could see a couple of parked cars. They were so old and broken, they looked like they had been abandoned since the Soviet years. A border policeman stood outside the crumbling office, smoking a cigarette.

We found a grit box on the side and sat there as we thought about our next plans. The weather wasn't exactly making my idea of roaming through the Armenian outback look appealing. There was a road sign ahead that pointed towards the capital.

'Are you sure you don't want to go to the city?' Andy asked again. We'd heard Yerevan was modern with cafes and wine bars. I knew he was desperate for a hot shower and to wash his clothes. I wanted that too. I could no longer face cereal bars. I craved a burger, pasta or a cheese toastie. Anything warm. I longed for a cappuccino and would kill for a bottle of wine. The thought of stocking up on tampons and pads felt luxurious. Yet going to the city felt like defeat. I didn't know exactly when I'd want this hiking journey to end, but we'd only just stepped foot in Armenia and I wanted to see more of it before heading straight to the capital.

'Yes I'm sure,' I said, albeit reluctantly. 'I just feel like we're doing it more authentically if we explore some of the towns and countryside en route. Going straight to Yerevan feels like we're giving up.' Through the corner of my eye, I could see Andy pull a face, but I turned away from him and walked towards the road.

We walked for an hour down a narrow, paved road. It seemed to disappear into the mountains. I looked back and forth, but there were no cars in sight.

'Not quite as easy as Georgia, huh?' said Andy.

After a failed few hours of hitchhiking, we walked along the road, aimlessly, until we found a trail that led into a valley with a river flowing through it. We hiked down to the riverbank. Cows and horses grazed, unbothered by the forbidding weather. We made our way past them until we found a shelter from the rain in a clearing underneath the trees.

I set up our tent as Andy went to collect firewood. My hands automatically knew what poles went to each peg. Having never so much as built an IKEA lamp, I was impressed that I could now do this so quickly. A year ago, I would have never imagined that I'd be camping in valleys.

I was now eating and drinking out of a single mug, which I'd wash out with cold ash and river water, before filling it up with broth, pasta or coffee. Anything I had in the mug seemed to have the same taste: chicken noodles with a hint of musty Nescafé.

I watched Andy walk towards the river where the powerful current took over the noise of him blowing his nose. He stripped down until he was fully naked.

'What are you doing?' I called after him, quickly glancing over my shoulder to make sure we were alone.

'Getting in.'

I followed him, wincing on his behalf as he walked in, looking at the contrast between his tanned legs and white thighs.

He caught me glancing and looked down. 'I think it's a good look.'

I laughed.

'Are you going to keep looking at my arse, or are you coming in?'

I took my clothes off, crossing my arms over my chest, my hairs standing on end. I could see green pebbles, tiny fish, an army of tadpoles and watched as my white toes sunk into the mud. I scooped up a handful of water and splashed it over my face. It felt glorious, although the stones beneath me pricked my feet. I walked in deeper, careful not to wet my hair and shoulders, feeling too cold to go any further. Andy waded over and wrapped his arms around me. He planted a kiss on my cheek, his wet stubble feeling spiky and rough. A splash of water drenching my hair made me squeal.

'Got you,' he grinned, turning me around. 'Come on, you wuss. Get in properly.'

I took a deep breath and submerged myself fully into the water. For the first time in a while, I felt clean and refreshed.

~~~

That evening, when the rain finally stopped, we explored our surroundings. A vast forest stretched down the valleys for as far as my eye could see. I could hear waterfalls, birds and the wind ruffling the autumn foliage. We watched the skies turn from scarlet to red to a misty pink, until the milky sun disappeared behind a hill.

There was a sensation that we were completely alone here. It seemed so easy to camp for as long as it pleased us, with no one around for hundreds of miles to disturb our peace. I tucked my cold hands into my pockets, breathing in the fresh air.

This was more than I had imagined when we first bought that one-way ticket to Georgia. Here I was, in one of the world's most beautiful nature spots, wholly removed from a life that I'd been part of a month ago.

It was the furthest east I'd ever been, a part of the world not known to most, tucked in between the Caucasus and Asia. On the other hand, the trees, valleys and mountains resembled Scotland

and the south of Chile. I wondered if it reminded Andy of home, too. I felt completely connected to the landscape around me.

I was testing the water temperature on the stove when Andy came over, held my chin and kissed me hard on the mouth.

'What's that for?' I laughed, wiping my lips.

'Just seen the date. It's our anniversary.' He looked down at the noodle broth. 'Three-course meal, huh?'

I giggled. 'Ha. Just missing some champagne.'

Andy squeezed my arm as he stood up. 'I'll get us some water from the river.'

I watched him stroll down. Most people my age, who'd been together as long as we had, were buying their first flat, securing a career or having babies. And we were here, in the Armenian outback, cooking up chicken noodles.

Andy came back with our two canteens filled to the brim. He handed mine over and clinked his against mine. 'Cheers, Antonia. Five years and plenty more to come.'

I smiled at him. 'Cheers.'

I dished the noodles into our cups and looked over at him, the flames from the fire forming shadows on his face. We took a few minutes to slurp and sip our chicken noodles, watching the twigs popping in the heat.

Andy put his mug down first, the clink of metal breaking the silence. 'I can't wait to get to Yerevan,' he said.

'Oh yeah? What's the first thing you're going to do?' I asked, envisioning my white wine.

'Find wi-fi.'

I felt my smile disappear. 'Why?'

'Work emails.'

'Can't you just forget about that for now?' It came out meaner than I intended.

'Come on, we've been through this. I actually enjoy my job. I'm looking forward to eventually going back to it.'

I bit my thumbnail before speaking again. 'Would you ever think of doing your job somewhere else?'

Andy looked at me, his eyes running over my face. I noticed he seemed almost nervous. 'Yeah. Yeah, of course.'

My eyes widened. 'Really? What if we did move abroad then? You could try and get a job in Malaysia, or Ecuador, or South Africa.'

Andy laughed. 'I meant more like London or Dubai.'

My smile faded. Neither of those sounded appealing. The thought of huge cities made me feel claustrophobic.

'Let's not talk about all that work stuff now. It feels like a different world, doesn't it?' He kissed the side of my head. 'Is this the travel dream you were hoping for?'

'Yeah. Although I can't help thinking we're not quite there yet.'

'How come?'

'I think we need to think of places to go that are really going to challenge us.'

'So not rat-infested bothies and glacial crossings?'

I ignored him. 'I just keep imagining caves hidden in mountains and hilltop monasteries.'

Andy pulled away and tugged on a piece of grass. 'You need to start appreciating what's in front of you,' said Andy. 'We're in the Armenian wilderness, and it's pretty amazing.'

The river rippled in the background, and I could hear crickets. Andy slurped the last of his broth. The flames warmed my feet, flooding my body with heat. I could hear him scratching his beard. He was right. We were living the adventure right now. Still, I couldn't help but keep thinking what was next. I was finally starting to feel fitter and stronger, and could enjoy hiking without wanting to collapse. The tent was feeling more like a haven and less like a plastic bag. My back was not breaking anymore in the mornings after sleeping on solid ground. I wanted to continue exploring and moving. What was next? Would we walk towards the east of Armenia? Go into Azerbaijan? Or were we done with the Caucasus for now? I was hungry for more.

# 11

The next morning, we crawled out of the tent to rain. I'd heard it fall again all night, battering the canvas, but found comfort in the safety and dryness of our shelter. I could see a few cows that must have wandered our way overnight, grazing. I mumbled good morning, then brewed up coffee on the stove while a tired Andy dragged himself to the river to wash his face. I watched him walk back, his hair wet and tousled. He had dark eye bags, although his face had a healthier glow from the fresh air. His stubble had slowly turned into an auburn beard.

'No luck sleeping?' I asked.

'There was a rock underneath me,' he mumbled, trying to stretch out his back. 'I feel like a ninety-year-old man.'

I handed him some coffee. 'Guess now's not the best time to tell you that I think we should walk twenty kilometres.'

Andy glared at me. 'Where to?'

'Dilijan isn't too far away.' I held up our guidebook. 'They call it the Swiss Alps of the Caucasus. There are some lakes and monasteries. I don't think we'll make it there today, but we'll find another camping spot. We can walk and try our luck hitchhiking again.'

Andy forced a laugh. 'I swear I'll become a monk in exchange for a bed.' He winced as he stretched his arms out again.

I followed his uncurling fingers and noticed some barbed wire attached to the trees next to him.

'What's that?' I asked.

He glanced over. Andy followed the wire, and as he did, I realised that the cable was connected to a fence surrounding us from almost all sides.

'Must be to keep the cattle in,' I said, stifling a yawn.

I sipped my coffee as Andy came back walking oddly, his steps slow and cautious.

'What?' I asked.

'Don't make any sudden movements.'

'Why?' I looked behind me. 'What's going on?'

'We're camping in a minefield.'

'What?' I scrambled to my feet.

'Stop! Move slowly,' he was breathing quickly. 'It's meant to be partially deactivated.'

'We need to get out of here.' I started to pull down the tent. 'Come on, help me.'

Andy yanked the pegs out. 'We've been walking around this camping area all of yesterday and today. I think it's okay—'

'I forced those pegs into the ground, they could have blown up in my face!'

We quickly packed up in tense and scared silence, haphazardly stuffing our tents and kit into our packs as swiftly as possible. We carefully followed the fresh animal tracks out. With each step, I reasoned to myself that if a hundred-kilogram cow had just stepped on this soil, I'd be okay.

With my heart pounding, face covered in sweat and limbs aching from trying to widen each step according to the cattle, I finally managed to walk the five kilometres out on to the road. We collapsed into a heap and started laughing hysterically.

'Oh my God,' I gasped, 'I can't believe we made it out alive.'

'Fuck's sake,' said Andy, 'this place is absolutely mental.'

'Well, I guess we're going to have to walk the whole way to Dilijan.'

'Yerevan,' he said firmly. 'One month of wild camping is enough. We're going to the city, and I'm sleeping in a bed.'

He marched up the road, tightening his backpack without looking back. A couple of cars came past, but each one roared on past us, splashing water, rendering us invisible. I didn't have the heart to argue. He was determined to get a lift.

It was an hour later when a lone car rattled forward. Andy stood in the middle of the road and stuck his hand out. This time it stopped.

## 12

We drove past Lake Sevan, the largest freshwater lake in Eurasia, then Mount Ararat and I could see Turkey in the distance. As we neared Yerevan, the skies cleared. I had imagined a mismatched, dated town—something out of the film *Argo*—but was surprised to see quite the opposite. Coming into view were skyscrapers, modern hotels, cafes and wine bars. The city's main square was flanked by a clock tower as well as galleries and museums all housed in dusty rose buildings, reflected through enormous sprays originating from a fountain in the centre.

After our experience in the remote mountains, the bustling city came as a pleasant change of scenery. It was a city of contradictions. The sleek and Westernised city centre gave way to the older part of town, which was marvellously bohemian. There was street art, buskers, students walking hand in hand, shops stacked high with textbooks and vinyl collections.

Smokers drifted in and out of cafes, engaged in stern conversation, sipping strong black coffees, jotting Armenian script on their worn leather notebooks. Markets lined the streets selling Persian carpets; nuts and dried fruit wrapped in colourful syrups dangled from the stall roofs. Books spilled out of boxes, in Russian and Armenian writing. Wooden carvings, religious icons and paintings decorated each stall. Vendors called out prices for dried meats and a whole range of sweet and sour wines.

The locals had a distinct, dignified look about them; curly, wavy hair, olive skin, green eyes and a hooked nose. What would be considered hipster in the UK seemed authentic in Yerevan. Craft beers, indie music and retro fashion were the norm.

Ironically, the local Irish bar was the hotspot for live music. We walked in there and saw that the bar was full of posters of Paddy O'Malley's, U2 and Sinead O'Connor, yet when Andy asked the bartender for a Guinness, the staff looked at him blankly. A glass of red wine in hand later had me shrugging logic off and listening to an amateur Armenian rock band.

As they performed, we both connected to the wi-fi and scrolled through our phones. The news headlines were all about Prince Harry who'd just gotten engaged to Meghan Markle. I signed into my travel blog, updating it with my photographs, captions and route, while Andy FaceTimed his parents, apologising for missing so many of their calls.

I opened my emails. Mum had sent me a handful of pictures of my nieces sending me love from everyone at home. I noticed there were no questions about my whereabouts or my trip. Still, at least there was some communication. I wrote a long email back, detailing our journey on the Caucus Trail, attaching photographs of the valleys and glaciers, and of us carrying our tents and backpacks. Maybe they'd respond to that one.

Once I'd sent it, I turned to Andy, but he seemed deep in thought on his phone, his eyebrows furrowed in concentration.

I began researching Armenia. There were many monasteries, a National Archive full of ancient manuscripts, a whole gallery dedicated to Caucasian art and Mount Ararat, where Noah was said to have landed his ark.

'We could easily spend a week here,' said Andy at last, sipping on some wine and looking up from his phone. He placed it face down on the table next to his glass.

'Yeah, well, I was just researching the east of Armenia, and there are some cool places to visit. We can see Mount Ararat up close and go all the way to Tatev monastery,' I said.

Andy put his glass down on the table and leaned back in his chair. 'Enjoy the city for a bit. We just got here.'

'I think we should spice up our plans a little,' I continued. 'We could fly to Nepal in a couple of weeks and from there try to hitchhike through the country to India. We'd need to get visas, but I think we can get them in Nepal. I was looking up this incredible hike called the Annapurna Trail. I know Everest Base Camp is the one everyone does, but that's why I think we should do something a bit different. Plus, the Base Camp trek seems to be very crowded and commercialised. This one's a bit more authentic. It's about a month long and you sleep in teahouses—the locals' houses—and there's plenty of other hikers around. So it could be quite fun. You get pretty high up, and I think there are pills you need to take for altitude. I'll need to do more research.'

Andy tipped the contents of his wine glass back into his mouth until it was gone.

'Well,' I asked, 'what do you think?'

He stared at his empty glass. 'I think you've watched too much *Indiana Jones*.'

'Andy, this could be great.' I reached over the table to grab his hand. 'We'd be hiking the Himalayas for a month. How epic does that sound?'

He laughed. 'Antonia, you hardly enjoyed the hike through these mountains. I just can't really imagine you hauling your backpack up the Himalayas.'

I reluctantly smiled back, trying to keep him on my side. There'd been sweat and tears, but I thought I'd done pretty well overall. 'I feel a bit stronger. And I've pruned my backpack.' This last part was true. I'd thrown away a book, an extra pair of shoes, as well as most of my toiletries. 'I'll show you pictures of the Annapurna Trail. I really think you'll like it.'

Andy grimaced. I reached out for my phone and started to share the research I'd found. He was silent, nodding occasionally. After a few minutes of explaining the trail in more detail and showing it to him on the map, I realised he wasn't paying attention.

I put my phone down. 'Look, you don't have to decide today. It was just an idea. We can just go to Nepal and figure it out from there.'

## 13

After a dinner of hot kebabs from the market, we checked in to a hostel. To our dismay, it was a miserable, damp room. It was too late to try and find somewhere else. There was no wallpaper, just thick grey slabs of concrete. Bunk beds were pushed into the walls but, fortunately, were empty. The shower was more of a cold trickle from a pipe in the wall. As I sat down on the bed, I could feel the sharp springs prick my thigh. Andy was looking out of the tiny window at a view of a dumpsite or car park—it was hard to tell with the sheets of rain. A constant drip coming from the ceiling fell into a bucket in the corner. The room smelled of damp and rot.

'Fuck me,' muttered Andy, 'we'd have been more comfortable in the minefield.' He kicked the edge of his bed. The mattress had a frayed grey blanket with a thick layer of dust, and I was terrified of bedbugs. I lay my sleeping bag and liner out, careful not to touch the fabric underneath.

'It's just one night,' I said, 'we'll book somewhere better tomorrow, or we could just continue hitchhiking and camp somewhere nicer than the city.'

'Antonia, stop it.' Andy hadn't touched his backpack. He glanced miserably at his bed and shook his head. 'I don't want to keep moving around.'

'So you want to stay in this hostel?'

'Fuck no. I want to go home.'

I stared at the back of his head. 'What?'

'I've just had enough,' he repeated. 'I'm sorry it means cutting the trip short, but—'

'What are you talking about? We've been on the road for barely over a month. We've only just started.'

Andy scoffed as he turned to face me. He had dark eyebags that looked puffier as he looked around the empty room and gestured at it with his hands.

'This isn't exactly my idea of fun.'

'I know that. That's why I'm looking at our options,' I raised my phone to him, 'and as soon as the wi-fi picks up, we can change our hostel. It's just one night.'

'No, I don't just mean this shithole. I mean everything. We've been hitchhiking and trekking for a month. We've done the camping, the fire, the whole sleeping outside with the stars, but…I'm shattered. I'm done.'

I swallowed, but there was a hard knot in my throat. He was talking out of tiredness now. We were both exhausted. Since crossing the border, we'd been unlucky. People were wearier of hitchhikers here, the rain seemed relentless and we were going into winter. I wanted a change of scenery. I thought Andy wanted it too.

'What about Nepal?' I asked him again. 'We can continue our trip there.'

Andy sat down on the bunk bed in front of me, and the whole setup groaned loudly. A pillow fell to the ground. He kicked it to the side, muttering under his breath.

'Fuck's sake. I just want a hot shower and some real food.'

'I know,' I emphasised. 'Me too. It will get better.'

'I don't get it. I'm trying to understand it, but I don't. It feels like I've given up everything to be here, and I'm not getting anything from it.'

'Because we've only just started.'

'Why don't we just go back? We can finally get married, get back into our jobs and save up for a holiday in Japan or Jordan or whichever exotic place you want to obsess over next.'

I could feel the rage building up inside me. 'Andy, you promised you'd do this for me.'

'Well, I'm allowed to change my mind.'

'That's not fair. Not when we're just a month in.'

He clenched his jaw and then ran a hand over his face, rubbing his eyes.

'Okay.' I tried to sound calm. 'Look, why don't we just sit down and go through our options. I'm sure we can come up with a new plan that we can compromise on.'

Andy was quiet. He was looking at the floor in concentration, a hand resting on the bunk bed's post.

'Do you have any thoughts?' I asked. 'We could look at going back to Europe, or even further, to Southeast Asia.' I sighed. 'Are you sure you don't want to go to Nepal?' I felt gutted. 'Let's think of something together.'

Andy grimaced, nodding slightly at my list of options and then slowly shook his head. He looked up at me.

'Antonia, I'm really sorry, but I want to go back to the UK.' He pressed his knuckles into his thigh. 'I got an email from my boss. The company's offering me a promotion in the London office. It's an amazing opportunity, and the pay is almost double the Edinburgh role.'

I searched for my voice. 'What?'

'I know how you feel about London, but we could get a flat near Richmond or Wimbledon, somewhere with parks around, so it doesn't feel claustrophobic.'

I could feel the colour leaving my face. 'Are you serious? Did you reply?'

'Not yet. But I want to take it.'

My stomach felt cold. I opened my mouth, trying to find the right words. 'So that's the reason you want to go back? You're just going to take it? What about all of this?'

'Well, what if you continued travelling on your own for a bit? That's what you wanted to do in the first place—'

'That's not fair.' My cheeks felt warm. 'We agreed we wanted to do this together. I didn't plan on you leaving me on my own. I want to be with you.'

'Then come back with me.'

I was quiet.

Andy shifted and stood up straight. He moved away from the bed and walked towards the window. 'I wasn't keen to come in the first place. Yeah, I got excited, but I guess I thought it would be, I don't know, *easier*. But every day I'm thinking about the stuff I could be doing back home.'

'You promised you'd do this for me. I've been there for you for the last few years. Now it's time we do my dream for a bit.'

'Is this really your dream?' he gestured around the room, half-laughing. 'Is this what you envisioned?'

I glowered at him.

'I didn't mean it like that,' he said quickly. 'Look, I'm sorry. I really am, and I love you, but you're trying to recreate some wild fantasy from the stories you read.'

I shook my head.

'I get it,' said Andy, this time more softly. 'I see how passionate you get when you read those books and watch those documentaries. It made me fall in love with you. But there are ways you can explore that dream without dragging us through minefields. In London you could get a new job, you could teach Geography, or get a PhD in, I don't know, imperial travellers. Or we could plan a big trip once a year, you pick where.'

A tear fell on the back of my hand, and I watched it slide through my fingers. I felt Andy sit next to me, his weight making the bed creak.

'I know this isn't exactly what you want. But we'll find a way to make it work. Okay?'

He squeezed my hand, and I wiped my face before looking up at him. 'I'm going to Nepal.'

He sighed and then shrugged. 'Okay.' He let go of my hand. 'Fine. But you're on your own.'

I could feel my heart starting to hammer against my ribcage. I laughed. 'Thanks a fucking lot.' How was this even happening? This was the guy who'd never let me walk home alone after the pub. The guy who wouldn't let me walk on the side of the road nearest to cars. 'Is this what you're going to do when our marriage gets tough? Quit?' I threw him a glance. His lips were pressed together, his eyes big and anxious.

'Antonia.' His tone was firm. 'This doesn't have to be a big deal.'

'This wasn't the plan.' My voice started to break. Rage bubbled up in my throat. 'Why did we leave everything if we were only going to travel together for a month? What was the point?'

'I'm trying to support you, Antonia, I really am, but you're so...' He shook his head, eating his words.

'What? I'm so what?' I challenged.

'Unprepared,' he snapped. 'I've haven't wanted to say this but... how can you be so naïve? You'd think that after years of reading and watching travel documentaries, you'd have been a bit more clued into what all this is about. Instead you could hardly handle the hikes, you overstuffed your bag with shite, you completely lost it when we slept with those rats—'

'Stop it.' My voice trembled and I felt furious at how weak I sounded. 'Yeah the beginning was rubbish, but I can do this now. You know I can!'

'Stop yelling,' he muttered, glancing warningly at the closed door. I could feel his eyes on me. 'I think we're just learning that we want different things from this trip, and that's okay.'

How was he sitting there looking so calm? 'Do you really think this is okay? Because right now, it feels like you don't care about me at all.'

A wrinkle formed between his brows, and he shook his head. 'That's not true. I love you.'

'If you did, you wouldn't do this to me.'

'If you loved me, you'd support my decision!' For the first time in the fight, his voice rose to an angry outburst. 'You know I've worked my arse off for this promotion. I wish you'd let me do this without making me feel like I'm the world's biggest dick!'

I looked at his face. His dimples had disappeared, replaced with red patches on his cheeks. There were lines around his eyes and tufts of hair upright from all the times he'd ran his hand over it.

I walked across the room, closer to him.

He was breathing quickly and loudly. For a split second, he looked at me with faint hope. He looked at me with a face that indicated that I'd quash this whole fight by wrapping my arms around him. Instead, I walked past him to the adjoining bathroom, closing the door in his face. I imagined his eyes, crestfallen, looking back at his empty hands.

I leant against the door and slid down to the cold floor, feeling my cheeks grow wet. I wiped my face with my sleeve. How dare he do this to me now? Our relationship was meant to become stronger on the road. We were meant to stay together, not go our separate ways.

Andy knocked on the door.

I ignored him.

My heart pounded against my chest. This wasn't the plan. I couldn't believe Andy was telling me this now, stuck in the middle of bloody Armenia.

If he'd told me before we left, then I could have come up with new ideas, booked tickets to countries I felt comfortable travelling alone to.

My throat felt tight.

Andy knocked on the door again. 'Antonia, come out, please. I'll stay here all night until you do.'

I wiped my face again. I couldn't stay in here forever. I needed to change my plans, all of them. I needed to figure something out. But who was I kidding? I didn't want to travel without Andy. I didn't want to be without him. I didn't have the guts—and I hated Andy for making me realise that. As much as I hated him right now, and as much as I would resent him for doing this, I knew deep down that I would end up going to London with him.

I took a deep, shaky breath and unlocked the door.

## 14

The next morning, I lay in bed with my eyes closed. I could hear Andy getting up but feigned sleep.

'Antonia?' he whispered.

I heard footsteps and then the creak of the bed. I opened my eye a fraction and saw him fully dressed, sitting on the edge of the bed, studying his phone. I wondered what he was doing. Probably sending the email confirmation to his boss. Maybe sending his parents an update. Where would we stay in the meantime? We'd probably have to rent an Airbnb for a couple of weeks. Unless he wanted us to go straight to London. The thought of it made my stomach heavy. It felt so unfair. But what if Andy had a point? What if I continued travelling on my own for a bit? Nepal sounded daunting to go solo, but what if I went somewhere else? I still had my savings. I could buy a ticket somewhere that felt safe. I could put the Nepal plan on hold, even though I was desperate to see the Himalayas. There had to be options.

I got up, determined to do some research. Andy looked up at me. His hair was dishevelled, and he appeared exhausted.

'Want to get coffee?' he asked.

I shook my head. 'I think I need a morning to myself.' I put on my clothes, pulled my hair up into a ponytail and picked up my phone. 'I'll meet you in the market at one for lunch.'

I wandered over to a cafe that overlooked the Yerevan market. Bookshelves of used Armenian books surrounded me. Students bent over their laptops, studying or reading. A lazy waitress sat on a stool, looking at her phone.

I sipped on my lukewarm coffee and logged on to the wi-fi.

I opened the world map and stared at it. I wouldn't survive a day anywhere on my own. I glanced at my book instead, *The Bookseller of Kabul*, by Åsne Seierstad, about a female journalist who'd set off to the Middle East on her own and lived with an Afghan family for a year. It sounded terrifying.

I thought of the other books I'd read. Maybe I could walk the Pacific Crest Trail, just like Cheryl Strayed had done. I could go to America, Australia or Canada, but none of those options made my heart sing. I could go back to Europe. That felt safe, but it didn't feel exciting or brave. I thought of the travel blogs I'd researched before coming, the itinerary I'd planned for us. I'd been thinking of the Himalayas for so long, of the hiking trails, pagodas and monasteries. The idea of going on my own was terrifying—but maybe that was my only option.

~~~

I was sitting on the steps by the flea market watching intense negotiations taking place over jewellery and cigarettes when I saw Andy walking towards me, carrying what looked like two kebabs.

'I've been looking for you.' He handed me one of them. 'I was told these were the best kebabs in Armenia,' he said, licking some sauce off the top.

I bit a piece off. To my surprise, it was delicious—a huge contrast to the cereal bars and noodles we'd had most days.

He chewed on his own one as he sat down next to me. 'Did you have a good morning?' he asked.

'I've booked my flight to Nepal.'

I watched as he put his kebab down. 'What?' He stared at me. 'Are you serious?'

I nodded.

He looked at the crowd ahead and then back at me. 'Antonia...'

'What?'

'I just... I thought you were joking when you said you'd go on your own. You should've told me.'

'Would it have made a difference?'

'We could have discussed things first.'

'London doesn't sound like a discussion,' I muttered.

He stared at me and then wrapped most of his kebab back up in the tinfoil. He folded it with precision, in corners and triangles and then smoothed out the wrapping.

'How long do you want to go for?'

I shrugged. 'I don't know. A month or two. I'll see what it's like when I'm there.'

'It's not a safe place to be on your own. It's not like here. I'm not sure if a woman travelling alone is—'

'You've never been. You have no idea.'

'I just think there might be better options for you—'

'Look, if you were that concerned about me, you wouldn't be leaving me.'

Andy stared at my hands. I crushed my own kebab into the tinfoil until it looked like a punctured silver ball. Neither of us said anything. We watched the men continue to negotiate, their voices loud and energetic.

His posture sagged, and his hand reached out to scratch the inside of his arm. He started to get up.

'Where are you going?' I asked.

'Think I need some time to myself.' He grimaced. 'That okay?'

I nodded. We made plans to meet at a pub in the evening.

He slid his kebab into the bin and sauntered into the market. A tiny part of me felt sorry for him. He was worried about me going on my own. I wondered if he was nervous about London and the job. We hadn't spoken about that either. It was a big career move that came with high pressure, late hours and stress. He'd be leaving his friends and the whole life we'd set up in Edinburgh.

I lost sight of him in the crowds. He'd only been gone a few minutes, and I missed him already.

# 15

I was starting to wonder if Andy was lost when I saw him walk into the underground bar. I'd been checking my phone to see if I'd missed a call and wishing I'd listened to him back when we were preparing for the trip when he'd suggested we install a 'Find my Friends' App. I breathed out as I saw him ducking under the doorframe and hid my bitten cuticles under the table. I glanced at my phone again. He was only fifteen minutes late, but I felt jumpy. The beer I'd ordered for him was warm and flat. He caught my eye and smiled before strolling over. He stood out, probably as much as I did. People were wearing tight jeans and shirts. The girls wore hoop earrings and eyeliner, and the men had gel in their hair. Almost everyone had a cigarette. Andy and I wore our green khaki trousers, grey T-shirts and large walking boots. I noticed some people looking at Andy curiously. He was taller than most, with almost ginger hair rather than black. Instead of olive skin, he was pale except for his sunburnt nose.

He reached me, kissing me on my temple before reaching thirstily for his beer. 'Popular place.'

'How was your afternoon?' I asked.

Andy's jaw clenched before he lifted the glass to his lips and took a big sip. He slammed it down next to mine, and beer poured over the glass onto the table.

'I'm coming with you to Nepal.'

'What?' I looked at him, wide-eyed.

'I've spent the last hour in a meeting with my boss.' He shook his head. 'I'm not going to take the job.'

'But...no. No, Andy, that's not right.' I shook my head. 'Come on. Call him back. You want this. We're doing this. I'll only be away for a month, maybe two, and then I'll come to London with you.'

He nodded, looking at his beer. 'Yeah. I know you'll do it for me. So let me do this for you.'

I frowned. 'I still think you should take it. You might not get this chance again.'

He grimaced. 'I'm coming with you. I've already made up my mind.'

'No, wait. I don't want to feel like I've taken this promotion away from you.'

'I've already thought this through. And there are always going to be other jobs. There's not always going to be another you.'

'But you're not going to lose me.' I gripped his hand. 'I'm coming back.'

'Yeah, well, I'm not going to risk it.' He smiled. 'Female solo traveller sounds way too hot for my taste.'

I laughed and moved over to kiss him. 'Oh, Andy, thank you.' I kissed him again, holding his cheeks and pressing his face against mine. 'Thank you, thank you, thank you.'

# PART 2

# NEPAL

## 16

The rickshaw jerked through the narrow streets, headed towards Thamel. The pollution was thick and heavy. I spluttered and coughed as the smog drifted into my lungs and burned my eyes. I couldn't see more than five metres ahead, let alone the infamous Himalayas. Tar no longer existed, dirt roads adding to the dusty clouds enveloping the city.

Poverty lurked in every street corner, half-naked children playing with dogs outside broken-down buildings, plenty of damage still visible from the earthquake of 2015. None of it seemed to have been rebuilt. Litter lined the streets. Goats, cows and chickens were tied outside shops amongst the dead remains of others.

Had we taken the wrong turn? Where were all the quaint neighbourhoods and temples I'd shown Andy on my phone? I had visions of men painting mandalas outside their homes, women drinking chai in saris and children playing in the streets to the sound of pagoda bells.

The rickshaw spluttered into a labyrinth of alleyways and ejected us and our backpacks out.

'Thamel,' yelled the driver. He gestured at the maze of dirty alleyways and sped off.

We wandered dazedly through the streets, down narrow alleys, where there were glittering gold-topped pagodas and small shrines. Women, dressed in embroidered, silky saris, walked by prayer wheels, rolling each one in turn. I breathed relief. This was looking more like it.

Thamel was a backpackers' melting pot. Hikers who'd just finished Everest Base Camp hung out over a celebratory beer. There were gap-year groups coming from India who hung out in Irish pubs. Old vagabonds who'd been travelling for decades lived in corners of Kathmandu. Shop after shop sold harem trousers, embellished with elephants and paisley prints—the staple uniform for any traveller here; pirated hiking books; leather notebooks and all sorts of useless but colourful trinkets for a tenth of a pound. Pickpockets and street sellers swarmed through groups of backpackers. Dogs ran past to join up with their gang or hung expectantly around food stalls. Steaming dumplings filled with buffalo meat, known as *momos*, were sold everywhere.

A Canadian couple helpfully pointed us towards our accommodation. We arrived at Hostel Zostel, a ramshackle building turned into everything Western. There were blackboards with breakfast specials written in chalk: banana pancakes, vegetarian sausages and smoothies. The lounge had stacks of books ready to topple over. I saw that many of them were the same, mostly copies of *Into Thin Air* by Jack Krakauer and *Seven Years in Tibet* by Heinrich Harrer. If we were going to be hiking in the Himalayas, I wasn't sure I fancied reading either disastrous attempt.

The receptionist showed us around. It was still dorm rooms packed with bunk beds, but this time they had working lights in place and a cleaner balcony. Justin Bieber's voice echoed through the speakers. There were half-empty jars of Marmite and Skippy. There were empty packs of Marlborough Lights and American Spirit. Most encouragingly, there were English-speaking backpackers. It was the first time we'd seen other travellers since the Israelis, and these ones seemed slightly less intimidating. They were lounging on bean bags, reading and playing cards.

I quickly learnt there were two types of travellers in Nepalese hostels. One was the hippie, guitar strumming, stoned out nature lover. The other was the ultra-keen hiker, dressed head to toe in Berghaus gear, carbon fibre walking sticks tied onto their ultra-sonic, compressible-in-three-parts, North Face 6549 backpack. Andy and

I were a highly sceptical version of the first combined with a budget version of the second.

'This is great,' said Andy, grinning, as we followed the tour.

We checked in for a week.

~~~

I unpacked my bag in the usual fashion, checking for bed bugs and laying out my sleeping-bag liner. A guy lay awake on his bed at the back of the room. He mumbled hello to Andy and me. Another one came out of the shower. In fact, I realised there were many Westerners, ready to settle in for the day with their books, iPhones and guitars. I'd only seen one older man venture out to the streets below. I wondered if this was what backpackers meant when they said they'd enjoyed Kathmandu. It was easy enough to love it from the rooftop, sipping a lassi in the shade, listening to a ukulele version of Ed Sheeran and getting high.

There was a group on the balcony drinking beer and watching the smoggy sunset. Andy left his bag on his bed and quickly joined them while I stayed in the room unpacking.

I was desperate for the bathroom and stood up and walked across the room, pushing the door open. To my dismay, there was a hole in the ground and a bucket, but no light switch. I'd heard of these types of toilets but never seen one before. I closed the door, but it left me in complete darkness. I was holding my breath, taking tiny gasps through my barely open mouth. I closed my eyes, then opened them to a slit, trying hard to avoid the repulsive hole in the ground. There was no toilet roll or flush. How the hell was I meant to aim?

I grabbed my phone and lit my torch, only to see an enormous cockroach scuttle over my sandal.

Someone knocked on the door. 'Hey. Are you okay?' came a voice.

I pulled up my pants and pushed the door open.

A guy about my age looked at me, standing a couple of metres away from the door. He had light brown hair that was overgrown. A pendant dangled onto his Henley shirt, and I noticed mud stains on his jeans.

'First time using a squat toilet?' he asked with a thick New Zealand accent.

I sniffed.

'They're all like this in Nepal. This one isn't too bad. The worst one I ever had was in Laos.'

He was taller than me and stocky. His sleeves were rolled to his elbows, and his arms were dark with tanned golden hairs.

'I'm Tom.'

'Antonia,' I mumbled.

'Get back in there,' he gestured at the bathroom, walking towards it.

'What? No…'

'Are you going to hold in your piss for your entire trip?'

'I thought I'd just find a bathroom in a cafe or—'

'You won't find a normal toilet unless you fly back to where you came from.'

'Maybe—'

'Get back in there. I'm going to talk you through it.' He opened the door for me, waiting.

'I'm not going to pee in front of you.'

Tom laughed. 'As much as you think that will turn me on, I'm just going to explain what you need to do and leave you to it.'

I looked at him. He seemed well-intentioned. If I didn't act soon, my bladder would take over.

'Look, it's up to you. I'd just like to go back to chilling out without interruptions. I'll just put earplugs in when you start crying again—'

'Fine,' I mumbled, pushing past him. I closed the door and used my phone for light. How the hell would I do this when my period arrived? I tried to push that thought out of my mind.

Tom's voice wafted through. 'Put your feet on the foot holders next to the hole and squat as low as you can.'

Was this actually happening? Where the hell was Andy? A complete stranger was telling me how to pee.

'...the bucket next to you has water in it and a scoop. When you've done your business, scoop up the water and pour it down the hole. Scoop it up again and clean yourself up. And don't go overboard because there's nothing to dry yourself with.'

## 17

After the world's most self-conscious pee, I came out feeling triumphant.

As I unpacked, Tom sat on his bottom bunk, chatting away.

'I thought I heard a Scottish accent earlier,' he said.

'Yeah, that's Andy. He's outside having a drink.'

I asked Tom about himself. He was twenty-seven, from New Zealand, the South Island. He'd quit a job and had since been travelling for almost two years. He'd been to every country in Europe, nearly all of South America, half of Southeast Asia and plenty in between. He'd spent the last month travelling on a motorbike around Kyrgyzstan and had arrived in Kathmandu yesterday morning.

He then told me he'd lived in Santiago for six months.

I grinned. 'I'm Chilean!'

'What a coincidence, *weon*,' he replied.

I laughed at his use of Chilean slang.

'It was my favourite country,' he continued. 'I was only meant to go there for a week, but I ended up staying in Santiago and teaching English.'

We talked about the neighbourhoods he'd stayed in. He'd been to beaches and the mountains that were familiar to me, as well as farms in the south.

He looked at me curiously. 'I wouldn't have thought you were Chilean, just with your accent. I thought maybe Scottish, but...'

I shrugged, resisting the temptation to roll my eyes. Growing up, my frizzy hair and pale skin set me apart from my Chilean peers. Yet in Scotland, I didn't feel Scottish. My hybrid accent and untamed mannerisms made me a foreigner. I could barely understand the local Scots, and it dawned on me that my parents' accent must have become diluted throughout their years in Chile. I didn't know where I belonged. I felt like a damp piece of a jigsaw puzzle that had frayed at the sides and swollen in size.

'My parents are Scottish. I'm a half-Scot, half-Chilean. Or a half-nothing, depending what way you look at it.'

Tom laughed. 'I'd rather be a half-nothing and have no labels than hear another fucking joke about kiwis and sheep.' He put his book aside. It was thick, and the title read *Bhagavad Gita*. 'Everyone in Chile was warm. I used to be invited to someone's family barbecue every Sunday. I've seriously thought of going back to live there.'

I smiled at him. I felt a small pang of homesickness in the depths of my stomach as I envisioned Mum sipping hot milky tea by the pool and Dad humming old Gaelic songs as he barbecued some Chilean wagyu. I quickly changed the subject.

'Where else have you been?'

He'd travelled through Uruguay, the Galapagos, America and Egypt for months on end. He had no plan on stopping.

'How can you afford it all?' I asked.

He shrugged. 'You know, savings. And when I'm running out of money, I stay put and work.'

'What kind of work?'

'Oh, just anything that's offered. Bartending or teaching, mostly. Although I prefer the outdoor stuff. I was a scuba diver instructor in Thailand. That was fun—a lot of first aid training. And I did some farm work in Wyoming, which was fucking freezing.'

His life sounded so unpredictable. I wondered what that freedom felt like.

'What about you?' he asked. 'What brings you to Nepal?'

'The Himalayas, mainly. We want to hike The Annapurna Trail.'

'Oh really? Same here. Need to get the permits for it first. Some backpackers came back from there yesterday and were raving about it. They sent me some pictures.' He showed me his phone screen. 'Here, check it out.'

The walk looked breath-taking. There were photographs of emerald valleys with cascading waterfalls and low-hanging suspension bridges. There were pictures of waymarkers—red and white stripes painted on stones—unlike the lack of signposting in the Caucasus.

'Have you hiked before?' I asked him.

Tom nodded. 'Yeah, I actually hiked Machu Picchu not that long ago. It's got similar altitude conditions. It's the right time of year to do this trek too, any time between September and November, because the monsoon season is over and it's not too cold. As long as you take altitude pills to adjust and have the right gear, it's fine.'

He seemed to know what he was talking about, more than Andy and me, anyway.

'What if you're not used to the altitude?' I asked.

'The Annapurna circuit is one of the best hikes for adapting. You start in the lowlands and every day you get a bit higher. So when you reach the highest parts, you're already quite used to it.'

He stood up from his bed and walked over to his yellow backpack, where he put the book back inside. As he got back up, I noticed him flexing his arm and saw a hint of a tattoo on his shoulder, some of it covered by his rolled-up sleeve. I could see part of a symbol about thumb-sized, black, that looked like a cross, with at least two bars across it instead of one. I wondered if it was a masonic reference, not that I knew much about it, only what I'd read once in *The Da Vinci Code*. He caught me looking and I quickly averted my focus to his bag.

'When are you going?' I asked.

'Probably next week or so.' I side-glanced and saw that he'd rolled his sleeve back down, so the tattoo was out of sight. 'I'm going to explore Kathmandu for a few days.' He zipped up his bag. 'Coming for a drink?'

~~

We ordered some beers in the rooftop balcony which was shaded by low-hanging, colourful canvases undulating in the wind. Fairy lights were strung over railings and frayed mats covered the floor. We spotted Andy with a group of three other backpackers. They were the same ones that had finished the Annapurna Trail and were finishing telling Andy about it.

One of them dug his hands into his pockets and pulled out a map and a booklet of the trail. 'Here, you can have this.' He passed it over to Andy before heading back to the bar.

Andy pocketed it, and Tom and I took the backpackers' empty beanbags and the two of them shook hands.

'So where in Scotland are you from?' Tom asked Andy, sipping on his beer.

'I grew up in Edinburgh, which is where we live now.'

'Oh, awesome. I've heard amazing things about Edinburgh. I've always wanted to go. What's it like?'

'If you like crap weather, dingy pubs and darkness for six months of the year, it's the right place for you,' joked Andy.

Tom half-smiled. 'Then what keeps you there?'

'My job. Well, for now. But the city's tiny. It gets very boring after a while.'

That wasn't the impression I had of Edinburgh at all, and it irritated me to hear Andy say that. Edinburgh had been my home for the last seven years. We had special memories there. I'd lived in both Old Town and New Town. I'd made little homes on the way, leaving trails of books, herbs and spices and charity shop furniture behind. We'd danced in the streets of Leith and had a yelling match on Blackford Hill. I'd met his parents in the New Town. We'd spent Christmas walking up Arthur's Seat and Hogmanay on Princes Street. I thought back to my walk by the Water of Leith, the trees bare and frosty and the trails carpeted by red and orange foliage.

'What do you think about it?' asked Tom, his voice interrupting my thoughts.

I looked past Andy. 'I think it's one of the most beautiful cities in the world.'

~~~

Over more beers, and after Tom had briefed Andy on his own travels, the three of us pored over the Annapurna map Andy had acquired. We'd be hiking in the north of Nepal, bordering China, in the remote mountains.

He told us that the hike's starting point was a town called Besisahar, a day's journey on a rickety bus to the north-west of Nepal. From there, we would hike for a month. About three weeks into the hike, we would reach the Thorong La Pass, at 5,416 metres.

'You know that's higher than Everest Base Camp,' said Andy to me, looking at his phone. 'It says here that base camp is at 5,364 metres.'

I said nothing, my chest feeling a bit tighter. Surely if we'd done the Caucus Trail, we could do this. I turned back to Tom.

'You'll see world famous mountains on the way, some of the highest in the world, like Annapurna I, II and III.'

The thought of seeing the Himalayas up close gave me a rush of excitement.

There would be no medical help and few places for food, so we needed to stock up on supplies beforehand.

'There's a lot of hiking equipment in Thamel,' said Tom. 'Everything from hiking poles to boots and jackets. They're North Face rip-offs, but they do the job, and for a fraction of the price. Those guys told me about two stalls which sell decent kit.'

'Sounds great,' said Andy.

'You also have to apply for hiking permits. I think there's an office downtown. Costs about eighty dollars for each one. I'm going there this afternoon, you guys want to come?'

Andy glanced at me. 'Yeah, why not.'

'You been around Kathmandu yet?' he asked.

I shook my head.

'Right. Keep your valuables locked up here, don't wear anything fancy except for good shoes. It's mental out there.'

~~~

Tom had an international SIM card which gave him access to directions. He moved so quickly, I was terrified we'd lose him. It was over an hour's walk, battling through traffic and squeezing ourselves through alleyways. Traffic noise was deafening, buffaloes and cows abundant, hundreds of tuk-tuks, people yelling, babies crying, animals bleating, fruit sellers calling out and hundreds and hundreds of people. Swarms of dust made my throat clog, and sewage smells made my eyes water. Every single one of my senses was hyper-stimulated.

I glanced a few times down alleyways to see glimpses of red temples and glittering white pagodas. I saw painted eyes on top of golden bells and men walking without shoes, kneeling in prayer. A bald monk dressed in an orange robe looked down at his mobile phone as he walked past me, oblivious to the chaos.

Andy tried to grab my hand a few times, but we moved so quickly we kept losing our grip. I could hardly hear him amid all the noise.

He kept turning back to face me, his forehead dripping in sweat and dirt. 'Just follow me, hold on to my shirt if you have to.'

We crossed a bridge that looked to be made out of plastic bottles, milk cartons and cardboard. I peered over the side, expecting water, but instead saw what seemed like a mudflow.

At a closer glance, it looked like the debris had gathered down a slope and was somehow moving back up.

Andy glanced over at me and gripped my wrist. 'Close your eyes.'

'What—' I realised in horror that it was hundreds of black rats. My body shook in disgust.

'Come on,' he urged. 'Just keep walking, come on.'

I was walking so fast I was almost running in the heat and dust, stepping on rubbish, cow and animal waste. If I stopped focusing for a second, I risked losing sight of Andy and Tom, who were charging ahead.

My shock was quickly replaced by incredulity as we reached a square with an enormous wooden red temple. It looked familiar. Monkeys were jumping from steps to windows, cackling down at people.

'Durbar Square!' yelled Tom. 'One of the famous temples.'

I stared at the hundreds of prayer flags scattered around the temples like stars, fluttering like birds in the wind and noise. I recognised it now from the pictures I'd seen on blogposts and guidebooks. Except in pictures it had looked so peaceful. There was nothing still or calm about Kathmandu. Everything felt like it was in constant motion. I saw women in saris chasing after children who were trying to run up the temple stairs. A little boy ran his hand over a prayer wheel, laughing at the movement. A monk waved him away.

'Antonia, come on!' said Andy. I realised he and Tom were standing a few metres ahead of me, waiting. I must have stood still.

~~~

The permit office was small, hot and stuffy. We gathered in the corner closest to the door to feel some of the tepid air circulate and stood in a lengthy queue. We soon learned that anyone wanting to go on any kind of hike in Nepal had to get a permit. The line moved at a snail's pace and I flapped my passport in front of my face like a fan.

A couple of hours later, we reached the front desk. A small man surveyed the three of us.

'You need travel insurance, a guide, and a Sherpa to carry your bags,' instructed a high-pitched voice behind the desk. 'Please sign these forms and join the second line.' He pointed to the swarm of people behind him. 'Next!'

'I don't think we need any of these things,' said Tom, in a low voice. Andy agreed.

I gave him a look. 'If they say we need a guide—'

'Nah, they want money,' said Tom. 'They're just opportunists. It's not a legal requirement.'

'But how well signed is the trail?' I asked.

'Probably well enough,' Andy reasoned, 'and we have a map.' He held up his little booklet and grinned.

Tom laughed.

I was less impressed. 'Fine, what about a Sherpa?'

'That's definitely a scam,' laughed Andy. 'We're fit enough to carry our own bags.'

'Speak for yourself.' I touched my shoulders which were still scabbed from the last hike. 'And travel insurance? What if we have an accident?'

We all looked at each other.

'I've got a first aid kit,' said Tom.

Andy fought to suppress a smile.

~~~

Tom took the piece of paper and scribbled on it. I watched as he made up a number for our travel insurance and wrote down invented names for our Sherpas and guide.

He went back to the officer and handed it in.

The official took one glance at us and issued three stamps, and then stamped another paper which he passed over to us.

'Permit issued. You three travel together.'

'Oh, uh, no,' started Tom, 'We're not together, we—'

'Then you go to back of the first line and start again.' He pointed at the entrance.

'It's fine,' said Andy. 'We'll sort it out.'

We walked out of the office into the noisy street.

~~~

On the eve before the trail, the three of us shared beers on the roof of our shabby hostel. The balcony overlooked the dark streets of Kathmandu, growing marginally quieter by night. We'd filled our bags with winter gear for the weeks ahead: fleeces, gloves, thick socks and sleeping-bag liners, as well as sachets full of altitude sickness pills. I stocked up on sanitary pads in anticipation, having learned my lesson the hard way in the Caucasus. Tom had also convinced us not to take our tent and mats, stove and cooking supplies, removing an extra few pounds from our load.

The rooftops were so close together, I could hear families cooking, watching television and snoring. Out in the distance, beyond the hazy, dark smog from the city, stood Everest, Annapurna I, II and III, mountains that had taken the lives of so many explorers – and would continue to take them.

# 18

The heat of the lowlands was sticky and heavy. Even this early in the morning, the tropical air seemed to add another layer to the warmth. We moved sluggishly through the stifling marshes, our heavy backpacks weighing us down. We'd arrived here last night after a gruelling eight-hour bus ride from Kathmandu to Besisahar.

We'd read that the first day was twenty kilometres long. There was only one way to go, and that was up. I was pleasantly surprised by the trail's signage. There were arrows and markers every kilometre or so, and most of the paths and bridges were intact. Compared to the remote Caucasus, this hike seemed well-trodden and busy. In the Svaneti mountains, we'd hardly seen another person. Here, there were plenty of hikers, some going on day trips on different trails, and the hills were bustling with locals moving from village to village. I saw women in saris carrying wooden logs roped to their backs. Men led cattle and goats down the trail, and we'd have to leap out of the way to avoid getting trodden on. Children coming back from school skipped and zigzagged their way expertly up and down the trail.

Villagers were used to hikers and waved us on. We ran into some other walkers as we began. There was a couple from Australia, a few Canadians and a girl my age from Dublin. I'd taken a fancy to her: like me, she always seemed out of breath.

The day was long, humid and hot. During the infrequent times where I walked on flatter ground, I managed to take in my surroundings. There were rice fields, women tending to their crops and plantations, cows and goats roaming free, small wooden houses painted in bright colours tucked into the sides of the mountains, ubiquitous rivers and refreshing waterfalls. I did wonder if I'd appreciate the landscape a whole lot more if I'd been walking downhill.

As we fought our way up the hill, we each faced our own challenges. Tom's stomach was struggling to keep down the questionable curry from last night. With non-existent toilets, he was on the lookout for bushes. Andy had brought thick hiking trousers for warmth and was battling with them in the heat. I complained the most, fighting to keep up with them both. They sped on, chatting away, sitting at the top of the hill while they waited for me. The second I arrived, in pools of sweat and gasping for breath, they would bounce back up, rested and ready for the next hill.

After weeks of walking in the Caucasus, I could not understand how my body couldn't keep up. I'd dropped a clothes size, and I knew my legs were hard as nails, yet it was an effort to pull myself up the mountains.

As the sun started to set over our first day, we dragged ourselves to the nearest village. Tom and Andy negotiated with the locals and asked them for a space in their home. A man led us to a tiny mud and wooden built shack where the whole family lived in one room. We ate with the couple and their baby at a table. They stared at us in silence as we gobbled down fresh naan bread, hot spicy lentils and rice.

After dinner, we were taken to our room. It looked like an old shed. The floor was made of loose slabs of wood, with nails and jagged ends. Tom found a thick yak rug tucked into a corner and lay it over the floor. We placed our sleeping bags on top. I wearily noticed an increasing number of bugs crawling on the walls.

There was no option of a cold shower; instead we shared a bucket of recycled water. Andy realised there was soap left by past walkers, and he crumbled it into pieces for each of us to use.

We slept in a cramped space on the floor, our sides touching, drenched with accumulative sweat, but too exhausted to care.

I woke up to a yell. Tom was sitting up, his hands clutching his groin. 'There's a fucking rat on my crotch.'

Repulsed, but in fits of giggles, I struggled to fall back asleep. Andy snored loudly, but I could feel Tom twitching. After a while, he got up and fumbled for his shoes.

'Where are you going?' I whispered.

'Outside. Can't sleep.'

I lay there for another fifteen minutes before giving up.

~~~

I tiptoed outside. The garden was alive with crickets. It was humid, but a cool breeze shook the trees and shrubs around us. Tom sat on some steps with a book on his lap.

'Mind if I join?' I asked.

He moved and gestured at the space beside him. 'Sit here. The grass is soaking.' His eyes were bleary, and his hair ruffled from lack of sleep. I didn't want to imagine what I looked like. My curly hair was out of control in the humidity and sweat. I scooped it up into a bun as I sat next to him.

He pointed at my book. 'What are you reading?'

I glanced at the tattered book I'd picked up from the hostel in Kathmandu. '*Into Thin Air*.'

He gave a low whistle. 'Incredible story, right? Though the whole part of paying hundreds of dollars to climb Everest was a bit uninspiring. Mountains should be free to climb, at your own peril.'

'It's a good book,' I agreed. 'I just can't imagine anything worse than dying from hypothermia.'

'Yeah, I think the journalist got away with a couple of frostbite scars.'

I winced. In tonight's humidity with the bushes alive with insects, it was hard to think about how cold we might be in a few weeks' time. I resented the warm clothes we were hauling around and were taking up all the space in my backpack, like dead weight.

'What do you think of his other book, *Into the Wild*?'

'When I first read it, I loved it,' I said. 'I was obsessed with Eddie Vedder's voice in the film.'

'Weren't we all.'

'But now I think Christopher McCandless was just selfish.'

'Oh?' said Tom, raising an eyebrow.

'All he had to do was leave his parents a note to tell them he was on a forever adventure, and send them a postcard every once in a while. But he became so obsessed with his need to leave home and his passion to be on the road, he didn't think of the consequences. He ruined his family's life at the expense of his own dreams.'

Tom was quiet for a moment, thumbing the bind of his notebook. 'I'm not sure if he had a responsibility to make his family happy, especially if he'd grown up in an environment he didn't feel comfortable in.'

'Maybe not happy per se, but I think all parents deserve respect. Even if they're unsupportive of your dreams. It's not malicious, I don't think. I think they just want the best for you, and maybe that means something different to them.'

'Take it your folks didn't give you their blessing to come travelling then?'

'What?' I snapped out of my Christopher McCandless analysis. 'Oh. No. They didn't.' I glanced back at the dark shed. I hadn't exactly shared this with Andy. But it was easier to speak to someone I hardly knew.

'I thought my dad would be all over it. He used to travel all the time. But when I told him, he just freaked out about my career and gave me a whole lecture on savings and money and Andy...' I shook my head. 'Nah, he wasn't keen at all. My mum didn't say much. I think they pretty much realised I was going anyway, but kept saying I was making a huge mistake.'

'Ah, that sucks.'

'Yeah. I keep thinking something shit will happen and they'll be waiting with a big, fat, told you so.'

Tom laughed. 'Well maybe that's why it's easier not to stay in touch while you're travelling. Spare them the shit stories. Send them the glossy ones.'

I wondered if that was his tactic, but I didn't feel confident enough to ask.

'What are you reading, then?' I looked at him.

'It's a notebook,' he said, tapping on the cover and quickly flicking the pages with his thumb. I could see ink doodles and the occasional flash of colour.

'You sketch?' I asked.

Tom put it aside. 'Not really, it's a stupid thing I do when I can't sleep.'

'Is it about your travels?'

'It's nothing, honestly. I'm a bit of a nerd. I just sketch some stuff from books that I've read.'

'That sounds fun. What book are you reading now?'

'One called *The Songlines*. A guy who travels around Australia but with a spiritual twist. It's a bit slow, if I'm honest.'

'So you're working from that?'

He shook his head and tapped his sketchpad. 'Nah, it's more like old favourites, you know. Books I read when I was a kid. *Lord of the Rings, Indiana Jones, James Bond* stuff. And no, before you ask, I'm not into Comicon stuff. I just like the stories.'

'Well, I think that's awesome. Can I see some?'

He glanced at the sketchpad and then slowly tilted it over and flicked quickly through the pages. I noticed a heavily detailed drawing that covered most of the page.

'Wait, can I see that one?'

He stopped leafing through the pages, and I chose the one that had caught my eye.

He'd drawn a landscape with mountains, burrows and trails. There were hundreds of painstakingly small trees covering hillsides and a river in the foreground. Must have taken him weeks. A smudge of blue paint outlined a river. On the right-hand corner were some initials, followed by a symbol resembling a cross with a few bars.

'I messed that one up,' he said quickly, closing the pad.

'That's incredible.'

He shrugged. 'Helps me sleep at night.'

'What book was that from?'

'*The Hobbit*.' He gave a small laugh. 'I'm pretty basic.'

'I used to be obsessed with *Harry Potter*.'

He glanced at me sideways. 'Okay, you're even more basic.' The corners of his mouth turned upwards, and I laughed. 'Yeah, you won't find any kid wizards in there.'

'Your loss.'

He skimmed through the pages quickly to close the pad. More flashes of colour and ink, with the same signature initials and crosses in the corner. I wanted to see them in detail, but he closed the book.

'Do you always sign them?' I asked.

He laughed. 'Only when I'm really bored.' He put the notebook away. 'So, what made you want to travel?'

I digested the abrupt change of subject and let the question sit there a moment. 'They say Chile is the end of the world. It looks like it's falling off the map. On one side you get the ocean, and on the other we have the Andes. You can't even look at the sky for a view because it's mostly covered in thick smog. And I always felt like I would miss out on the rest of the world if I didn't leave.'

There was silence and I looked up to see Tom appeared amused.

'What?' I asked.

'Nothing,' he shook his head. 'It's just funny you say that. I used to feel the same way. The town I grew up in is at the end of New Zealand, near the Southern tip. I once read that it would take one strong earthquake to wipe out my entire town—' he snapped his finger, '—just like that. We'd be removed from the map.' He shuddered. 'I used to freak out about earthquakes when I was a kid. Normal kids go to sleep making sure they've got their favourite book or toy. I used to check every door frame and wall before going to sleep and had an earthquake survival box under my bed.'

I started to smile. 'But why did you come to Nepal then? It has earthquakes all the time. Did you bring the box with you?'

He snorted and sat forward, rolling down his sleeves. 'Wish I had. Could've used some of the soap.'

I laughed.

He picked up his notebook and started to get up. 'I'm less scared of earthquakes now that I'm no longer at the end of the world. I'd be happy if I died here. I'd feel like I at least existed.' He walked backwards a few steps towards the room but so that he was still facing me. 'Do you know what they call Nepal?'

I frowned. 'What?'

He took a few more steps back and grinned. It was a boyish grin, one that made his eyes smile and cheeks shine, as if he was about to get up to no good. He stretched out his arms, extended them fully and pointed towards the sky. 'The roof of the world.'

# 19

Next morning as we hiked, we came across a school. A group of kids were playing outside. I noticed that only some of them wore uniforms. Others wore ragged, loose tops or saris. Most were barefoot. As we came closer, they started to run towards us.

They fought for our attention, with not a word of English spoken. Some of them stared at us, frightened or in awe, but others ran up to us, asking for money and tugging at our bags. They had big grins on their faces, were of tiny stature, and burst into laughter when we said hello. Although I felt intimidated, I loved their presence. Andy saw the more cynical side to it.

'They just want money,' he muttered, looking self-conscious and uncomfortable.

There was a bit of that, but most of them seemed fascinated by us foreign hikers. A little girl touched my hand, tugged on my hair and talked fast and happily at me, not thinking for a moment I couldn't understand her.

After a quiet lunch of boiled noodles and chocolate, we set off for the afternoon, conversation dwindling. As the sun went down, we stopped to decide how much further we would walk. The villages were now close to each other, and as we stopped in one to evaluate our sleeping conditions, a fresh bunch of children ran towards us. As I talked to the kids, I realised my smile was now forced, and my patience was waning as I clutched on to my backpack. I pressed on, I could see Andy ahead of me, but glanced back to see where Tom was.

I first saw his yellow backpack on the floor and I stopped in my tracks. Tom was around the corner, crouching down, talking to the children. He reached for his bag and pulled out a packet of apple rings. He handed one out to each child, delighting them.

Tom caught my eye and grinned. 'It's the easiest way to handle these little rascals,' he said, ruffling a girl's hair.

I glanced back at Andy, but he was already gone, up ahead and lost in the woods.

~~

The evenings in the lowlands were long. We tried charades, had exciting rounds of twenty questions and played card games. I taught them *carioca*, a Chilean version of rummy, and Andy taught us Blackjack. My favourite nights were when we sat in silence outside. Andy read his book, Tom sketched and I wrote in my journal.

Tom introduced us to the local hash. There was a process of grinding and wrapping it up into tobacco papers. I tried it sometimes, but it gave me a headache and an early night.

Andy, however, took a liking for it. He eventually bought his own stash and took it out most evenings. Tom taught him repeatedly how to roll until, after a week or so, he'd got the hang of it and was doing it for the two of them.

Back home, Andy had always been interested in fitness and food. He'd trained himself into healthy habits. Aside from an occasional weekend of binge-drinking pints, he'd never touched cigarettes or drugs. It amused me watching him with glazed eyes, staring obliviously at the sky.

~~

The higher up we went, the more rugged the landscape became. I began to notice some local men carrying immense sacks of bags on their back, wearing little more than flip-flops and old shirts. As they drew closer, I saw the bags they were carrying looked brand new, branded Osprey and North Face. They were all tied up with ropes, each backpack stuffed to the brim.

My jaw dropped as I saw one of them hauling three forty-litre backpacks. Cords attached the bags to his forehead and he was doubled over as he continued to drag himself up the hill.

'What's that about?' I asked the boys, shocked. They looked equally confused.

About a half hour later, a group of ten young hikers, roughly our age, strolled up the hill carrying nothing but walking poles. They stared smugly at our bags, talking loudly as they strolled on with ease.

We stopped that evening at a purpose-built lodge for hikers. We sat huddled on wooden benches, next to the large group, while the light bulbs flickered in tune with the icy winds whooshing through the roof cracks. I still had my jacket and hat to combat the cold, and as I tucked in to the warm and spicy *dal baht*, I resented the unspoken rule of not asking for seconds.

I learned through their loud voices that these were the Sherpas we had heard about. Hikers paid for them to transport their heavy baggage throughout the whole trek. The Sherpas would walk ahead to their accommodation for the night so that when the hikers finally arrived, their bags would already be there. They were paid an equivalent of a dismal UK salary, which was a fortune for them in the rural mountains. Since hikers did not actually have to carry their bags, they would stuff them with more than they needed. I was astonished to see Sherpas dragging around hairdryers, stacks of books and feather pillows.

After dinner, Tom and Andy went to the fireplace where a few Sherpas had just arrived with the baggage. Tom gestured at the bags.

'Can we try those on? We want to see how much they weigh.'

One of the Sherpas grinned and passed the bags over. He was a petite boy in his late teens, about half the size and stature of Tom. By the looks of the grins on all the Sherpas faces, they'd obviously been asked this before.

Andy tried first. Purple veins protruded from his neck as he tried to pick the bag up from the ground. It didn't budge.

'Come on, can't be that bad,' said Tom. He leant over to grab it. It stood still.

The Sherpa laughed at their scrunched, red faces, then the petite boy stood up to lift it.

## 20

We were clocking in over thirty kilometres a day now. Used to each other, tired of each other, but having to push on, we walked in a military line, often keeping conversations to a minimum. Every couple of hours, we'd reconvene in a huddle to discuss logistics.

Now that I was picking up speed, the dynamics were shifting. Earlier it had been Andy and Tom upfront. Now I moved between the two of them, Tom upfront, Andy at the back. With Tom's yellow backpack, Andy's green one and my red one, we must have looked like a moving traffic light zigzagging our way around the mountain.

I preferred to chat with Tom in the mornings. My brain was more switched on, and we could share thoughts on the books we'd exchanged with each other. He ran me through the principles of mindfulness, teaching me about breathing, organising thoughts and trying to focus only on the present. He asked if I could speak to him in Spanish, so he could practise the language. He laughed at the Chilean slang and compared it with the dialect he'd learnt in Colombia.

When I grew testy, which was usually before lunch, his teasing would start to annoy me, and I'd slow down my pace. After lunch, tired and drowsy, I'd trail back down to Andy. I could just be myself around him. Sometimes we chatted non-stop about our Fitbit records, the books we were reading, the hike here compared to the Caucasus, or what we'd be doing if we were back home. Other times we walked in comfortable silence. I liked slipping my hand into his.

~~~

One morning, as we climbed around the mountain, the views became particularly scenic. I could see frozen waterfalls, suspension bridges and yaks grazing against the backdrop of the glistening snow. A third suspension bridge led us to a gravelly hill. I focused on each step, making sure not to trip, when a sudden wave of nausea overtook me. I stopped where I was, my feet unbalanced, as if I was riding a wave, and threw up on the ground.

'Are you okay?' I heard Andy's voice.

I glanced up and saw him coming back down. Tom was too far ahead. I could just about make out his yellow backpack turning around a corner.

'I'm also starting to feel the altitude,' said Andy, wiping sweat off his brow.

I breathed in fresh air, feeling better after vomiting, but held onto a rock. 'My period is late.'

Andy stared at me. 'What?'

'I think it is. I mean I can't tell for sure because I haven't been tracking it, but I think it was due a few days ago.'

'Are you…do you think…did we…'

'I don't know. The last time was in Kathmandu. It's been a couple of weeks, so the dates could match up.'

'But surely the pill would work.'

'I don't know if I've taken them every day.' I held the back of my neck. 'It's not exactly been a priority when we're setting up camp or waking up at five in the morning.' I curled my fist up into a ball and tapped it against the rock. 'Shit, shit, shit.'

He twisted his way out of his backpack and set it down. 'Come, take your bag off. Just sit down for a bit.'

I let him lift the bag off my shoulders and we leant against the rock. We could see the snowy peaks fading into the distance. Prayer flags littered some of the villages below, a blur of colour in the constant wind. Brown tracks showed the path we had followed so far and the way that we'd follow tomorrow, which disappeared even higher into the white mountains.

He planted a kiss on my head and I gave him a side-glance, only to see him smiling.

'It's kind of exciting,' he said.

'Seriously?' I pulled away. 'Andy we're not ready. I'm not ready.'

'We're never going to be ready.'

'Stop, I'm not even going to entertain this. I'm just a bit late, that's all we know.'

I heard him sigh, and I swallowed back my frustration. The silence felt heavy and emphasised by the fact that there was stillness all around us. My eyes flickered to the trail we'd been on, and I looked to see if there were any other hikers, but all I could see was a lone yak in the distance.

Andy shifted and broke the silence. 'When are you thinking we should go back?'

'Where? To Edinburgh?'

Andy gave a nod.

My chest felt tight. 'Do we really need to talk about that now? We're in the middle of the Himalayas?'

'I'd like to, yes. What are you thinking? For our next plans?'

I sighed. 'I don't know. It's, what, November now? I thought we could go to India after this.'

'You mean if we're...if you're not...'

'Yes,' I said hastily.

'Okay, so we spend a few weeks in India. What about after that?'

'I don't know yet. But I want to keep travelling.'

'So, give me an estimate return date.'

'Maybe next summer?'

Andy's eyes widened. 'That's a while away. I was thinking a couple more months.'

This was irritating me. 'Why? What's the huge rush?'

He shrugged. 'I don't know. This is fun, but it's all sort of an escape. I feel like our lives can properly start when we get back.'

'But our lives have started. We're living more on this trip than most people do in a lifetime stuck at the office.'

'I'm not just referring to my job.'

I frowned. 'What do you mean then? The wedding? Because I don't think we can put in a date just yet.'

'I was actually meaning starting a family. We could see what happens.'

I stared at him. 'Andy, I'm not pregnant. I'm just late.'

'You don't know that. But even if you aren't pregnant now, maybe we could think about it.'

I gave a half laugh.

'Just hear me out. It's not like we're going to have a crying baby in our arms tomorrow. Maybe you could stop the pill, and we can start the process. It can take a while. I've just been thinking it might give you a different purpose when we go back, rather than having to job hunt all over again.'

I swallowed. We'd discussed having children a year or so ago. We both wanted them, but it felt so much easier to say that when it was still so far away.

'Look, I can deal without having a wedding the minute we get back,' said Andy, 'and if you want to postpone the wedding for a few years, I can also come around to that. But I don't want a wedding to be in the way of us moving on with our lives.'

I looked at the view of the mountains. I could see tiny hamlets tucked within blankets of forests. I wondered if I could bring my future children up these mountains. That was the kind of life I wanted for them, full of travel and outdoor adventures.

I slowly nodded. 'I think I need to figure out what my own purpose is before trying for a baby.'

Andy grimaced, and I noticed something twitch in his jaw. 'I thought *this* was your purpose.' He gestured around. 'Aren't we doing this so that you can get it out of your system?'

I inhaled. 'Well, yeah, but it's not the only dream I'm ever going to have. When we get back, I'm going to find new ones.'

'I think...' Andy shook his head. 'It doesn't matter.'

'What? Tell me.'

'I think you have no idea what you want. It's like nothing ever satisfies you. You're always looking for the next best thing. It's exhausting. What are you waiting for, Antonia? When *is* a good time to get married? When *is* a good time to start trying for kids?'

'I don't know,' I raised my voice, 'but this is not helping.' I grabbed my backpack off the ground and put it on my back, clipping it around my waist.

'Is it about your family?' asked Andy, his tone softer. 'Are you having second thoughts about settling down so far away from them? Because we can talk about that—'

'Look, can we talk about this another time?'

'That's not fair.' He was standing still, his arms crossed over his chest. 'I'm allowed to ask. You're my fiancée. We need to discuss these things. And you seem to get a panic attack or run away every time we do. It makes me wonder if you're really invested in this.'

I stopped at that. He was right; this was running away. I faced him again.

'Yeah. Okay fine. This chat freaks me out. But it's not because of you—it's because of me. I have no idea what kind of job I want, where I want to live, or when we should get married. But I want you. I know that. So, I just need you to help me answer these questions, because I'm too scared to.'

'Okay,' said Andy, breathing out. He gave a soft laugh. 'Okay. Thank you. That's the most you've ever spoken about it. Yes, I'll help you.'

I nodded.

'I think you should take a pregnancy test as soon as we find a pharmacy.'

'Yup.'

'And I think we should get married when we get back to Scotland. We'll give your family some notice. We can do something small, like you wanted, just our families, in Edinburgh. You've always wanted them to come over. We can book a chapel, and we can have a nice meal after that.'

'Yeah. Okay. That sounds good.'

'You can wear any colour you want, and you don't have to look like a cupcake.'

I winced.

'And I think we could maybe start trying for a baby when we get back. You can still look for a job, and if it happens sooner,' he glanced at my stomach, 'it happens.'

We started to walk back up the hill. As I followed Andy, I looked down at the little diamonds sparkling on my ring and turned it around my finger. It felt slightly looser up in the mountains because of the cold. I'd shoved another silver ring I bought in Thamel in front of it to make sure it didn't slip off.

I thought back to the day Andy had proposed. I was twenty-five and we'd spent a holiday in Chile with my family. He'd been in awe at the haze of languages and cultures erupting from my childhood home. He'd come in time for the Chilean national holiday, nicknamed the *dieciocho*, which my parents liked celebrating alongside Burns' Night. Fried pastries, mainly *empanadas* and *sopaipillas*, were served up with *pisco sours*, alongside haggis, neeps and tatties. Dad began the lunch reciting a broken verse from Rabbie Burns, insisting that Andy join him by wearing a kilt in the thirty degrees heat.

After seeing them, we'd taken the car to a beach up north, a place called Cachagua. We were on the coastal trail that twisted through rock pools. Andy walked behind me while I chatted to him about childhood memories and showed him an island inhabited by penguins.

As we sat on the sand getting sprayed by the waves, he handed me a black velvet box. I'd sensed it coming, even seen the box back home, but the moment had still caused us both unexpected emotions. Andy, who I'd never seen cry, wiped his eyes and hardly managed a sentence. I cried into his shoulder, and then we laughed and cried some more and covered each other in kisses and tears. I couldn't believe how happy he made me; how lucky we'd been to find each other. Andy was safe. Having felt rootless for so long, I now had someone who felt like home.

I still felt all those blissful feelings when I thought of the proposal, but they didn't seem to transfer to the thought of a wedding. Why was I so afraid of it? Maybe signing the paper that made me Andy's wife felt like I was giving up my freedom. Becoming his wife and then mother to his children, felt like I was ticking all of *his* boxes. But what about mine? I probably would never be able to travel this freely again or use my savings to fly home spontaneously. Those savings would now have to go towards a deposit for a house and children. And I'd need to find a financially secure job. I didn't want to depend on Andy. The thought of going back to a cramped office all day made me depressed. If we went back to our old routine, Andy would hardly be home. Even less so if he eventually got his promotion. I could only imagine how lonely the days and long evenings would feel with a baby.

I didn't want these thoughts ruining our travels. So I kept on walking.

## 21

As the trail gradually rose to higher altitudes, we started leaving the green rice plantations, colourful houses and waterfalls behind. We were now faced with a more alpine landscape which occasionally opened up into expansive miles of unsheltered land and rubble. The teahouses looked like mountain huts, made out of brightly painted wooden planks, balanced on towering stilts which were wedged between rocks.

One morning we walked through tundra; the endless flat wasteland opened up ahead of us, no end in sight. It felt like we were rooted in a bowl of dust, winds blowing us in all directions. The gusts were unforgiving and vicious, dust blew steadily into our faces. We trudged on, our buffs around our faces, the plastic of our cheap market sunglasses rattling, still feeling the constant gravel piercing our cheeks. The wind was so strong, we couldn't hear each other from metres away. Tom went up ahead while Andy stayed closer to me.

Hours later, the gravelled tundra gave way to a frozen valley. Tom stopped ahead, and as soon as we could hear him, he pointed towards a narrow track. 'There's a goat trail that way,' said Tom, gesturing at a narrow path up the side of the mountain. 'It's off-piste, but it will take us out of the wind.'

We followed him, the wind relentless. When we reached the valley and its trees that offered us shelter, the wind ceased. My ears were ringing, and my head was thumping.

We were all tired now, but there was no village in sight. Tom walked fast, determined to escape these conditions, and we lost sight of him. Andy slowed down, occasionally looking over his shoulder at me.

The goat track was narrow. As we followed it higher and higher, into the mountainside, it became dangerously thin. No more than one foot fitted into it at a time. I realised I would have to walk sideways to keep my balance. As I repositioned myself, I cast my eyes down and noticed how high up we were. The tundra lay a couple of hundred metres below us, with hostile-looking shrubs being the only thing that might save a fall.

I could hear Andy calling out for Tom. 'Hey!' he called out, 'where are you? Does the trail get any wider?'

I slowly side-stepped the track, trying not to look down for almost half a kilometre, until I realised that up ahead there was a crevasse dividing the valley. The only way to continue would be by grabbing on to a shrub and having to take a sizeable calculated step. I drew closer, breaking into a sweat, but saw Andy on the other side, waiting for me.

'It's okay,' he said. 'Take your bag off and pass it over. It will be easier without it.'

I did as he said and hauled the bag over and he placed it precariously on the cliff edge. He stepped closer to the side, instructing me on my footing as I tried to contain my panic. I grabbed his arms as he helped me over.

'There.' He let go of my arm. 'Well done.'

I crouched as I put my backpack on. One bad step and everything would go terribly wrong.

'Where's this path even leading to?' I asked.

'I don't know.' He was looking up through the thick shrubs and trees. 'Tom said it could take us to a road, but I don't think that's looking likely.'

A few steps later and we were facing the same challenge, except the crevasse was wider. I was going to have to jump.

'Oh no…'

'Let's do it the same way again. Just be really careful.'

As confident as he sounded, I could see the frown on his forehead and the constant glances up ahead, hoping for a glimpse of Tom.

I started to prepare for the jump.

Andy put his hand out. 'No, wait, stop. This is a stupid idea. It's way too dangerous.' He was studying the crevasse, walking to the edge and looking at the other side. 'Stay here. I'll see if I can find him.'

He took his backpack off, leaving it with me, and I watched, terrified, as he made the jump over. The impact of his feet landing on the other side set stones flying down the cliff. Pumped with adrenalin at having landed on both feet, he gave a nervous laugh.

I could hear him calling out for Tom, as I perched on the thin trail clutching both bags. About twenty minutes later, both of them came back.

Andy readied himself for the jump back to me, and I moved backwards to give him space. Loose gravel sprayed my trousers as he landed.

'Gets worse higher up,' said Andy. 'More big jumps and the trail ends. The only way to a road is straight through the shrubs. It's too risky.'

'Yeah, but I saw the road at the top,' said Tom. He stayed where he was, on the other side of the cliff, ready to continue. 'It's a bit of a climb, but it'll get us there.'

'There's no way,' snapped Andy. 'Look at where we are. Antonia can't do it.'

'Well, we don't have a choice,' said Tom.

'It's okay, Andy,' I said quickly. 'I'll try.'

'No,' he shook his head. 'Let's turn back.'

'That's going to take us hours,' said Tom. 'Honestly, it's just a few more jumps and we're on the road, with no wind. It's a massive shortcut. You really want to go back through that windstorm?' He was looking at me.

I looked from him to Andy. I could do the jumps. I just needed to concentrate on my exact footing.

Andy grabbed his backpack in silence and looked at me. 'I'm going back down. I'd like it if you came with me.' He clipped on his backpack.

'It's just a couple of big jumps,' I said. 'Come on, it's not worth going all the way back.'

'She's right,' said Tom.

Andy moved past me. 'You guys do as you please. I'd rather not die on a goat track.' I watched him as he started to climb his way down, his green backpack crunching the shrubs behind him. Was he really just leaving?

'Well, come on then,' said Tom, gesturing. 'We'll meet up with him this evening.' That one's an easy jump.' He pointed at the gap between us. 'It's much easier than it looks. Just don't overthink it. You got it, right?'

'Yeah,' I mumbled.

'Come on, let's get going.' He started walking. 'There's a pretty cool view from up top.'

I looked over my shoulder. Andy's backpack had disappeared. I felt my chest tightening. How dare he leave me on my own? I slowly took a step forward. Tom was moving through the track. If he moved any faster, I'd lose track of him too. I broke into a sweat. How the hell was I going to do this on my own? I walked towards the edge. I could no longer seen Tom. Pebbles fell kilometres through the dark abyss. I could just about make the jump, but what if I didn't go high enough? What if my backpack weight stopped me?

I took my bag off. It wobbled and tilted towards the edge, so I turned it over, so that the weight would lean towards the rock. I looked back at the empty trail and then at the path resuming after the crevasse. Without the bag I could easily jump it. It was just getting it over. What if I threw the pack over first? I went back for it, lifting it with both hands, and walked back. Something clamped the top of my boot and I flew face forward, my bag saving my nose from smashing against the ground.

'Fuck's sake.' I pushed my bag aside and saw that my foot had become tangled in a tree root and I strained to pull it back out, untying my laces as I did. I knelt forward to do them up again, and as I did I knocked my bag with my elbow. It began to topple at the edge of the cliff. 'Shit, no, no, no,' I reached for it, but it was too late. It tipped over and I watched in horror as it plummeted down the cliff.

'No!' I yelled. 'No! Fuck! No!'

'What the hell are you doing?' I heard Andy panting as he climbed back up the trail towards me.

'My bag! My bag!' I pointed at the cliff edge, covered in shrubs and trees, no sign of a red smattering. 'It's gone!'

'Fuck, Antonia. Seriously? What the hell did you think was going happen?' He walked by the edge, peering over the shrubs, trees and bushes, shaking his head and swearing.

'It's fine, it's going to be fine,' I muttered, trying to calm my breathing. 'Dammit!'

'What have you got in there that's important?' he asked.

'Everything!'

'Okay, you've got your passport, visa, some money, debit cards—'

'My phone, journals, all my clothes—'

'Shit,' he muttered. 'This wouldn't have happened if you had listened to me—'

'Or if you hadn't played it safe and left! You could have helped me with my bag.'

'Helped you be an idiot, you mean? And maybe we could have both lost our fucking bags.'

'Oh, shut up, what am I going to do—'

'Don't,' said Andy, turning on me, his jaw clenched. 'You don't get to freak out this time. This is on you. So get over yourself and follow me the fuck down.'

My stomach felt cold and I could feel the wave of nausea hovering again. But I'd rarely heard Andy sound so furious, so didn't say anything. I started to follow him downhill. I wondered where Tom was, and when he would realise we'd turned back. My ankle felt bruised from where I'd pulled it out of the root. I swore inwardly to myself. How could I have been that stupid? What was I going to do without my bag? It had everything I needed.

'You're so selfish,' I could hear Andy muttering. 'You should've listened to me. Or just had some common sense. Now the whole trip's ruined. We're going to have to go back to Kathmandu, and fly back to the UK.'

'Your dream's come true then,' I mumbled.

He stopped in his tracks and turned around. His eyes were wide. 'Are you serious?' His words felt still and piercing. I took a step back, feeling uneasy.

He said nothing after that. Neither did I. We kept walking, heads down. I wiped my face a couple of times, when I was sure he wasn't looking. I wasn't used to walking without a backpack, and I felt unbalanced. Were we really going to have to fly back home? Had I ended our whole trip? I was close to hating myself.

~~~

Our detour added at least another hour to our trek, but we found the original trail and this time stuck to it. The winds had calmed down and I could just about hear Andy's footsteps ahead. Despite having no load on me, I walked well behind him, looking at my shoes. I was so determined not to look up, that after some time, I almost crashed into him.

'Hey.' His voice sounded calmer, and his swollen jaw was softened by a tight smile. I gave a tighter one back. 'We'll fix this, okay? Let's just find somewhere to stay tonight, and we'll figure things out.'

I nodded. 'I'm sorry,' I said quietly.

Andy started walking again. He tightened his backpack straps. 'You need to know your limits, Antonia. You need to know when enough is enough. And enough is when there's a huge crevasse in a mountain that you expect me to watch you jump.' He shook his head. 'Just thank the universe only your backpack went over that edge.'

~~~

With only the moonlight to guide us, we reached a tiny hamlet, distinguished by a few dim lights in a window. As we came closer, I noticed it was the only house that was lit.

A woman emerged from her makeshift house. Two cows followed her out onto the road. She pulled her woollen scarf around her shoulders.

'Can we stay here?' asked Andy.

'Money,' she said.

It must have been 9 p.m., and now the cows were busy mooing, waking up the other hamlets around her.

'We'll pay,' he said.

She led us into her home, where she made up a room for us by laying woven mats onto the floor. There was a squat toilet in a room off the side. We laid Andy's sleeping bag out and cleaned up while she prepared us a meal. In the bathroom, I scrubbed my face and armpits with the small dribble of water that reluctantly left the tap. I wriggled out of my trousers and grabbed some shorts that Andy had lent me to change into. As I pulled them off, I noticed a blood stain on the seat and gave a cry of relief.

'Andy?' I yelled out. 'We're not pregnant.'

~~~

The two of us sat in silence as we hungrily slurped our broth in the woman's kitchen. There was a loaf of bread so stale it was hard, but we were too hungry to care. Andy tore some bits off and I chewed on it until it was soft enough to swallow. The woman came through again, holding one more bowl of broth and propping it in front of me. I thought she was going to join us for supper, but I heard her speaking to someone outside the door. I looked up, and saw Tom walk through.

'Oh hey y'all,' he grinned.

'How did you get here?' asked Andy, his mouth still full.

He made a point of rolling his eyes. 'You were right, the crevasses became too wide to jump. I didn't go much further up to be honest. I got stuck going up, so turned back. I thought I could hear you guys further down. Once I found the trail it took me a few hours. Thank fuck that wind calmed down, made it a lot easier to walk. This was the first place I found with the lights on. Food any good?'

'If you're hungry,' I said.

'Famished.' He started eating the soup and Andy tossed him the last bit of stale bread that sounded hard as it landed. He eyed my bread. 'You should give me yours too,' said Tom, 'seeing as I carried your backpack the whole way here.'

I opened my mouth. 'You what?'

He started to smile, his mouth full, and took a moment to swallow. 'Saw it between some shrubs as I was coming down. Hard to miss an enormous red backpack. Pretty fucking happy to see you both, to be honest. I thought something might have happened.'

'You've got my backpack? You've been chatting to us this whole time and you're only telling me now?' I scrambled to my feet and started running up to the room.

'Take it I'm eating the rest of yours then?'

~~~

With better moods, fuller stomachs and warmer toes, we wandered out into a cramped veranda covered in boxes and baskets and sat amongst them. The air was crisp and frosty, but we sat in our jackets and hats, looking out at the silver mountains lit up by the moon.

'I can't believe you carried both backpacks,' I said, laughing.

'Yeah. You owe me.' Tom started rolling joints. Andy lit one up almost immediately, not saying anything.

My legs were cramping. We worked out that we'd walked thirty-one kilometres, an impressive feat considering most of it was uphill. As we chatted about the distances for the next day, I noticed Andy's chat was still short and monotonous.

'Hey,' I said, squeezing his hand. 'I'm sorry about today. We won't go up a goat trail again.' The ends of my mouth threatened to go up, but his stayed put.

'I'll just say one more thing,' muttered Andy. 'I do think you guys need to have more awareness about you. You're not fucking invincible and I, for one, do not have a death wish.'

'Okay, fine,' I said quickly. 'You've made your point.'

Andy glared at the view, a frown settling in between his eyebrows.

I glanced at Tom, who grimaced at me and gave a small shrug.

'No worries, mate,' said Tom. 'Promise we'll stick to the path tomorrow.'

'Whatever,' he muttered.

We were silent for a while, and then I tried again. 'Andy, come on. We're over it. Let's move on, or tell us what's going on.' I wasn't used to being the rational one and I realised I was waiting for Andy to snap back at me. Instead, he looked at us.

'Fine,' he agreed. 'Last night, after dinner, I heard the Sherpas talking to another hiker. They told him that this time last year there was a snowstorm.'

Tom and I stared at him.

'It wasn't predicted, and it caused avalanches. It killed a whole lot of hikers like us, doing exactly what we're doing now.'

Silence. I could tell on the look on Tom's face that he was only learning about this now too. The end of the joint fizzled.

Andy shrugged. 'I don't know, it just…got to me.' He looked away. 'Could be us, you know? These were young guys and girls, amateur hikers. They were from Israel, Germany, New Zealand, even the UK. The stories were…horrible. Watching their friends die. People trapped for days, buried alive, slowly freezing to death, panicking…'

I wondered why he hadn't told me this until now. It must have been weighing on his mind the whole time.

'I…I had no idea.' My voice interrupted the silence like static. 'How many died?'

'Over forty. They keep finding bodies. I think a lot of them went missing.'

Tom inhaled some more of the joint and then cleared his throat. 'It must have been a hell of a mess. I can't imagine the search and rescue teams being quick here. And by the time a helicopter comes, they can only fit a few people inside…' His voice trailed off.

I took a deep breath and took the joint from Tom. It was too awful to think about. I couldn't remember reading about it on the news, and I was surprised we were only finding out about it now. No one at the permit office had mentioned it either.

Around us the mountains looked still, the air peaceful, the moon bright. There seemed no sign of immediate danger. But then again, these hikers had probably thought the same thing.

I glanced at Andy, his eyes were glazed over, and his face was sunburned. His beard was the bushiest I'd ever seen. The sun had turned it auburn. It was wild and shaggy, disappearing into his mane of ungroomed hair. It was a stark contrast to his past work appearance, where he'd have a clean shave every morning and smooth it over with sharp smelling creams and aftershave. His usually defined jawline was hidden, making his face look warmer and approachable.

I squeezed his fingers through my glove. 'Thanks for looking out for me.'

## 22

We were walking at almost 3,000 metres, Annapurna II in full view. The landscape was spectacular, but the altitude was starting to affect me. I got more and more out of breath and kept having to stop to catch it back. A few times, we saw people walking the opposite way, back down the trail. The boys seemed more subdued. Whether it was the altitude symptoms starting to get to him, or because of the discussion we'd had about the goat trail, Tom seemed a little less headstrong and set a more reasonable pace.

One day, just after we'd stopped for a break by a frozen waterfall, I saw a girl from Dublin I recognised from when we began. She was walking the other way, towards us. I thought she was wiping the sweat off her face. As she came closer, I realised she was rubbing her eyes. She stopped as she reached us.

'The altitude is too much. I feel sick. My headaches won't stop. It's still another 2,500 metres. It's not worth the risk,' she explained. 'I'll come back again one day when I'm fitter.'

I watched her, slightly envious of the downhill she faced, and wondered if she ever would come back.

I trailed on more cautiously, and in the next few days, I saw more people turn back. Altitude didn't discriminate. There was an experienced Austrian hiker who lived in the Alps and a forty-year-old American who'd walked most of the Appalachian Trail. Each of them had altitude symptoms, and none of them thought that pressing on was worth it. With each person turning back, my pace became slower, my mind desperately analysing every single bodily symptom.

~~~

The air was thinner, and to say the nights were cold was an understatement. I wrapped myself in everything I owned: thermal tights, leggings, snow trousers, gloves, all my socks, scarves and hat. I then crawled into my sleeping bag, tucking it around me tightly.

Where shower facilities had previously been a bucket of water, these were now a bucket with large ice chunks. Already struggling to cope with the freezing temperatures of minus ten degrees, the last thing anyone felt like doing was washing their armpits. The only cleanliness habit that I could stand was brushing my teeth by melting some ice. On the plus side, my towel was unused and dry, and I'd wrap it around my face to protect my nose against the cold.

~~~

One night, we stayed in a wooden mountain lodge, a large communal room where we all slept on mats. A small fire hidden by a grate was the only heat source for the icy cold room. I woke to go to the bathroom. It took a good ten minutes to get out of the sleeping bag with all the layers that I'd meticulously laid on. I fumbled through the dark, careful not to step on anyone.

The air outside was frozen, but there was a surreal aspect to being in the middle of the Himalayas. The enormous mountains were outlined underneath the enveloping sky, the vast moon as bright and big as I'd ever seen it. The silence was eerie and infinite.

I spluttered as the icy wind pierced my lungs and burnt my eyes that watered and caused me to blink out solid ice tears. The jagged ends clung to my eyelashes and painfully grazed my retinas. Scared of slipping on black ice, I crawled to the toilet, a thick ice glaze over everything. It was too cold to remove my two layers of gloves.

I stood outside for an extra few minutes, each breath fiery and raspy, marvelling at where I was and the grandness and stillness of it all. Tucked up, deep in the mountain, the roof of the world, with gigantic peaks around me, snow-caps gleaming in the moonlight, I thought about how many people these very mountains had buried. I wondered how many souls were resting here, and if it had all been worth it just to feel the unquestioning significance of nature over man.

## 23

The higher we went, the shorter the distances we travelled. We were now aiming to achieve altitude rather than distance and the tracks were steep and torturous on the calves. We decided we'd take an afternoon to recover. We reached the village of Chame just after lunchtime—a pleasant change to our usual late arrivals—and indulged in some time off. Andy was desperate for a shower and a nap, but Tom and I stayed outside. We sat on plastic chairs on a wooden veranda overlooking the carpet of thick forests we'd be walking through tomorrow.

The village looked straight out of a fairy-tale. Narrow street alleys snaked around stone houses with neatly piled stacks of firewood amongst young Buddhist monks in their orange robes.

Two French hikers were staying in our same hamlet. They were in their early forties, with more expensive equipment on their feet than we had in our three backpacks. They joined us on the patio outside.

I was sipping on water but watched as the Frenchmen took out their high-tech stoves and started brewing up some powdered Nespresso, which they offered to us. The smell reminded me of the Georgian and Armenian countryside. Over a warm cup of coffee, we started to chat.

'It must be tough carrying all that equipment,' I sympathised.

One of them chuckled. 'We've got two Sherpas and a guide. It would be impossible to do this without them.'

'We're just taking our own bags,' said Tom, 'although we didn't bring too much stuff.'

They looked at him, surprised. 'With no Sherpa? Why?' One of them started laughing. 'You must be going very slow.'

'It's too expensive,' I said, trying to hide my irritation. 'Plus, we don't really need it. We're not pressed for time.'

One of them shook his head. 'It's not expensive. Nepali prices compared to the European ones, pfff,' he scoffed. 'We're paying eighty dollars a night, and that includes pre-booked accommodation.'

I raised my eyebrows. 'What do you mean? The accommodation on the Annapurna is free. You just need to pay a donation each time.' I could feel Tom nudging me under the table but thought nothing of it.

One of them frowned at me. 'How much are you paying for this one?'

'Antonia...' said Tom.

I ignored him. 'It depends on us normally. We leave them a couple of dollars each when we leave.'

'But how did you book it?'

'We didn't. We just show up each night and ask.'

I looked over at Tom, but he shook his head at me, a look of warning on his face.

'I think you're wrong, girl. We were told it's eighty dollars per person a night for everyone.'

'I don't think—'

'Hey,' snapped Tom. His hand clutched my arm. He looked at the angry men. 'We're on different trips. Your one probably includes things ours don't.'

But the men had already realised they were being ripped off. They were talking to each other in French, their tone loud and angry. Presumably, they couldn't believe they'd let the locals get away with it for this long. They yelled angrily to each other before storming off to find their guide.

'Come on, let's go for a walk,' muttered Tom. 'I don't want them back here with their angry guide.'

I pulled out my camera, and we went to explore the village. The homes were made mostly out of stone. Women carried wicker baskets overladen with groceries back to their homes. The smell of firewood wafted through the town as the early evening home routines began taking place. We walked and talked, wandering around the monastery, watching the young Buddhist monks finish their lessons. Boys as young as three sat crossed-leg on their mats, weighed down by orange robes, their heads closely shaved, bent over their work. My serene picture was jiggered by one of the little monks pulling their tongue out at me as we walked past them. We pulled faces back and waved and they giggled behind their teachers' backs.

We reached the top of the monastery and continued up a staircase that led to a rooftop. We could see men tending to their cattle, yaks grazing and children playing on the roofs, dogs barking up at them wanting to join. We watched the sunset, wishing we had a beer but content with a brilliant pink sunset encasing the mountains we'd just been climbing.

'We used to climb up to the rooftop of our building in Edinburgh,' I said. 'You can see all these old tenement buildings from the nineteenth century or older, for miles. The skies there are amazing, I've never seen anything like it, not even here. The clouds are purple and enormous, and on foggy days the whole city looks like it's coated in candyfloss.'

'So, you want to go back to Edinburgh after this?' asked Tom.

'Yeah, of course, eventually, but I'm not thinking that far ahead.' I rested my chin on my knees. 'I don't even know what I'm doing next week.'

'And Andy's on the same page, I'm sure?' His lips twitched and I rolled my eyes.

'What's he said to you?' I asked.

'Nothing.' He chuckled. 'He doesn't have to. It's pretty obvious that you're leading this whole thing. The only thing keeping that poor guy trekking through the Himalayas is you.'

I shook my head gently, staring out at the view. 'He almost went back home when we were in Armenia,' I admitted. 'His job offered him a promotion, and I really thought he was going to take it. Anyway, he ended up turning it down. He came to Nepal with me instead.'

Tom raised his eyebrows. 'Yeah, that's commitment.'

'It's not like we'll stay on the road forever. The deal was that I would stay with him in Edinburgh for a few years while he built up his career, and now it's his turn to support my dream. Afterwards, we'll go back to Scotland.'

'Makes sense I guess,' said Tom.

I smiled, but it felt forced and anxious. 'You really think he's having that shit of a time?'

'What? No, I was joking. I just meant, well, that he's maybe more cautious and serious than you are. I like him and I think it's cool that he's putting himself out there for you. I respect that. I don't know if I could do that for someone else, maybe I'm too selfish.'

'If it's the right person…'

'Ah, don't start giving me that spiel, Shakespeare.' He elbowed my arm and we laughed.

'What about you then?' I asked. 'Are you on the road forever, or is going back to New Zealand in the works?'

'No. I don't think I'll ever go back there. I feel a lot freer on the road.'

'Would you ever settle somewhere?'

Tom shrugged. 'I don't want to be anywhere for longer than three months.'

'That's specific.'

'It's just enough time you need to get to know a place and its people, without it rooting you down. You can leave without feeling a sense of attachment.'

'Why wouldn't you want that attachment, though? Surely that's what makes it more special.'

He shrugged. 'Getting attached to a person or a place just makes things complicated. I want to continuously live like a nomad and get to know as much of the world as I can.'

I thought about it for a while. 'If we're being honest, I think your plan doesn't sound sustainable.'

Tom chuckled. 'How come?'

'It'll grow old after a while. You'll get tired of living out of a suitcase. You're not going to still be travelling when you're an old man.'

He stretched his legs out and surveyed the villages beneath him. 'Ah, but that's where I have a plan.'

I looked at him expectantly.

'At some point, when I get tired, I'll move to South America. Somewhere like Colombia or Ecuador. I'll set myself up there, in a remote village. I'll build my own house and a botanical garden for the community, maybe even a library. I can help at a school or build one up.'

I had a vision of children running around tropical gardens and Tom sitting outside on a veranda of a grand wooden house. I smiled. It was out of a storybook. I wondered how much of this was just a dream to help justify his travels.

'What about your family?' I asked.

His eyes averted. 'We don't really speak.'

'Oh.' I wanted to ask why, but it felt too invasive.

'Don't they worry about you?'

He gave a short laugh. 'I don't think so.'

I nodded, not knowing what to say. 'Where do they live?'

Tom pulled more weeds out. 'New Zealand.'

'Do you have any siblings?'

He bit down on his thumbnail. 'I had a brother.' He added his name as an afterthought. 'Charlie.'

'What was he like?'

Tom smiled. 'A complete nerd. I mean he was the most irritating human alive, you know. But he was still cool. My mum homeschooled him, so he was probably two years ahead of his classmates. He even did my homework sometimes.' He laughed.

'So you got on?'

'Yeah. He was a few years younger than me so we grew up close. Our parents didn't let us have television or anything like that in the house, and there was fuck all to do where we lived. So we spent most of our time outside exploring and making shit up, mostly playing *Indiana Jones*.'

I thought of his elaborate drawings of the books he read. 'So that's where your sketching comes from.'

'Yeah, sort of. He loved reading but I'd get too bored. Drawing was more fun.'

'What happened to him?'

He looked back down. 'He got leukaemia quite early on. Had it for most of his life. Died when he was twelve.' He swallowed. 'Almost, yeah, ten years ago now.' He forced a laugh. 'You'd think ten years is enough time to get over it, but it still sucks.'

'Tom, I'm so sorry.'

'Yeah. It's a shitty story.'

'And I guess in your case, it didn't exactly bring your family closer.'

Tom shook his head. 'After Charlie got diagnosed, Mum basically forgot I existed. My dad occasionally made an effort, but he got the whole financial brunt of it. And I get it, you know? You get this cute, smart kid who is slowly dying in front of you, and, as parents, you feel helpless. It cost them all their savings just to keep him in hospital. Fuck, I would have given anything too. Dad had to work extra hours, and Mum quit her job to become his carer.'

Tom kept on pulling at grass. 'When he died, we all just dealt with it on our own. Mum was so depressed she ended up in hospital a few times. And I hated myself because I just felt jealous of Charlie. When I was a kid, I kept on thinking that if I was sick or dying, maybe they'd talk to me more. And once he was gone, I realised he was the only one in the house who I actually spent time with.'

I nodded, staring at my boots. 'It sounds horrible.'

'Yeah, well. I left home when I finished school. I went to university for a bit, but after a while, I figured that all I wanted to do was leave New Zealand. So I worked. Saved up enough to go travelling, and then I fucked off.'

'Were your parents okay with it?'

Tom chuckled. 'I don't know. We haven't really spoken since I left for university.'

I thought about my own parents. I still felt guilty about not having their blessing to be on this adventure. I wished I could share these views with them, tell them that I was days away from reaching Thorong La Pass. Part of me thought Dad would be so excited.

'Where did you go first?' I asked Tom.

His frown started to disappear as his face brightened slightly. 'I went for a long walk through France and Spain. Have you heard about the Camino Santiago de Compostela?'

'Yeah, I have,' I said, glad to be able to focus on something less personal. 'Doesn't it take a month, even more?'

'It does. Best thing I've ever done,' he shrugged. 'The Camino sort of brought me back to life.'

I stared at the rooftops in silence, thinking of the long hiking trail through Europe and imagining Tom walking for weeks on his own.

'Where are you going after Nepal?' I asked.

He stretched out his legs. 'Think I'll go to India for a couple of weeks. I'll cross overland, spend some time in the north. And then I want to go to Sri Lanka.'

The thought of saying goodbye to Tom made my chest feel tight. 'We're thinking about going to India next too,' I said.

He glanced at me and raised an eyebrow. 'Well, maybe we can time it so we go together. It's been great travelling with you guys.'

I felt a small rush of excitement at the thought and contained a smile. 'Yeah. That would be really nice.'

## 24

We stayed on the rooftop until the sun had completely disappeared and started walking back in the dark. We climbed back down the narrow stairs, past the top of the monastery, past the now empty classroom and down to the dark village. The smell of firewood no longer hung heavy in the air, and the breeze felt icy. There was a single light from a nearby stone home, which meant I could just about see my breath as we descended the last of the stairs.

I turned into a narrow alleyway, the one that led us back to the teahouse. The children who'd been playing in the streets earlier were probably fast asleep now. There wasn't even a yak in sight.

'Let me just get a torch out,' I heard Tom saying behind me.

We heard some footsteps but couldn't see anything, and then a few more.

'Stop, one second,' said Tom, his voice quieter. 'Need to turn this on.'

I turned around, heard a click, and then a bright light coming from his phone. I realised I'd been holding my breath.

I looked up and recognised the flags on one of the houses. 'We're only a minute away—'

Tom's hand suddenly gripped my arm. He held me back so forcefully that I couldn't move.

'What are you—' I glanced in front of me.

Four men.

Locals.

All eight beady black eyes on us.

'Can I help you?' asked Tom. There was no friendliness in his voice.

'You're the ones at the homestay,' said one of them, his eyes narrowing. He pointed at me. 'You told my group not to pay me.'

I didn't say a word. Tom pulled me back as he stepped forward. He was taller than all of them and bigger. He broadened his shoulders and looked at the short, squat man square in the face.

'We can talk about this.' His voice oozed steady calmness. 'Let me take her back to the house first. Okay?'

'Wait,' I glanced at Tom, 'where are you going—'

'Okay?' Tom repeated.

The guide looked at us. My heart was racing. What the hell was going on?

Tom held onto my arm as we moved back. They followed us closely. I tried to talk, but he wasn't letting me. As we reached the teahouse, he gestured at me to go in.

'Just be quiet,' he said quickly. 'Don't speak to any locals. Go inside and stay in the room. I'll be back soon.'

I tried to make eye contact, but he'd turned around and was walking back to the group of men waiting for him.

Shakily, I walked back to the room.

Andy was awake. He listened to my version of the story. He seemed as worried as I was, and we waited for a couple of hours. Andy went for a short stroll around the area but came back with nothing to report.

'What if they do something to him?' I fretted. 'This is all my fault. I shouldn't have said anything.'

I was restless and kept looking out of the window. We didn't have a way to contact him. Andy was quiet, both of us feeling helpless. There was no chance of us sleeping, and we agreed to go out looking for him if he didn't show up in the next hour. I was close to tears. We were sat on our sleeping mats, looking expectantly at the door and out of the window when we heard footsteps.

The door opened, and Tom walked in.

'Oh, hey,' he said quickly. He seemed surprised to see us up and walked hastily over to the other side of the room, near the bathroom, sitting next to his sleeping bag.

'Where have you been?' I asked.

'Why are you still up?' His hands were stuffed deep inside his pockets.

'What happened?'

'It was fine. It was nothing. I told the guide we wouldn't say anything else to the French guys and reminded him who was the bigger one.' He winked.

'Why did you take so long?'

'I found a guy selling hash,' he grinned. 'I chilled out for a while.'

I watched his face as he chuckled, but my eyes darted to the unusual position of his hands. When I glanced back up, he avoided my gaze.

'Should've told us,' said Andy, perking up. 'Right then, drama over. Antonia made me think you were a goner.'

Andy crawled into his sleeping bag.

I followed suit, lying down on the mat and feigning sleep, listening as Tom lay down next to me. He turned his back towards me. I heard him flicking through the pages of his book.

A while later, I heard him move. I opened my eyes a slit. The lights were off, but moonlight shone through the curtain-less room.

I watched him take his hands out of his sleeping bag, and I silently swore. Both his hands were in ruins. They were covered in dry blood. Pieces of skin were hanging off by his fingernails, and a large chunk of thick skin detached from his palm looked like it needed urgent medical attention. He studied them, his arms stiff, his hands shaking.

I listened as he went to the bathroom and waited as he stayed there for a good hour. When he came back, he glanced over at me. My head was on the rug, but this time my eyes were wide open.

'I'm so sorry,' I whispered.

He lay down on his mat. He moved his butchered hands out of sight. I was too scared to say anything or even move, afraid to wake Andy up.

'It's not your fault.'

His face didn't show an ounce of pain. He lay on his back, his eyes open and alert. His hands were tucked away under his sleeping bag, his bare shoulder peeking out over the top. I could see the other half of his tattoo now, the black, angular ink jarring the curves of his shoulder. His breaths became more even and he gradually turned to his side, his eyes now closed. A gentle shift made the sleeping bag slide down further, enough that I could see the full tattoo. I could see a cross clearly now, the three bars, predominantly black and subtly outlined in red. Was he a mason? Was it a weird sect thing? For all I knew, it might have just been a drunk rite of passage when he was eighteen. I did realise one thing: it matched the crosses in his sketchbook. Like a sort of signature he had at the corner of every drawing. I made a note to ask him, but I wondered if it was too private an answer.

Slowly I moved my fingers. My hand slid out of my sleeping bag. I stretched my hand out and placed my hand on his shoulder. I slowly traced his tattoo with my thumb and felt his muscle tighten beneath my fingers.

## 25

We set off walking the next morning, bleary-eyed and heads down. We were now walking at over 3,800 metres. Ben Nevis, the highest mountain in Britain, was 1,345 metres, and we were aiming to walk five times that. There was no pleasant scenery on either side anymore. As we left Upper Pisang behind, the wooden shacks faded into the distance until they looked like tiny black dots in the snow. Soon they'd disappeared entirely, and we moved onto stark, barren land.

The whole trail ahead of us was empty, except for previously trodden footsteps. We walked through a snow-covered valley, where we could see for miles ahead.

It was hard to get the full story from Tom with Andy around, but after a few quiet conversations, I pieced together what had happened. He'd gone to meet with the group of locals, where they'd demanded he paid for what they'd lost from the Frenchmen.

Tom refused to pay them. On his way back to the teahouse, he was followed. They tried to start a fight with him. Knowing better to try fighting with someone twice their size, they resolved to push him into a dry ditch made up of stone rubble. He'd wrecked his hands by trying to protect his landing. The men had run away, leaving him there.

Laughing it off, Tom had said the hardest bit had been finding the teahouse in the dark.

~~~

Six bitterly cold and quiet hours later, we reached Low Camp at 4,450 metres. It was the last camp before reaching the Thorong La Pass. The camp was defined by a wooden lodge built purposely for the hikers who would be summiting the next morning. I noticed there was barely a temperature difference inside the lodge, and I kept all my layers, including my gloves, on. A wood-burning fire crackled and hissed, the flames fighting to stay alive. Four other hikers were already there, sitting on a wooden bench in front of the fire. A couple of Sherpas sat nearby on a wooden table, drinking black coffee from metal mugs.

The Sherpa running the camp came over to us with a small bowl of broth. He recommended eating as little as possible as a heavy meal would make the altitude effects worse. He told us to expect little sleep. We were not used to these low oxygen levels, and we'd spend most of the night out of breath.

We were huddled around the fire when a loud and disturbing rumble penetrated the echoing silence. We all looked to the windows, except the Sherpa who sipped on his mug.

'Helicopters,' he explained. 'They come most days.' He looked out the window, a frown passing over his face. 'Hikers get stuck at the Pass. It's too high for them.'

'What happens to them?'

'Some get a headache. They keep walking. It gets worse. They start coughing blood. That's dangerous. Very dangerous.' He shook his head. 'If they don't get a helicopter straight away, their brain starts to swell. That's the end. Every year people die.'

I immediately thought of the forty hikers who'd died trekking the Pass last year. I'd thought of it most days since Andy had brought it up, but it now felt very real being in low camp, feeling the cold in our bones and sitting in the exact spots they must have sat on last year.

We listened to him with rapt attention as his threat turned into instructions for the hike tomorrow.

'The way to the Pass is difficult. It is very steep. You will have to climb sometimes on your knees. It will be very, very cold. Minus twenty degrees, and that's before the wind comes in. Do not stop walking. There is no shelter or stop on the way. There are no trees, shrubs, nothing. The only way to recognise the summit is by the prayer flags. You will see many of them, on top of each other, and you will know you have reached the Thorong La Pass.'

I glanced over at Andy and Tom, whose focus on the Sherpa was every bit as intense as mine.

'You will leave tomorrow no later than 4 a.m. You need to reach the summit before 10 a.m., because that's when the winds start and there is too much danger. You must walk fast. Do not stop walking. If you stop, you will get too cold, the altitude sickness will start, and you will not make it to the top. If you have to stop, you must come back, and try again the next day. If you reach the summit before 10 a.m., you may continue to the descent. If you reach it after 10 a.m., you must come back. Remember, there will be no help there. You must make good decisions.'

I noticed it was only men around me. There was a Spanish athlete; a Swiss man who'd just motor-biked through Pakistan; and an experienced fifty-year-old from Denmark who'd just climbed Base Camp. Even without the altitude being a factor, I knew I wouldn't sleep a wink. I didn't want to tell Andy how I was feeling. What if I couldn't make it? I hated the part of us having to walk fast against a timeline. I couldn't walk quickly without one, let alone with. Outside our camp was the steepest trail I'd ever seen. We were going to have to climb it. It faded about a kilometre up, into the mountains, only going north. It was barren, just snow and rocks, no sign of anything that would cast a shadow.

~~~

I was already awake when the alarm went off at 3.30 a.m. It was so cold the night before that we'd slept in our full gear, shivering in our sleeping bags. We began to pack up. Bleary-eyed and scared, we dragged ourselves outside into the freezing cold. It was pitch black. Andy and I only had our phones as torches, but we followed the others who had head torches and began to climb the mountain.

The air was as thin as it could be. I gasped as each freezing breath hurt my lungs, our breathing wheezy and raspy. The only other sound was our footing against the rocks, and occasionally someone stumbling as they tried to blaze the trail up ahead.

Unsurprisingly, I was last. Wearing all my layers, including my towel around my face and my hat over my eyebrows, the only thing peeking out was my nose and eyes. Although my pack now had barely more than my sleeping bag—since I was wearing everything in it—it felt heavy, and the straps seemed to dig into my shoulders more than ever. The more we walked, the more I felt fear and fell behind.

It wasn't until I realised that the torches were gone and my own light was dim, that I saw the rest of the group were a few hundred metres ahead of us. I could only discern them by the flash of lights and could no longer hear their breathing or footsteps. Andy was just ahead of me, going slower, but the more we went uphill, the further away the men got until finally they were out of sight. I looked up and saw the blackness of the mountain. There were still hours to go until the sun rose, hours left of walking in the freezing cold and darkness. I had no confidence in myself to do this. I thought of the people who'd turned back, the people who had been taken down in a helicopter.

Through raspy, panicky breaths, I burst into frightened tears. Andy couldn't hear me from up ahead, so I yelled and asked him to stop until I caught up with him. Out of breath and doubled over, I unsuccessfully tried to regain my composure before freaking out again.

'I can't do it. I can't do it. I'm so sorry, I can't do it,' I sobbed. 'We're not going to make it before the winds hit, and then we'll be stuck. Everyone is going so fast. We're never going to catch up.'

I waited with my eyes closed for Andy to argue with me or get pissed off. Instead, I felt him hold my gloved hands.

'You can do this.' He squeezed my hand. 'I know you can. Remember the glacial water in Georgia? Remember the really steep hills we did then? You can do this.'

'I don't think I can. They're going too fast, I can't keep up—'

'So we're going to go slow. We'll go slow and steady. Okay?'

I met his eye and shakily managed a nod.

## 26

A few hours later, we were deep in the mountain. An icy light suggested the sun was creeping out behind the thick fog. In the white mountains, I could see the dark outline of hikers ahead of us and thought I could recognise Tom's green jacket. With little talking and consistent footing, their figures became clearer.

'We're catching up,' I said, astounded.

As we continued, I realised that wasn't entirely true. We hadn't sped up; they had stopped. We first saw the Spaniard. He was clutching his stomach, resting on a rock, sipping water. He looked pale and sweaty, and there was a frozen yellow pool of what looked like bile beneath him.

'Are you okay?' asked Andy.

'*Si, si*. It's not much longer. I can do it. I just need a minute.'

We stopped next to him, but he quickly reassured us that he was just taking a break. '*Dale*, keep moving, don't get cold.'

I realised what he meant. Within seconds, I felt my hands start to freeze, even beneath two layers of gloves. I groaned in pain.

'Take them off,' said the Spaniard.

'Are you crazy?'

'Take them off,' he repeated, 'and blow into them, hard.'

I did as he said, and after blowing into my gloves and trying to move my hands and fingers around, I finally regained some sensation in them.

We continued walking once we'd seen the Spaniard getting up and slowly following. We saw Tom next. His usual grin was forced, and he reluctantly admitted he had a headache.

'Do you want to go back?' I asked.

'It's not too much further. I think we'll be there in half an hour. At this point it's better to get there and start going downhill.'

He trailed slowly behind us.

We were not surprised to meet the Swiss man, tending to the Danish man who was also throwing up. We stayed back, offering altitude sickness pills and water, which they took. They concluded the same as Tom—it was better to reach the summit and start the steep descent than go all the way back.

I trudged on, trying not to think about my cold, throbbing extremities, looking mostly down at my feet.

When I finally glanced up, I saw what seemed to be the most beautiful thing in the world: a scattering of colourful prayer flags beating against the winds of the Himalayas.

'We've made it!' I yelled. I looked back, but Andy was further away than I thought. His face was pale, and he was moving slowly with the rest of the gang. Despite all the elements that had been slowing me down for weeks on end, I managed to jog towards the flags, whooping in delight as I touched them.

I looked at the wooden carved sign:

*The Thorong La Pass, 5,416 metres*

Arms outstretched, I cheered and looked up into the blue skies. The rest were slowly catching up, momentarily forgetting their discomforts against the triumph of reaching the summit. I watched as Andy heaved himself up the last stretch. As he came closer, I realised he was beaming. He was speechless as he touched the flags.

He turned to face me with his arms outstretched, and I smiled as I hugged him back.

'We did it, Antonia, shit, we did it!'

I kissed him, our cold lips touching. 'We did!'

'I just want to say that this,' he gestured at the flags and the summit, 'this makes all our travelling completely worth it.'

I gripped his hand and then watched as he walked over to the flags to take pictures of the other hikers who'd made it. He was laughing and cheering, the smile on his face so big, there were dimples and lines on his face I hadn't seen before. I wondered if I'd ever seen him this happy.

Before I could think further, I felt someone hugging me tightly from behind and lifting me in the air. Tom was grinning from ear to ear.

'And who would have thought you'd be the first to reach it?' He laughed, squeezing me. 'I've never seen you walk that fast. Well done!'

He lowered me to the ground. I hugged him tightly. I smelt the mustiness of his jacket and could feel his arms holding me. They were different from Andy's. He was a bit sturdier and broader. I felt his hand rubbing my back, and I suddenly pulled away. Had I lingered? Had he noticed? Had he felt me touching his shoulder, tracing his tattoo? I avoided his eye as I quickly glanced over at Andy. He was still taking photographs. My face felt warm. I wondered if it was the accomplishment or the confusion that made my cheeks flush.

## 27

It took us another week or so to climb down the mountain to the city of Pokhara. As we left the high altitude behind, the days became hotter and humid. There were suspension bridges, cattle crossings and villages, each larger settlement indicating we were almost there. As we came back down to rice paddies and waterfalls, the Himalayan mountains seemed further away. They could be seen at a distance, through the haze and fog, like reliefs in a painting: intangible and divine.

There was noise again, and a sense of sadness at leaving the tranquillity behind us. Through the roar of motorbikes and clouds of dusty roads, the mountains seemed a distant memory, a figment of the imagination, almost like we'd never climbed them at all. But we'd been there, in the thick of the snow, gasping for breath and wiping sweat off our brows.

The trail gradually turned from dirt into tar. We trudged onto the roads, dodging traffic.

At long last, we reached the city of Pokhara.

~~~

Pokhara was the ideal place to relax after almost a month of hiking through the Himalayas. There were running cold showers, coffees and restaurants. There was a large, peaceful lake with beach shacks on the sides selling ice-cold beers and coconut water. Backpackers were playing the guitar, sketching, reading or smoking joints. It was a hippie's paradise.

We checked in with our families and sent them emails with our updates. I could see Andy pacing around the cafe garden, chatting to his parents, recognising the impatient monotone answers he saved for his mum's tirade of questions. I noticed Tom didn't even reach for his phone, pulling out his book instead, waiting for us to finish up.

I'd received an email from Mum telling me a cousin had got married, and photos of my nieces as flower girls. Dad had sent me a link to earthquake statistics in Nepal. I was about to delete it when I saw his message at the end: 'Send me some pictures!' I felt a small thrill. Maybe he was coming round to my travels.

I thought I'd treat myself to a pair of colourful pants with elephant designs and a fresh, black T-shirt. After wearing my two T-shirts for over two months, it was time to feel clean. We'd all shed some pounds, but we quickly made up for it by eating large meals of fried dumplings at the Nepalese version of a McDonalds, renamed YakDonalds.

One evening I sat in the hostel courtyard. Fairy lights decorated the tropical trees around us, and the bushes hummed with crickets and mosquitos. I sat writing in my journal and sipping on a beer when Andy walked through. He glanced behind him to make sure we were alone and pulled out a chair next to me.

'Did you tell Tom he could come to India with us?'

I looked up. I thought back to the chat we'd had in Chame on the rooftop some weeks ago. 'Oh. Yeah. He told me he was going. I said we wanted to go too.'

'And how long is he planning on sticking around?' There was an edge to his voice.

'Not long. He's planning on going to Sri Lanka.'

Andy pulled a face, but the lines on his forehead softened slightly.

'What's the big deal? You spend almost every night smoking or drinking with him. I assumed you liked him.'

'He's all right, but I don't need to spend the rest of my life with him. You want to bring him home with us too?'

I rolled my eyes. 'For all we know, we'll just cross the border, and he'll meet another group of backpackers.'

He was silent and turned to open his daypack.

'What was I meant to say anyway? That he couldn't come with us?'

'Yes.'

'And how would I tell him that?'

He pulled his phone out of the bag and turned to me. 'Cheers, Tom, nice to meet you. My fiancé and I are going to continue travelling alone.'

'Look,' I lowered my voice, 'the guy is resourceful. You said it yourself. He knows how to negotiate and get visas and cross the borders. He can save us that hassle.'

'Well, he's busy doing that now. And he's trying to plan some camel trek for us in the desert, some place called Jaisalmer.'

I started to laugh. 'Think of him as a free travel guide.'

Andy didn't return the smile and glanced back at his phone, raising it to the air to get signal. 'I'll deal with him as long as there's an expiry date.'

'There is,' I nodded. 'Hey, why don't we make a plan for when he leaves?'

Andy's phone started buzzing. 'Not now. I've finally got wi-fi.'

As the bus crawled out of Pokhara, I watched for the last time the sun rising over the sprawling dirty city, where dogs were stretching, and monkeys waited for humans to fill the squares. For the first time since we'd arrived, the city actually felt calm. In the distance, past the red clouds of dirt, I could very vaguely make out the outline of the snow-capped Himalayas.

Nepal had been more chaotic and challenging than I had imagined. My legs felt a bit stronger, my arms a bit tauter and my backpack a bit lighter. My face was smattered in freckles and tan lines—or was it dust?—from where the buff, sunglasses and hat had pressed against me. I could use a squat toilet without having a panic attack and manoeuvre myself through the loose planks and small hole. I could sleep in minus fifteen degrees and knew what angles gave me the most warmth. My stomach had now conquered food poisoning and I could eat *momos* from street vendors and *dal bahts* from teahouses, no problem. Hell, I'd managed to survive a 5,416 metres mountain pass without completely collapsing.

I felt tougher.

~~~

I thought Kathmandu had been as chaotic as it came, but I was in for some shock when we finally reached the Indian border. It was madness.

Streets were lined with crowds of heaving Nepali people trying to push through border control. Cars, buses and taxis crammed the road. Most of them were stopped still. Only motorbikes were able to weave themselves slowly through the masses. Then there were the lorries—painted in bright colours with psychedelic designs—that backed up for kilometres. Across the vast, flat landscape, I couldn't even see where it ended. A taxi driver later told me that it could take a whole month for a lorry driver to pass the border—that is, if his permissions were approved.

We were the privileged ones; Western tourists, who had their own queue. We got through the border in ten minutes. Not that it was pleasant. Tom and Andy added extra stress as they struggled to let go of the leftover hash they'd been carrying with them. They finally tossed it, while I breathed out shaky relief.

The guards gave us one brief look before ushering us forward. A vast, towering Indian flag cast a shadow over us as we took our first steps into the country.

# PART 3
# INDIA

## 28

We travelled in a rickshaw to the station to begin our first Indian train ride, a gruelling two-day trip, to Udaipur. We would be sleeping in berths. As someone who'd never taken a sleeper train even in the UK, I had no idea what to expect.

The train station was chaos. There were no signs, only platform numbers that were impossible to see through swarms of people. Beggars were abundant, barely clothed, sprawled on the ground, and had their eyes on foreigners. I moved closer to Andy, keeping my bag where I could see it. One of them, a mother with a baby, grasped Andy's wrist. He started telling her to let go, raising his voice to no avail. It was only when he forcefully removed her hand that she stepped back.

We were quickly shuffled into our compartment. As we walked through, I saw the train was already full of people. I wondered how far they had come. I sank back into the seat, now staring out of the window. It was almost noon, and I watched the scenery flashing before my eyes. The snow seemed to melt into wheat fields, then blossom into forests, giving way to small villages. Cattle grazed peacefully in meadows. Children balancing on fences waved up at the train. Women washed clothes by the riverbanks while men bathed in the murky water.

I was transfixed. We were in India! The view unravelled like a film in front of me. There were hundreds of cows in the street, no lanes or rules, just constant fluxes of people, motorbikes, cars and noise. Dark-coloured youths, with white tunics and barefoot, moved through fields with haystacks balanced on their heads. Women in bright saris worked on textiles, woven baskets at their feet. Small boys snaked their way between cows, grabbing onto their horns, with no fear in the world. There were so many smiles, so much chatter, as if the Indian countryside was its own contained world, protected from modern times.

I watched in awe as the enormous sun began to set over the villages, a scarlet sky blazing over its tired people, wiping the sweat away from their day.

'That's the biggest sun I've ever seen in my life,' I said. Andy didn't answer so I squeezed his wrist.

He sighed before looking up from his phone. 'What?'

I repeated my comment.

'That's impossible,' he said, quickly glancing out of the window. 'The sun doesn't change its size.'

He went back to his phone and I took out my book. I was painfully trudging through *Shantaram*, Tom studied a battered copy of *War and Peace*. After battling to find a stable network connection, Andy flicked through *Sapiens*. I could hear them both huffing in their seats, and it didn't surprise me when moments later, they suggested a walk through the train carriages.

'I'm craving samosas,' said Tom. Andy followed.

I stayed put. I was happy reading and watching the landscape flicker through the window like a movie. The train paused by a large white temple. A crowd of people were gathered around it. I wanted to know what the temples were and what kind of ritual was taking place. I wanted to know exactly where we were in India. I took out my phone, hoping for some signal, but as I opened Google Maps, it died. Irritated, I grabbed Andy's out of his bag. He had an almost full battery. As I typed in the search bar, his latest search popped up on his phone:

*How to know if she still loves me*

My heart sank. I inhaled sharply, but the air didn't seem to fill my lungs. Why had he typed this? I glanced over at the empty hallway. I wanted to leave all my bags here and find him. I wanted to throw my arms around him. Of course I still loved him.

I thought back to the trek. As much as I hated to admit it, I had some sort of feelings for Tom. But it was purely platonic. Tom was the kind of character I read about in all my travel books. We had so much in common and he was living out my dreams. I envied his life, his courage to show up in a new country completely on his own and discover it, without worrying about money, a career or a biological clock. I loved that we'd read the same books and that he was also secretly a dork. It also helped that he had nice shoulders and an easy, cheeky smile. But Andy was my everything. He was my home, best friend and fiancé wrapped into one. I loved him in a ferocious, unconditional way. I just needed to show him that.

~~~

It was half an hour before Andy came back. To my relief, he was on his own.

'Where's Tom?'

He sat down in front of me. 'He got chatting to some Italians. They've got the guitar out. I just came to check on you.'

I put my book away and reached out to close the carriage door behind him. 'I need to talk to you.'

'What's going on?' I could smell hash, and then noticed his eyes were shiny and red.

I swallowed. 'Look, I'm really sorry. I picked up your phone because I wanted to look up some temples we just passed. I…' I flashed his phone at him, showing him his Google search instead.

He barely read it, and his eyes flickered down at my hands.

He smiled awkwardly and forced a laugh. 'It's nothing. I was probably drunk when I typed that in.'

'Well, okay, but let's talk about it.'

'No, it's fine. It was a stupid, passing thing. Don't worry about it.'

'Andy, of course I love you.' As I said the words, I noticed how little I said them, compared to how often I thought them. We'd been more affectionate in the beginning of our relationship. Over the years, the declarations of love and feelings had settled. There was a 'love you,' at the end of a phone call or before bed, but not a face-to-face explanation of our feelings. We'd been together so long, no clarification had ever seemed needed during our daily routines.

Andy looked quickly over his shoulder to make sure we were out of earshot and then back at my knees.

'What made you think that?' I asked.

'Honestly, Antonia, it's nothing. Just get over it.'

'No, come on, please tell me.'

He sighed and looked out of the window, shifting in his seat. 'Yeah. Fine then. Why don't you want to be on your own with me?'

I frowned. 'What?'

He clenched his jaw and then breathed out. 'You dragged Tom along with us because you're avoiding me.'

'Where's that coming from? Why would I be avoiding you?'

'I don't know.' His voice rose slightly. 'Maybe it's because you don't want to speak about the wedding, or kids, or jobs, or anything that spells out a future for us.' He sniffed and stood up, still looking outside.

'Andy...'

'When's the last time we slept together?'

I thought back to the last month or so. I knew we hadn't had sex in a while. The last time must have been in Kathmandu. I looked down. 'It's just because we're sharing rooms, and we're in hostels.'

He grimaced. 'Kind of a lame excuse. We could find a way.'

'It's nothing personal,' I said, feeling my cheeks go warm. 'Look, I've been wearing the same clothes for months, and we've been hiking thirty kilometres a day. I haven't washed my hair properly since we left Scotland. I feel gross and sweaty. The last thing I'm thinking about is sex.'

'Yeah, well, maybe that's the problem.'

I half laughed. 'Andy, you forget that any time you have a minute to sit down, you're on your phone. It's not exactly great foreplay.'

Andy scoffed. 'Come on, you're as bad as me. Maybe not with your phone, but you're always reading, or you've got your head in your journal.'

'And isn't that okay? We spend every second with each other, and it's impossible to be alone. It's the only way of giving each other space.'

'I think there's probably too much space between us right now,' he muttered.

I fell silent and looked at his jeans. His head was turned towards the window. He walked over and sat back on the bench.

'Are you still happy with me?' he asked.

I felt my eyes sting. 'Of course I am.'

He grimaced. 'I feel like we've run out of conversation. Or maybe that's because you're always busy chatting with Tom.'

I felt my jaw tighten. 'That's not fair. And it's not true either.'

He crossed his arms over his chest and looked at me expectantly.

I breathed in. 'Okay, maybe we haven't been having hugely deep conversations, but it's not because I don't want to chat to you. You don't bring up any ideas for our trip. I only saw you truly happy when you got to the top of Thorong La Pass. And now you're back to being moody, and I keep thinking you're counting the days to go home.'

Andy nodded slowly. 'Yeah, okay. And I feel like every time I bring up the subject of going back home, you cut me off or don't want to speak about it.'

'Because I want to enjoy our trip now. I'm dreading going back.'

'Well, I'm not. I actually enjoyed the life we had together.'

I swallowed. 'I didn't mean it like that. I just meant the whole idea of getting a job and going back to a nine to five routine,' I mumbled.

Andy gave a short laugh and shook his head, looking out of the window. He pressed his lips together and crossed his arms over his chest. He opened his mouth and then shut it, thinking of it again, and shaking his head.

'What?' I said. 'We might as well get it all out.'

'Fuck's sake, Antonia. I'm sorry I gave you such a miserable life back in Edinburgh.' His Scottish accent became thicker, I could hear it in the rolling of the 'r's and the speed he spoke. 'You seem to selectively forget any good times you did have with me, even in our routine. This time last year we were driving all over Scotland looking for a bloody dog to bring home. I don't remember you being so bored on that trip. And your life at the flat wasn't exactly grim. Every morning I bought you a cuppa, every Sunday we'd have breakfast in bed for hours watching *Downton Abbey* and, you know, have sex. Good sex. And what about other evenings, drinking whisky, listening to Leonard Cohen or cooking with Frank Sinatra?'

My eyes were wet as I struggled to form words back, but I swallowed and did. 'You're right, I know you're right. We had lovely times, and I can't wait to go back to those parts of our lives. I just…I'm enjoying not having any commitments right now.'

Andy was quiet for a moment. He tugged on the zipper on his backpack and then pulled out a bottle of water, tapping the cap. 'You do have a commitment, by the way, and that's me,' he stated, 'and I'm not going to be on the road forever, and neither should you.'

'Why not? What's wrong with that?'

Andy blinked. 'It's selfish. It's indulgent. You're my fiancée and, without being creepy about it, you do have a responsibility to be with me, and share our lives, and build something together. And even if I'm out of the picture, you have a commitment to, I don't know, humanity, society, to give something back. A career, kids, a contribution to the world you're so obsessed with exploring. You can't just use it as a playground your whole life. It's…immoral.'

Heavy silence hung between us. Had Andy always been this highly principled?

I swallowed. 'It's easy for you to say that. You've known what you wanted since you were born. You have this clear trajectory in mind. You know exactly what you'll be doing in five, ten, fifteen years' time. Not everyone is moulded that way.' I felt my cheeks growing warm. 'Maybe someone can be on the road forever, and just enjoy life, just be, without a purpose, or creating a legacy or having a bullet-point list for every single thing they do.' I immediately regretted the last part, being carried away by my temper.

Andy broke my gaze. 'Well, then maybe you do have more in common with Tom.'

I said nothing back. Neither did he. I glanced at my book. I was itching to open it and read to kill the uncomfortable silence. Instead, we sat in tense silence for the next while until Tom came back in carrying a cardboard plate full of samosas.

As the carriage filled up with light conversation again, I went back to my book. The words swam across the page. I realised my heart was still beating fast. I tried to focus on a sentence, but my eyes felt blurry, and my mind was elsewhere. I hated that he was having doubts. It scared me how insecure he seemed. I was used to him being totally in control, level-headed and in charge of his feelings. I'd slowly become used to seeing him with a beard, out of his shirt and tie, wearing loose cotton shirts and jeans, a woven leather bracelet from Georgia replacing his silver watch, his hair messy and long. But insecurity…that threw me off guard. I was normally the anxious one, the doubter, the one that needed a filter, wearing my heart on my sleeve. He grounded me. If he was sinking, where did that leave me?

For the first time in our relationship, I felt scared. What if he decided to end this? I couldn't imagine life without him. Being alone terrified me. Andy was the best thing to ever happen to me.

There was no way on earth I'd ever find someone half as wonderful as him. No one would ever love me as much as he did.

But when he'd asked me if I planned on travelling instead of facing reality, something inside my chest had expanded. The heat from the carriage had dissolved, if only for a moment, and I felt like I could finally take in a full breath. There was something delirious about being alone on the road. I couldn't find the word for it—something about infinite possibilities, excitement and meaning.

It was only an hour later, when the skies had gone from orange to grey, that the word I was looking for appeared in my book.

Freedom.

## 29

The train crawled its way to the west of India, where within Rajasthan lay the sleepy town of Udaipur. We stiffly disembarked and walked into the centre with our backpacks, dodging motorbikes and dozing cows. We planned on staying a week in Udaipur and then moving to Jaisalmer, the desert, to join a camel trek for a few days.

Udaipur was also known as the city of lakes. It was where *James Bond* was once filmed. The centre was dotted with cafes and restaurants, and I started recognising signs in English. Flat Whitey Coffee. Spicy Acai Bowls. Avokado and One Egg on Sower Dow Bread.

There were yoga and meditation centres by the dozen, art classes, and plenty of posters saying, 'Find yourself', 'Discover your inner zen', and 'Change your life'. There were shops selling beads, leather necklaces and bags, mandalas, prints, watercolours and crocheted yoga mats. There were huts by the river advertising water rafting, rock climbing, mountain walks and motorbike expeditions.

Backpackers walked past us, talking in a flurry of accents. Each one had more dreadlocks and baggier pants than the next—all of them were most certainly high.

It was the perfect city in which to drink some 'flatey whites' and to spend Christmas.

The three of us checked into a hostel called Be True to Self. The hostel was on the lake, with a view of the scarlet sunset. Bookshelves weren't yet an invention here, so books left behind by thousands of backpackers were stacked tightly against the wall, in a dangerous Jenga style. Take one out, and you'd be drowned by hundreds of unread copies of *Shantaram*.

The hostel boasted its own entertainment. Bollywood dance nights, Bollywood karaoke, Bollywood cinema nights and morning yoga. The beds in the dorm had privacy curtains—privacy curtains!—night lights and drawers with locks. I briefly wondered if we could abandon our travel plans and just stay here for a couple of months.

~~~

The hostel lounge was busy with backpackers, mainly groups of friends, a few couples and a handful of lone travellers. A few people lay on couches on their phones or laptops. We sat down near them with our books. I was happy to be surrounded by English-speaking people. It was Christmas Eve, though there were no fairy lights, wreaths or 'Santa Claus is Coming to Town'. Still, we all pitched in to get a whisky-looking liqueur and a box of syrupy Indian sweets. When we felt tipsy and drowsy, Tom took out a wooden harmonica and gave the worst rendition I'd ever heard of 'It's beginning to look a lot like Christmas'.

I was the first to get up to head to bed. I could feel the liquor making my mind fuzzy, and I slowly wandered down to the dorm room.

As I reached the room, I heard Tom's voice. I turned around. He walked down the empty corridor towards me. 'Antonia.'

I stopped. My heart beat a bit faster, as it had done for the last few days whenever he talked to me.

'Merry Christmas.' He held out a brown package. I took it from him, carefully removing the string. It was a notebook. It was made of dark brown leather and handmade paper. The Hindu God of Elephants, Ganesha, was drawn intricately on the cover.

I looked up at him. I wanted to tell him I didn't trust myself being alone with him. I wanted to say to him that I was confused, all the time, about my feelings for him which were inextricably mixed with my feelings for Andy. I wanted to tell him he was making me doubt my choices and my future.

'Thank you.'

He gave me a small smile. 'It's for your writing. Maybe one day you'll write a book about your travels.'

## 30

We spent a few days exploring Udaipur, walking down its alleyways.

One morning we sat on the balcony sipping chai and sifting through Lonely Planet books. We put our heads together, ready to explore life out of the sleepy city. The other backpackers, with their excited voices and fresh energy, were starting to get on our nerves.

'There's a rat temple about an hour away,' said Andy. 'There're meant to be 25,000 black rats that live there, and they're honoured by the Gods—'

He caught the look on my face.

'There's also Ranakpur Temple and some hyped-up fort and waterfall. It's a two-hour drive from here. What do you guys think?'

I nodded. 'Let's do it.'

We hired a car and a driver. For the whole day, he would charge us the equivalent of seven pounds. The vehicle rattled out of the city, and snaked around cliffs, slugged up dirt roads and zoomed through the little bit of tar that existed. I was green and struggling not to throw up. When we finally arrived at the site, I shot to the bathroom and saw my breakfast before me.

At the entrance to the temple a large sign was tacked to a post: ENTRANCE IS FORBIDDEN TO WOMEN DURING MENSTRUATION

I stopped in my tracks, as Tom and Andy walked ahead of me. It took them a moment to realise I wasn't following. Andy looked at me questioningly and I gestured at the sign. They studied it.

Andy pulled a face. 'Surely it doesn't matter,' he said, quickly glancing behind him to make sure no one was around.

'Ah, shit. I think I've read about that in a book,' said Tom. 'The Hindus think periods are impure, and that it might upset the Gods or something.'

'Seriously?' I said, thinking of the early wakeup call and the hours it had taken us to get here. I looked towards the car park and could see a tiny makeshift shop and a cafe with taxi drivers loitering about.

Andy gave me a sympathetic smile. 'I'll take pics.'

~~~

I wandered through the car park, looking at the intrinsic stone-carved sculptures decorating the temple. Behind it was the abandoned fort, built on the edge of a cliff, with ladders, staircases and roof landings. It looked like an adult's playground.

Sure enough, I could soon see Andy and Tom roaming through it. I watched as they climbed precarious ladders, walking far too close to the edges and climbing through derelict windows.

The breeze was picking up, and I pulled my pashmina around my bare shoulders. I walked towards the little shop. I glanced and realised, to my immense surprise, that they sold Cadbury's chocolate. I bought a bar and wandered around a narrow concrete track that bordered the stone temple. Below the trail was a five-metre drop into a dried-out river, now mostly scattered with litter. I popped each cube of chocolate into my mouth, savouring the velvety texture of honey and toffee, home comforts seeping through.

To my right was the outdoor cafe, where a couple of families sat sipping chai. Up ahead on the track, I saw a small water buffalo grazing on a plastic milk container. It looked relatively small, almost cute. It was blocking my way ahead, so I started to turn back.

I could see Andy and Tom still clambering up ladders. I waved at Andy, who was gripping onto a rung. He was fumbling with his phone, trying to take a photograph of me.

'Move to your right,' yelled Andy. 'The sun's in your face. I'll take another one.'

As I turned for the camera, I suddenly realised why the buffalo was so cute. It was a baby. I looked to my other side and I found myself metres away from its gigantic mother. I was standing between them.

My stomach turned to ice. The mother's tail swished back and forth and she dug her front hooves into the ground. Before I could think, all five hundred kilograms of the beast charged at me.

I heard Andy scream my name. The chocolate bar fell from my hand. I jumped blindly, throwing myself off the cliff into the rubble below. My knee smacked once, twice, three times against the concrete edges. My arms whacked against the jagged cliff walls.

Falling, falling.
A yell.
A thud.
Black.

I lay on my back, the wind out of me as I gasped for breath. My heart was pumping. I could hear yells and footsteps coming from the cafe. I saw a couple of men hoisting themselves down the side of the cliff. There was a high-pitched ring in my ears. I tried to get up, but a handful of faces and hands were now in my way, instructing me to stay still.

'I'm a doctor,' a man reassured me. 'Your head is okay?'

'Yes…' I started. 'I think so.'

'Your knee not okay. Your arm not okay.'

I lifted my head and felt my leg shaking.

The man's hands pressed on my knee. I realised my leggings were ripped. There was a warm sensation on my shin. The men were talking fast in Hindi, watching me. I began to feel the waves of pain coming from my knee. I looked at it and cried out. I'd split my left knee open, and blood was gushing from it. I tried to reach my arm out but realised I'd cut my elbow open too.

'Don't move,' insisted the man. I felt someone tie something over my leg. Another man joined him and set something next to me. I realised it was my broken sandal. 'You go hospital.'

'Wait,' I looked up at the fort. 'My friends are there.'

They exchanged words in Hindi as they both looked at the trail winding down from the fort expectantly.

I saw Tom and Andy racing towards me.

Tom reached me first, looking at my leg and gripping my shoulder.

'Antonia! Oh my God. Are you okay? We thought it killed you!' He half laughed in shock. 'Andy, mate, she's okay!'

Andy reached me, kneeling down and grabbing my hand. I focused on his face, which had turned ashen. Even his lips had gone a weird grey.

'It's okay. I'm okay,' I said.

He nodded and gripped my hand tighter.

'We need to get her up to the car park,' said Tom.

He put both hands under my arms and lifted me up. Another man held my legs, and they carried me to a stairwell and lowered me down. Andy was next to me. I noticed that the cloth they'd tied over my knee was someone's shirt. Blood was beginning to seep through it, and as I shifted my leg, the shirt budged.

'Can you make the shirt tighter?' I asked Andy.

He knelt forward and tried to adjust it, but his hands were shaking.

I winced at his effort. 'Stop, don't.'

He pulled back and turned away from me. I saw him running a hand over his face.

'Are you okay?' I asked.

'Yeah. Sorry.' He turned back, rubbing his hands on his knees. 'I, uh, I thought it attacked you.'

I gripped his hand.

Tom came back, holding my phone and wallet, which someone had handed to him. 'I've just spoken to the driver. There's a hospital which is not too far. He's going to drive us there. I've got the directions on my phone. In the meantime, you just need to hold that shirt down against your knee. I tried giving them some rupees for it, but they're not taking anything.'

'Thanks,' said Andy, standing up.

'You all right?' said Tom, patting him on the shoulder. 'Gave us a hell of a fright, eh?'

'Yeah, fuck,' he muttered, straightening his posture. 'Could do with some of your hash.'

Tom laughed and winked at me. 'Let's take her to the car.'

~~~

By the time we reached the hospital, my hand was numb from pressing it against my knee. Andy's hand had covered mine the entire way. I saw the hospital entrance. There must have been a hundred or more people, mostly groups of families, crowded into disorderly queues outside. I wondered how long it would take us to get seen. What if my knee was screwed by then?

'What are we going to do?' I asked quietly. 'There are so many people. We don't even have insurance and—'

'It's okay,' said Tom, 'I'll go speak to the paramedics. There'll be an emergency unit.' He started to get out of the car, but the driver stopped him. He was demanding to go back to our hostel to sort out payment. The hostel was still another hour away, and we'd initially agreed to end the trip there.

'Can't he just wait for us?' asked Andy. There was an edge to his voice. I could see the blood from the shirt had stuck to his hands.

Tom grimaced. 'I don't think he wants to. He keeps pointing at the time.' Tom tried to negotiate a deal with him, but the driver kept shaking his head.

'For fuck's sake!' yelled Andy, banging the roof of the car. 'Antonia needs to see someone *now*. Just pay him whatever he needs.'

But the driver was demanding to go back with someone. He got paid a fee by the hostel, and the hostel wouldn't believe he'd made the trip if he showed up without one of us.

Andy had opened the door and was getting out of the car. 'Then just go back with him,' he snapped at Tom.

Andy walked over to my side and opened my door. He tried to help me out, but his hands were rough, and his grip pinched my elbow. I cried out and tried to get up on my own, but my leg was stiff and swollen. I felt the wound slit open again, and I collapsed back into the seat. Tom got into the backseat and helped me out.

'Come on,' said Andy. 'Just take my arm.'

'I can't. It's too sore to walk.' I grabbed onto the car door.

He looked at the large crowd ahead. 'How the hell are we going to do this?' He breathed quickly. 'This is a nightmare. For fuck's sake.' He smacked his hand against the door of the car.

'Mate, I don't mind staying here with her. I can go and speak to the medics at the entrance,' said Tom quietly. 'If you want to go back and take a breather, I don't think we'll be too long.'

Andy turned over to Tom, looking him up and down. 'I'm sure you wouldn't fucking mind. Just get lost.'

'Andy...' I said, my eyes widening at his temper, 'he's trying to help.'

'He's not. He's a dick. And don't take his side. Why the hell is he even still with us?' He shot a look at Tom. 'I told you already, *fuck* off.'

I watched as Tom raised his hands and shrugged, muttering something under his breath as he got back in the taxi.

Before I could say anything, Andy held me under my arms and lifted me up. I stared up at the dark skies grimacing, trying to think of anything but the throbbing pain. I could see the hospital lights getting brighter as he carried me closer to the building.

'Can you help us?' said Andy urgently to someone.

I was tended to quickly by a paramedic who lay me on a stretcher and disinfected my wound. Andy was sent to the waiting room when a doctor was called up. He spoke little English but had a kind smile. He looked at my injuries and gave me some injections and painkillers.

The slit on my leg was deep. The nurse sewed stitches in my knee, elbow and foot. There were only a couple of stitches on the rest of the wounds, but there were ten on my knee. I winced and sunk my teeth into my pashmina as the needle and thread yanked my skin back together, glad neither Tom nor Andy were there to witness the scene.

## 31

I stayed put for almost a week, my knee stiff and bruised. I was mostly on my own, as Andy and Tom seemed to be avoiding both me and each other.

I was worried about the camel trek. After the accident, Andy had tried cancelling, but the money was non-refundable, and our only option was to postpone it to a week later. The three of us had put down the money already. I wanted to go, more than either of them. They doubted the commercialised aspect of it, the inauthentic experience and the overpriced tickets. But I had insisted we pay. I was desperate to be in the desert, riding camels through the sand dunes and sleeping under the stars. Andy had been prepared to lose the money, and he wanted rid of Tom ('there's no way you'll be walking by next week, maybe the two of us can go to Darjeeling instead'), while Tom was more conscious of the expense ('I don't know, just feels like a huge waste of money if we don't go').

There wasn't much to do in bed except drink chai and read books. The heat was my enemy, adding to my already low levels of hygiene. I craved a shower with soap. I'd tried a few times to hobble around the tap and had used an annual supply of wet wipes to try to make myself feel a little less disgusting. I hadn't appreciated until then how access to a shower could affect my mood. The absence of one was making me dirtier and depressed.

Tom would occasionally bring me snacks but kept our conversations short. I wondered if Andy was giving him as hard a time as he was giving me. I knew they were also growing bored. They'd been visiting the same temples and lakes every day and were increasingly spending time in the hostel drinking.

Slowly I started to limp around the room, stretching my leg out and testing my footing. I felt comfortable enough one morning walking around the room and ventured outside. Andy and Tom were having breakfast and reading their books on the balcony. I noticed Andy was still speaking to Tom, although his tone was less friendly and more cordial. Maybe he didn't want to show him that he cared at all. Tom, however, was treating him more respectfully.

I joined them, excited to feel the fresh air.

Andy looked at me curiously. 'Better?'

'Yeah, I think so.' I sat down next to him. 'I think we should head on to Jaisalmer. I can walk. I'll just need to take it easy.'

We found a bus leaving the next night.

~~~

The night bus had actual bunk beds crammed inside it. We each claimed one, the bus jolting, thundering and creaking every two seconds. I plugged my headphones in, my head banging the ceiling. It was a fitful sleep, my arms and legs jerking with each bump.

I must have managed some sleep, for I woke up feeling groggy like time had passed. There was a cacophony of snores coming from Andy and Tom. We must have been getting more used to Indian transport than I'd thought.

A couple of hours later, the bus rolled into Jaisalmer. Tom pulled back the curtains. It was a desert, arid city with sand forts coated in a haze of golden dust. The view opened up to mud houses with open rooftops, men in light, long robes, women in colourful saris and market vendors. Every once in a while we spotted a backpacker. I saw one drenched in sweat, backpack on the floor, a bandana on their head, gulping down water.

We got off the bus. It was roasting, close to forty degrees. In this city, women weren't meant to show shoulders or anything above the knee. I wore light trousers and a sari over my T-shirt, sweating through it all. I should have worn a sari over my hair, but it kept falling down, and I was too warm. Sweat trickled down my leg into my bandages. As the trousers rubbed against the wound, I squirmed uncomfortably with each step.

We roamed the town until we found a hostel on the outskirts. As we approached the entrance, I stopped in my tracks. Two large cows slept in the shade outside the entrance. I stood still, my heart thumping.

'Come on,' said Andy.

'I'm too nervous.'

'It's okay. They're too hot to even move. Look, Tom's passed them already.'

'I can't.'

Andy's forehead was dripping with sweat in the heat. He had my backpack on his shoulders as well as his own.

He wiped his brow and gave me his arm. 'Come on. Follow me.'

I shut my eyes as Andy guided me around the beasts. I could feel my heart pounding against my ribcage. I dug my nails into Andy's arm.

None of them moved, too lethargic in the heat to pay attention to us.

We checked into the dorm. Compared to the Udaipur hostel, which had been so full of backpackers, and where I'd constantly been tripping over backpacks, toiletries and sandals, this room was empty. We hadn't had this kind of privacy for over a month. There was even a bathroom with a cold tap and a bucket all to ourselves.

As soon as we could, we went out into town to organise the camel trek. I was excited. We found the trekking agency in town, and we huddled into the office, getting the brief for tomorrow.

'We should get turbans and look the part. They're selling them for pennies in that stall.' I pointed across the street. 'Which one do you want?'

'I wouldn't spend money on that shite,' grumbled Andy. Tom agreed.

'Oh, come on,' I sighed dramatically. 'We're in the freaking Indian desert! We're about to go and ride jewelled camels through sand dunes. Think about Lawrence of Arabia, *The Little Prince*, *The Prince of Egypt*! We're probably never going to do this again.' I threw Andy a look. 'What colour are you getting?'

He raised an eyebrow, but his jaw had softened. 'Fine. Green.'

'I'll take black,' said Tom.

I chose a brilliant red.

## 32

After a day's walk, Andy insisted on having a drink in town. We found a bar a half hour from the hostel, crammed with backpackers, a group of which immediately invited us to join them. Beers were ordered on repeat. I watched Andy easily mingle with the others.

There was something wrong with my knee. It had been acting up, and it hadn't helped that I'd been trailing behind the boys all day. It could have just been because I hadn't walked that distance in a while.

A beer later, and it seemed to feel worse. Andy was talking to a Canadian backpacker about the Annapurna Trail. I lay a hand on his arm.

'Hey,' I said quietly, 'my knee is really sore.'

Andy sipped on his beer, his eyes still focused on the Canadian. I squeezed his arm.

He glanced over at me. 'Right. Okay. Just have some beer. You'll feel better in a bit.'

'I think I want to head back to the hostel.'

'Take some painkillers. You're fine.'

'I don't know, it's really uncomfortable.'

He studied my knee and shrugged. 'Look, we'll go back in a couple of hours. I'm waiting to play a game of pool.'

So I sat in a booth, drinking beer. There were a couple of Australian girls next to me. By the sound of their conversation ('Yeah, I loved Rishikesh. Did you do Vipassana?') they too had met on their travels. They tried a few times to include me in their conversation, but I hardly engaged, tired and too focused on Andy. I'd lost count of how many beers he'd had. Must have been five or six, at least. I could hear his Scottish accent booming down the table, getting louder with every sip. I couldn't remember the last time he'd drunk so much. Maybe back home with his rugby friends.

My head was starting to pound now as well as my knee. More than anything, I felt dirty. My whole body felt sticky, covered in grime. I watched Andy finish his pint. When he finally did, I thought we'd head, but then he ordered another one. I noticed Tom getting up to leave and jumped at the chance.

I went over to Andy again, interrupting his chat with the Canadian and another man who'd joined. I didn't care to introduce myself.

He pulled a face, irritated.

'Andy,' I tried again, 'honestly, my knee feels like shit. I know you're having a good night, but I'm not feeling great. Tom's leaving now, I'm going back with him.'

Andy turned to me, his eyes glazed over. 'No, you're not. You're going back with me.'

I laughed in disbelief. 'He's leaving now, I just thought—'

Andy stood up quickly. 'Either tell that dickhead to walk back alone, or I will.' His loud voice made some conversations stop and I saw the two Australian girls look over and then whisper to each other.

I bit down on my lip and pushed past him. Tom had heard Andy from a mile off and was already on his way out.

'See you later,' he said, walking away. I watched him go and leant against the door, trying to level my breathing.

'Antonia.' I heard Andy stumbling towards me. Why was he so drunk? What was he playing at?

He followed me outside, out of earshot.

I could smell the beer on his breath as he came closer to me.

'Why don't you have some water?'

'I'm done,' said Andy, 'I thought you were just trying to prove a point, to show me how I should be more like him, embrace the crap hippie life. *I get it.*'

I felt rage rising in my throat.

'What else do you want, huh? Do you want to fuck him? Would that make you feel better?'

'You need to calm down.'

'No. You need to stop giving me such a hard time for not wanting the exact same things as you. I'm doing this for you. I'm doing all of this travelling for you. Isn't that enough?'

'Yes, it is. You're blowing this all out of proportion. Tom was leaving anyway—'

'Don't speak to me like a kid. He wants to fuck you, and you're just leading him on. And what am I meant to do? Stand here like a right fucking idiot? You're humiliating me, and you know you are, but maybe I'm the bigger dick because I'm letting it happen, just because, somehow, fuck knows how or why, I still fucking love you.'

I wiped away tears. 'Andy, stop it—'

'And by the way, I really don't get it either, because he's some fucking hippie with no ambition who's going to end up working in a kitchen for the rest of his life. But that seems to turn you on, as long as he's washing dishes in Thailand or someplace Instagram-worthy.'

I couldn't find words to respond and rubbed my face with my sleeve.

'Aren't you going to say anything?' he asked.

I swallowed. 'Nothing has happened.' My voice was hoarse.

He grabbed his beer and walked towards the door. His Adam's apple bobbed up and down beneath his beard. When had his beard grown that much? It was as bushy as I'd ever seen it, brown with ginger flecks.

He held the door. I thought he was going to open it, but he stood still. He looked back at me. 'Are you…' He cut himself off short and clenched a raised fist which he then let hang limp. 'Do you love him?'

My stomach went cold. 'Of course not. He's a guy we met a few months ago in a hostel. We share some interests, and that's it.'

He stood still, slowly nodding. I watched as he clumsily tried to make up a joint. His eyes were glazed over as he tried fiddling with tobacco paper. My knee burned.

'I'm going back. Tom's already gone, and I'm not waiting for you any longer. I'll see you later.'

'Whatever,' he muttered.

As I left, I worried about how he'd get back. I wondered if I'd ever seen him that drunk. The camel trek was tomorrow.

As I walked down the dark road on my own, I felt the tepid desert air against my flushed cheeks. It was the first time since I'd met him that Andy hadn't walked me home.

## 33

When I got back to the hostel, my legs were covered in sweat, and my bandages were brown and wet with residue.

Tom was in the dorm room, reading his book. He put it down as I came in.

'Hey, you all right?' he asked. 'Where's Andy?'

'Still out,' I muttered.

I didn't listen to what he said next, too intent on getting to the bathroom.

I was determined to feel clean, even though it meant the bandages getting soaked. The small trail of cold water was a relief. The water was a light brown colour but odourless.

I stripped down to my sports bra and underwear. I used the dirty soap, unsure if it made much of a difference, trying to wet my hair and armpits. I grimaced as the dirty, brown water trickled through to the bandages on my knee. It burned—a lot. I gave a low groan as I realised it was too painful to continue. Angrily, I turned the tap off and wrapped my mouldy, damp towel around me.

I caught sight of myself in the mirror. Half my hair was damp, the other like a lion's mane. There were streaks of dirt on my cheeks. Whether it was the fight, my knee or the consistent lack of hygiene, I felt tears building up. I was too angry to cry. I wiped my face quickly, staining my face further with the muck. I reached for the soap to pack it up, but it fell and cracked. I tried to grab it, but the pain in my knee stopped me.

'For fuck's sake,' I snapped. I leant against the sink, trying to take a deep breath.

There was a knock on the door. Pointless, really, since there was no lock or handle on it.

'You okay?' asked Tom.

'No,' I muttered.

'Can I come in?'

'Whatever.'

He opened the door. Whatever I looked like, it must have been amusing, for he was trying not to laugh.

'You're a mess.'

I kicked the soap. 'I hate this. I hate this hostel. I hate India. I just wanted a fucking shower.' I sat down on the edge of the seatless toilet.

He was barefoot but rolled up his jeans and walked over the wet, murky floor. He picked up the soap from the floor and put it on the windowsill. He then squatted by the tap, where he twisted it open. The water came pouring out. He turned it back off.

'Seems to be working fine.' He got back up. 'Come on, this is luxury compared to that squat toilet in Kathmandu.'

'I know, it's just my knee. It's too sore.'

Tom glanced at the bandages and made a face. I knew what he was thinking. They looked rotten. They probably smelt worse. He rolled his sleeves back.

'What are you doing?'

'Changing your bandages. I think they might be infected.'

'But I don't have any to replace them with.'

'Good thing I've got a first aid kit.'

~~~

Tom brought the first aid pouch from his bag and set it up on the bathroom floor. I noticed he left the door half-open.

He knelt in front of me and looked at my knee and the mass of grey cloth. I wondered if he could smell the wound too. He probably could. It smelt putrid to me. The small bulb hanging from the ceiling gave a green, sickly light. The tap dripped behind us. A cockroach scuttled in the corner.

He bent over the few tools he had. His dark brown hair was matted with dust. I noticed he also had streaks of dust across his jaw and eyebrows. I could see a pair of small scissors, disinfectant, clean bandages and some pills. He held my forearm as he cut the bandage from my elbow. He removed the silver bangles I'd bought in Udaipur, setting them on the windowsill, and took my wrist as he cut the dressing wrapping my fingers. Then he held my ankle, undoing the anklet's latch, as he cut the bandage off from my foot. The wounds were red, and felt fiery as the damp air made contact with my raw skin.

He held my calf in his hands. My leg was covered in bruises. It was tanned and flaky and hadn't seen cream or oil—not to mention a razor—since we started travelling. I cringed at the sight. He focused on the large brown bandage covering my knee.

'So this is the painful one.'

'Yeah,' I mumbled.

His right hand slid up to my knee, the left one still holding my calf. He started cutting into the side of the bandage. The movement of the scissors against it caused direct friction of the material against the wound. I cried out.

His hand squeezed my calf. He continued. More slowly, this time.

'Does it hurt now?'

'It's okay,' I managed, my teeth grinding together.

He moved again. His hands were swift.

'How do you know what to do?' I asked.

'I was a trained first aider when I did my scuba diver stint in Krabi, remember? I used to fix coral cuts and infections all the time.'

The bandages were thick and damp, and he pried them apart with his fingers. I watched his brows furrow in concentration.

I looked down and swore.

He was right; the wound was infected. The smell made my eyes water. It was triple the size it had been, spreading all over my knee. Layers of congealed blood surrounded pools of yellow pus. My whole knee, right to the back, was an angry shade of pink.

'It looks bad,' I said, cringing.

Tom said nothing, which made it worse. We were in the middle of the desert. What if this really was serious? Could I go back to the hospital? Maybe I'd have to fly to Delhi.

My hands shook. I tried to look away from it. My jaw clenched, and my knee kept jolting in Tom's firm hands every time they threatened to move.

'Antonia, I need to clean it. It's going to hurt more if I don't.'

'It's going to hurt like a bitch if you do.'

He squeezed my calf. I watched in terror as he prepared the dressings. If the air was hurting it, I couldn't imagine what any other pressure would do.

He lifted a cotton ball soaked in alcohol up to it. He looked at me, and I looked back at him. I closed my eyes.

He pressed it in.

I screamed.

## 34

When I opened my eyes, my face was wet and my nose was running. My fingernails dug into the palm of his hands, and I gasped for breath, looking at him. He was panting too. His brow was wet, but he seemed immune to me almost breaking his hand.

'Well, that wasn't too bad, huh?' he said.

I met his eye. We both started to laugh.

I continued to squirm in his grasp as he cleaned out the infection from the wound. He scraped off the residue, mopping up the older pus until the liquid became transparent. My tears kept on splashing onto his arms, but he worked skilfully, hardly looking up.

When he was done cleaning it, he grabbed his towel and ran it under some water, adding soap. He came back over. My legs were still shaking. He sponged up the area around the wound and then travelled down to my calf. He did the same with my other leg.

'This is called an improvised shower,' he said.

I wiped my face as he rubbed my legs down.

'It'll feel a lot better tomorrow. I'll get you some antibiotics.' He gestured at the stack of pills in his pouch.

'Thank you.'

He moved up to wipe my arms. 'Hey, come on. Cheer up.'

I swallowed. Shouldn't Andy have done this?

We were silent as my arm fell limply in Tom's hands, and he patted me down. He picked up my right arm. He ran the towel over my wrist, and his hand moved up my forearm, around my elbow.

'I've never seen Andy lose his temper like that before.'

Tom said nothing. He rubbed more soap onto the towel and changed sides.

'I'm the one who goes wild. He's normally so calm.'

Tom's face gave nothing away. He worked on me with concentration.

I stared down at the top of his head. His hair was thinning slightly around his ears. 'You know, back in Edinburgh, he's the one who cooks every night. Even though he comes back late from work. He loves it. And he'll always put on Frank Sinatra, or something cringey and romantic, and light candles. Even on a Monday night. I miss that.'

I pressed my lips together, watching Tom scrunch up the old bandages. He put them in the bin and went back to cleaning my legs.

'I think I've pushed him to the limit. Maybe he's had enough. The way he was speaking to me…he's just never done that. He watched me walk back alone. This is coming from a guy who hardly let me walk in front of cars without him being there. I feel like I've broken him.' I breathed out.

He cleaned gently around the wound for a while and dabbed the towel in more alcohol. 'Listen, do you want to come with me to Sri Lanka?'

I stared at him and felt the silence grow tense around us. I watched his hand moving in slow motion around my knee.

'Well, the option's there if you want it.'

'I can't do that to him, Tom.'

He shrugged, not looking up. 'Guess I misread the situation then.'

'What situation?' I winced as I heard the words come out.

Tom raised an eyebrow. 'You need me to spell it out?'

I swallowed. 'Yeah.'

'I don't think you're happy. Neither is he. I'm no relationship expert, but I don't think it should be based on deals. You guys don't owe each other anything. I think you're both just keeping it going because you feel stuck.'

My stomach started to tighten. 'You don't know us,' I muttered. 'Yeah, it's been stressful travelling. But things'll be different when we go back to Scotland.'

Tom stopped moving his hand and glanced at me. It was almost with pity. 'You think he wants to go back to Scotland?'

I didn't answer. My chest tightened as his fingers rubbed my leg. I wished he'd go closer to the wound. I wanted him to touch it. I didn't want to think. Instead, he stroked my leg. I lowered my fingers on to his hand, and he slowly held them in his grasp.

'Can I say something else?' he asked.

I looked at him silently.

He breathed in. 'While I'm being honest, I...' He swallowed, 'I like you, Antonia. I think we could have a lot of fun travelling together.'

His eyes slowly met mine, and we looked at each other in silence. My heart beat fast. Why was he telling me this? What was I meant to say back? That I liked him too? That I liked him a lot and that it scared me? That I had more in common with him than anyone I'd ever met, that his travel lifestyle was my dream, and that I envied his spirit and his freedom and most of me wanted to go with him?

'Promise me you'll think about it,' he said.

I closed my eyes. Andy. How could I love him so much and want to leave him at the same time? The thought of leaving him was torturous. It would destroy me. It would break him. I couldn't do that to him. How could I even think that way? When had I become such a monster?

'Antonia?'

I opened them. 'I'll think about it.'

Silence filled the space between us, and I was relieved Tom was busy with the disinfecting process and we could both focus on that. Once the pus and gunk had been scraped out, fresh blood had pooled in, and he wiped that with more wet wipes. He then doused it with an antiseptic, dabbing on as much as he could. I practised breathing in and out deeply and methodically to distract myself from the burning and throbbing sensations.

I breathed in again and my eyes flickered to his tattoo, now fully revealed next to his rolled-up sleeve.

'What does it mean?' I said, gesturing at it. I hoped it would be enough to break the silence and shift the tension.

The corners of his mouth twitched. 'You're not supposed to ask someone that.'

'Oh…sorry…really? I thought it was just voting and age that were off limits.'

'I'm just joking.'

He was quiet, and I thought he was avoiding the question, but then:

'You're going to give me shit.'

'Oh my God, is it Comicon? Are you going to confirm you really are a dork?'

He gave a short laugh. 'No. But kind of. It's a sword symbol from *Indiana Jones*.'

I grinned triumphantly. 'I knew it,' I gave the air a fist pump, 'I knew you were a geek.'

He looked down at my knee and gave a small smile. 'Right, I think that's clean,' he said quietly, almost to himself, now looking around for a clean roll of bandages.

'So…' I continued, 'is there any meaning to said sword? Or was it just a really good franchise?'

He shrugged. 'You know I told you about Charlie?'

My smile faded. 'Yeah.'

'Well we used to play these games when we were kids, you know, pretending to be Indiana Jones.'

'So you got matching tattoos at age ten?'

He glared at me.

'Sorry.'

'In one of Charlie's surgeries, they left a bad scar on his back. It looked like the sword from *Indiana Jones*. I drew on it later with a sharpie. He loved it. Mum almost killed me. But we kept drawing it back on. I'd do the same on my arm. So yeah, then I got it tattooed when I left home.'

I pressed my lips together, watching him unravel white strips of bandages. 'That's...special,' I managed.

His eyes briefly flickered up at me in acknowledgement. I glanced at the black sword again, but now it seemed too private for me or anyone else to look at. It was interesting that someone who was so determined to estrange himself from his family had permanently scarred his brother's memory onto his skin. Tom was clearly still wrestling with past demons, probably still furious with his family.

'When's the last time you spoke to your parents?'

Lines formed between his eyebrows—I didn't know if it was a result of the question or the concentration—as he adjusted the strips and started to fix them around my knee.

'A long time ago.'

'I'm just...I guess I'm surprised that they've not been in touch with you. I mean you were their biggest link with Charlie, you were his best friend. How have they not tried to contact you or—'

'I didn't say they haven't tried. I just said we haven't spoken.'

He shrugged, wrapping the bandages on tightly and weaving them under my leg and over the knee. 'They tried to be in touch. I changed my phone number. Now they write emails. Mostly Mum sends emails asking where I am, telling me what they've been doing, asking if I...whatever. You know, all that usual Mum crap.'

He snorted without a smile and finished adjusting the bandage. 'She invites me for Christmas every year, even though I've never answered a single message.'

I stared at him dumbly. 'You've never answered? Since you left?'

'Just once. Told them I was leaving New Zealand.'

'But...wow...your poor Mum, I can't believe you won't—'

'Don't,' he snapped.

I flinched.

He looked up at me and it was the first time in a while that we'd held eye contact. His brown eyes looked darker under his furrowed brows.

'I've told you this crap in confidence because you asked, but I'm definitely not asking for your opinion.'

He grabbed the first aid kit and pushed through the door. I could hear him unzipping his backpack in the room. I'd had a vision of Tom as this carefree, rootless and genuine guy. But he was just running away, hurting people and being selfish. I couldn't bear the thought of his mother behind the laptop every morning, waiting and hoping for a reply.

I looked down at my clean, white bandage. I'd made my decision. I'd made it as soon as Tom had asked me, and this had only confirmed it. I didn't love Tom. I didn't want an adventure with him. I didn't want to live my life always on the run. I wanted a life with Andy. There were many journeys waiting for us, even though they might not always be in the form of travel. Our marriage would be our next biggest one. I needed to fight for him. I needed to save our relationship. I needed to give it all I had.

Tom pushed the door all the way open as I hobbled through to the bed.

'Why are the lights off?' I asked, turning them back on.

A pile of jeans lay on the floor.

I looked up to the bunk bed.

Andy.

Tom's eyes were on me. I moved towards Andy. Tom shook his head at me.

'He's passed out,' he whispered.

What if he'd heard Tom asking me about Sri Lanka? Or about our relationship? He had to be passed out. He had to be.

I lay with my eyes open, straining to make out a sound from Andy, a snore, loud breathing, sleep-talk, anything, to know he was asleep.

The night crawled on, and I detected nothing. How had we not heard him come in? Then a thought struck me, and my stomach was instantly cold; what if Tom had?

I felt alone. What if neither Tom nor Andy were on my side?

It must have been an hour or so that had passed when I realised that I didn't hear Tom's usual soft snores either. I wondered if the three of us were lying awake, hidden in the dark, haunted by decisions we had and hadn't made.

## 35

Sleep must have come, for the next time I turned around, sunlight flooded the room, and Tom's alarm was going off. It was six in the morning, and we needed to meet the jeep that would take us camel trekking in an hour.

For a blissful minute, I'd forgotten what had happened, and I blearily got out of bed. The swelling in my knee was going down and the redness was clearing up. It felt easier to stand on.

'Morning,' mumbled Tom.

My stomach twisted back into its knots as last night's events came back to me. I went to the bathroom to get ready for the day.

When I came back out, Tom was packing up his sleeping bag. He looked at me, his eyes pausing on mine, but I broke it off. Andy was still in bed, a T-shirt over his face.

'Andy, you getting up?'

A loud groan. 'Too much beer.'

'Come on,' I said, 'we've got camels waiting. We'll get you some water and a coffee, and you'll be good to go.'

A grunt. Followed by movement. He shuffled his way down the bunk bed. He looked rough. His hair stuck up all over the place, and he had dark bags under his eyes. He turned to walk past me to go to the bathroom but stopped.

'You've got new bandages.' He scratched his hair. Did he even remember our fight from last night?

'Yeah. Changed them last night,' I said, sitting down to fix my bag.

He hesitated, watching me pack. 'Is it still bothering you?'

I tightened the straps of my bag and shook my head. I watched his bare feet and hairy legs as he padded to the bathroom.

~~~

The three of us walked in weary silence to the jeep. We only had our day packs and water and left everything else in the hostel lockers. The tour manager came out of his office and rode with us. He was coming to drop us off in a desert village where some guides would meet us with the camels.

We left the golden city behind us, and the further the jeep went, the emptier and more vast the landscape became. I sat wedged between Tom and Andy, knocking our knees together. I stared straight ahead. We were surrounded by sand dunes and miles of desert. Andy was giving me nothing, his head hanging out the window.

After an hour, the roads stopped, and we continued on sand, the jeep wading through—just.

Two hours later, we were in the middle of nowhere. We stopped at a tiny hamlet, where three mud huts were built close together. A couple of children played in their white robes outside.

Two male figures walked towards us. We jumped out of the jeep and got our bags out. The manager spoke to us in English.

'Your guides are Dai and Rashi.' He gestured at them.

The two men stared back at us. They each wore long brown smocks and an expertly tied turban, which I wondered if they ever removed. Tom wore his in an amateur arrangement, and Andy used his to wipe the sweat off his face. Dai looked about seventy. He had permanent lines etched into his face and large, droopy, brown eyes. Rashi couldn't have been older than fifteen and was small and slight.

'Dai has managed the camels for many years. His family comes from a desert village. You must listen to the guides all the time. They will cook for you and set up the tent. The camels are carrying all the water for five days. You're going to the middle of the desert of Jaisalmer. There is nothing there. No town. No extra water. No hospital. If there's an emergency, we will send jeeps.'

I swallowed back nerves.

'We have one rule,' he continued. 'The desert is a holy land. It's a sacred space. There are many Gods here. No alcohol. No sins. You cannot make the Gods angry.'

~~~

'That was intense,' I muttered to Andy. 'Didn't realise it would be so strict.'

'Yeah, but I'm not going to miss the booze either.' He looked nauseated at the thought.

To my delight, our guides took our turbans from us and ravelled them expertly around our heads. They moved their hands with dexterity yet almost mechanically, tucking the folds neatly and smoothing out any creases. We then followed them through the sand dunes, and it wasn't long until we spotted three huge brown lumps in the desert.

I'd never seen camels in real life before. They looked like creatures out of *A Thousand Nights*. They were double the size of a horse and seemed twice as lazy. Dai woke them up like children, talking, singing and patting them until they were on their feet.

They had enormous eyes swarmed by flies, and pools of drool and sweat soaked the sand beneath them. Each one had a brightly coloured saddle—pink, green and blue—hand-knitted with silk and yarn, with beads and mirrors sewn into them. Their long necks were painted with intricate patterns in a dark coloured dye. They had floral designs, circles, spots and spirals all delicately drawn.

They had wooden pegs through their nostrils attached to leather reins, which we were taught how to gently pull to steer them.

Rashi, the young boy, helped me onto one of them. He tugged the camel by its reins to make it stand up.

The camel rocked its whole weight forward. I felt like I would slide down its neck, but it staggered back, making me grasp its reins until it was finally upright. I sat there, startled. I worried I was too heavy for it.

I said this to Tom, and he laughed. 'You see the panniers on its side? They probably each weigh about one hundred kilograms. It can't even feel you.'

'How do you know that?'

'I rode camels in Egypt….' He carried on, filling me in on his more authentic experience. I grabbed tightly onto the reins.

The camel's smooth steps through the dunes gave me the sensation of swimming through the desert. Its fur felt like velvet beneath my hands. The sun was up now, starting to beat upon us. I'd poured sunblock all over and changed my red turban for a red cap instead. I realised why we'd been advised to wear long-sleeve shirts. The sun was scorching every inch of skin it could find.

We trekked on through the dunes. Andy was slowly starting to emerge from his hangover.

He glanced over at me. 'You doing all right?'

I nodded.

I thought he was reaching out to stroke my camel's neck but realised he wanted to touch my leg instead. I glanced at his fingers. He squeezed my leg, but then his camel moved and he lost his grip.

We kept on moving. I tried to talk to Rashi, but he just looked at me with his huge eyes and a wide grin, so I spoke to Tom and Andy instead.

'Did you know Lawrence of Arabia died in a motorbike accident? After all the adventures in the desert, you'd think he'd have better luck.' I glanced back. Tom was staring at the view of the sand dunes ahead. Andy's eyes were on me, a small forced smile on his face.

~~~

Rashi might not have been able to talk to us, but he knew how to communicate with camels. He used his throat and tongue to emit guttural sounds. A 'chks' or some tuts, and the camel would turn or stop fidgeting. He must have learnt it from Dai, who was even gentler, if that was possible.

What most amazed me was that they both walked on foot. They had sandals that seemed a century outdated, with broken soles and torn straps. Yet for hours, they walked ahead, in the beating sun, their heads bent down.

They barely stopped to take water. Every thirty minutes, they would offer us some. Their bodies must have been acclimatised. It was well over thirty-five degrees, and they scarcely had sweat on their faces.

My camel moved towards Andy so that we rode side-by-side. He reached out for my arm and squeezed it.

'How's your hangover?' I asked.

'Better now. Listen, I think I remember being a complete asshole.'

I gave a wry smile.

He looked at me, and I noticed dark lines under his eyes. 'I'm really sorry.'

I reached out for his hand and squeezed it back.

'Me too.'

## 36

That evening we arrived at a secluded spot, just in time for the sunset. The sky turned a shade of light pink coral that I'd never seen before. The sun's mist seemed to light the sand up, and we were surrounded by dunes of glittering gold. The stars would look incredible tonight. There were no clouds or pollution, and to see them from the desert would be magical.

As soon as the sun went down, we were offered cups of chai while the guides went on to make our dinner: *dahl baht* and roti on hot stones. It was surprisingly cool, even though the sand remained warm on our bare feet. I was grateful for the jumper I'd brought.

The three of us shared a tent. The guides laid out some camp mats and blankets, and we curled up into our sleeping bags with our phones as torches.

An hour must have passed, and I lay wide awake with my thoughts. I wanted to speak to Andy. I wanted to let him know how I felt. It would be impossible to do it with Tom here. I wondered if we could go outside and look at the stars. I turned around in the dark. I could hear both of them snoring.

I slipped quietly out of bed and put my hand on Andy's arm.

'Andy,' I said, 'wake up.'

'What?' he mumbled.

'Can we go for a walk?'

'What, now?' He stared at me, groggily.

'Yeah. We can see all the stars. They're meant to look amazing from the desert. I thought we could go, just the two of us.'

He started to get up as he rubbed his eyes.

'Yeah, okay. Give me a minute to wake up.'

I grabbed jumpers and our blankets while he got out of bed. We crawled out of the tent into the dark skies. There was a cool breeze. The moon and stars lit up the sand dunes. I could see the camels sleeping together out in the open air. We trailed up a dune in silence.

By the time we reached the top, my heart was beating faster, and I felt warm again. We sat at the top. Andy wrapped a blanket around me, tucking the corners underneath my feet. He sat next to me, propping his knees up and wrapped his arm around my shoulder.

I looked up at the millions of crystals that decorated the sky.

'Where's Orion?' asked Andy.

I'd clocked it already. I raised my finger up and traced the outline, guiding Andy.

'Oh, I see it now,' he said. 'It's so clear. Better definition than the Edinburgh night sky.'

I tugged on my blanket. I hadn't thought of Edinburgh for a while. With sand dunes for miles around us, I felt so far away. I missed it and felt a rush of homesickness for the brewery smell and cobbled streets lined with tenement houses. Maybe it wasn't the worst idea to start thinking about going back soon.

I pulled away from Andy and turned around to face him.

'I'm sorry I've been distant,' I said. 'I know I've given you a hard time, and I just want to say that I do realise all you've given up to be here. I know this hasn't been easy. And I know I've been self-absorbed for a lot of it.' I put a hand on his knee. 'I don't know if you remember much of last night, but I need you to know that nothing is going on between Tom and me. You were right to point it out. I did get caught up in some platonic fantasy but, to be honest, it only helped me realise how sure I am about you.'

He lifted his gaze and finally met my eye.

'I love you so much, Andy. Nothing will ever come close to the feelings I have for you.'

He gave a small smile. 'Come here.' He opened his arms, and I shifted around so that I could lean against his lap and shoulder. He put his arms around me, squeezing me tighter than usual.

'Thank you for saying that,' he whispered.

I nodded.

'I've been a dick too,' he said. 'I behaved badly last night. Getting drunk and letting you go back on your own...I'm sorry.'

I kissed his neck. 'I think travelling together hasn't been the fantasy picture I painted, huh?'

'No. But I appreciate it. You've taken me on a trip of a lifetime.'

'I'm sorry for, you know, brushing off the wedding and baby chat. I just need some time to feel free and to do this. I honestly do want all of that with you. I don't know exactly when, but I do know I want it.'

He kissed me on the side of my head and let out a huge breath, pressing his forehead against mine.

He wrapped his arms tighter around me. 'I know.' He clutched at my arms. 'And I don't really care about that now. I just don't know what I'd do if I lost you.' His breath tickled my face.

I grabbed onto his arm and squeezed it. 'Neither do I.' I didn't have to look at him to see that he was smiling. I could feel his dimples underneath my fingertips and his teeth against my lips.

We kissed. Not like we kissed daily. But like we hadn't kissed for a while. His lips covered mine, and my fingers were in his hair. I pulled back.

I stood up and took my shoes and socks off. I pushed them aside and felt the sand beneath my toes.

'Am I getting a striptease in the desert?' he asked, propping himself up with his elbows.

'Bet you Lawrence of Arabia didn't get this treatment.'

'Not from girls he didn't.'

As he laughed, I started to unstick my tattered clothes.

I remembered back in the day where I'd come home with new lingerie, each set lacier than the last. Andy would tear it off in seconds.

Now, my T-shirt and shorts hadn't seen a washing machine for months, and my underwear was grey, broken, and the elastics had snagged months ago. I hadn't shaved my legs since I'd left the UK, and my hair—on a good day—added a good metre to my head width.

Still, Andy lay back and watched with a grin on his face—the same grin that had once made me feel like the most beautiful girl in the world.

As he took off his top, I lowered myself onto him. I felt the dent in his shoulders and the ripple of his backbone. I moved my legs. The wiry hairs on his thigh tickled mine. He rolled me over, so I was beneath him. The sand underneath me was hard. Andy's stomach was firm. He leant forward, hands outstretched on either side of my head.

I watched Andy's eyes open and then slowly close.

We lay side by side afterwards, breathless and stunned. His lips pressed against my tangle of sandy hair.

I ran my fingertips over his arm. I was too lethargic to get up. I pushed my hair back out of my face and lay it out behind me. Andy was watching me, his eyes flickering over my lips and neck.

'This would be such a nice photograph right now,' he said.

He kissed my collarbone, and I held his arm. I could feel his heart pounding against his ribcage. His arm draped over my shoulder, like so many times before. I traced his Saturn-shaped birthmark, feeling the rough edge beneath my finger. His arm was firmer, like his stomach. The hikes and the sun had made him stronger. There were more freckles scattered on his shoulder. He breathed quickly and loudly, each breath tickling my ear.

'This has been my favourite night of the trip so far,' said Andy.

I smiled. 'Mine too.' I'd missed this. I'd missed Andy. Travelling had challenged us, but this had made me realise that our relationship was still alive. We hadn't lost it.

I touched the back of his hand, and he shifted to kiss my temple, holding his lips against me.

I stroked his hair. 'I can't wait to start the rest of my life with you.'

My heart felt full. I lay in pure bliss, noticing how the starry sky seemed to be easing all my anxieties. We fell asleep out in the open, my head on Andy's chest.

## 37

'Fucking hell, seriously?'

I opened my eyes. The first thing I saw was pink skies above me and a heavy arm draped around my chest. I shifted and heard Andy grumble, moving aside.

A brown head of hair came into focus.

Tom.

I sat up, clutching at my blanket, feeling sand fall over my back. I looked around, but Tom was already walking down the sand dunes.

'Shit, Andy, get up. We fell asleep.'

Andy was already on his knees, pulling his T-shirt on.

'Was that Tom?' he asked.

'Yeah,' I turned around again but could only see the golden dunes. I started to pull my clothes on.

'They must be looking for us,' said Andy. His cheeks were flushed as he grabbed the blanket and clothes. 'Fuck's sake.'

He stopped for a minute and caught my eye, and we grimaced. 'Come on, let's go.' He stretched out his hand and pulled me up.

I was mortified when I saw Rashi and Dai watching us the whole way as we clambered down the dunes to the campsite. I cringed with embarrassment.

'Do you think we've offended them?' I asked Andy.

He looked as uncomfortable as I did and shrugged as we quickly climbed down. As exciting as sex in the desert had been for us, this was still a sacred space for them. I clung to the thought that they might not have known what we'd done. Maybe they just thought we preferred sleeping on sand rather than a mat.

I noticed the tents had been dismantled and the camels were packed and ready to go. It took me a moment to spot Tom. He was sitting behind the camels, reading his book.

Andy spoke to Rashi and Dai. 'The stars…the sky…we went out to see it. Must have fallen asleep.'

They said nothing but offered us each a cup of warm chai. We sipped on it gratefully. Tom didn't say a word. Neither did we. We drank in silence as the sun lit up the desert.

We needed to start the trek early before the sun heated the sand and roasted our pale skins. We climbed onto our camels. Andy's was upfront. Tom's camel stayed behind mine.

'How's your book?' I asked Tom. My tone sounded sheepish.

Tom said nothing. I glanced at him, but he was looking fixedly ahead. I rolled my eyes. I refused to let him make me feel guilty for sleeping with my fiancé.

A while later, Andy turned around on his camel and called out to us.

'Do you reckon we'll see any of the ancient forts?'

I saw Tom glance up. 'Hope so. This is the shittest camel trek I've ever been on.'

After a few hours of silence, the guides stopped the camels and began to prepare for a rest while we sat under the shade of some dry shrubs.

Tom didn't join us, opting to go for a walk instead.

'What's up with him?' asked Andy, still vaguely amused, 'he had to look for us for an hour—big deal.'

I shrugged, sipping on my water.

Andy lay back on the mat. I rested my head on his chest while he stroked my hair.

I opened my eyes to a shadow blocking the sun. Tom stood in front of us. His whole face was twisted. His eyes looked shiny and beady, and he was looking at us with contempt.

It was only when I sat up that I realised he was holding a bottle of whisky.

'Where'd you get that from?' I asked.

'Brought it with me. Just in case.'

I then noticed it was almost empty. I stared at it. 'You've had a whole bottle?'

His smile became more skewed, and he laughed. 'There was nothing else to do. This is shit.'

His voice sounded odd and slurry. He started to unscrew the lid. He ignored me and offered a swig to Andy, who shook his head.

'Mate, come on, it's not even lunchtime.'

Tom ignored him and tilted the rest of the contents into his mouth. He made a point of smacking his lips together before putting it down. Something was churning inside me, a mixture of fury and disappointment.

'I need to piss,' he said, stumbling over to the bushes.

The guides—who'd been tying the saddles back up—were calling us to continue the trek. We walked towards them, glancing around to see if Tom was going to follow us. Dai got Andy onto his camel first and strapped his bags in.

Just as Rai was going to help me, I saw Tom moving in the shrubs. He had thrown the bottle, which was now on display.

'Shit,' I muttered, moving away from Rai. I glanced at Andy. 'Distract the guides. I'll hide it.'

Rai motioned for me to get on the camel.

'Just one minute,' I said, gesturing an apology, 'I need to get Tom.'

I turned back and walked quickly the way Tom had gone. He was buttoning his trousers, the whisky bottle glittering on the ground.

'What the hell are you doing?' I asked.

Tom laughed upon seeing me. 'Pissing.'

I ignored him and glanced at the bottle at his feet. 'Give me that, now.'

'No.'

I lunged and grabbed it, but before I could move, he snatched it with force out of my hands.

'Don't touch it.'

My palms stung where he'd scratched them. 'Don't you get it? The guides are going to see you.'

Tom sneered at me, biting his bottom lip. 'You weren't too worried about them seeing you fucking this morning, were you?'

'You know what? Whatever.' I started to leave, but I heard him mutter something behind me. I turned around. 'What did you say?'

Tom clenched his jaw. 'I said fuck you, Antonia.'

I could hear Andy and the guides calling us back.

'That's not fair,' I shook my head, 'you can't throw a tantrum just because your plan didn't work.' I gave a quick glance behind me and lowered my voice. 'I thought about you, and I thought about

Sri Lanka, but you forget that Andy and I are engaged. We have too much history. I can't…I'm not going to throw that away.'

Tom gave a small laugh. 'Do whatever you want. Your relationship is dead anyway.'

I shook my head. 'You don't know anything about it.'

He raised an eyebrow. 'I know more than you do.'

'What's that supposed to mean?'

Tom shrugged. 'Your soulmate is going to London. He took the job. Never rejected it in the first place.'

The sand beneath me suddenly felt unstable. 'I don't believe you.'

He shrugged. 'Whatever. I thought you'd be smart enough to figure it out.'

I couldn't find my voice. It seemed to be hidden at the bottom of my stomach, covered by layers of rage. A hard lump had settled in my throat. I could feel it bubbling up, eager to turn into sobs.

I turned away from Tom, towards Andy, who was calling after me. There was only desert around us for miles. For a moment, I wondered what it would be like to walk away from the two of them.

'Where's the bottle?' asked Andy, who'd dismounted his camel.

I'd completely forgotten about it. I shook my head. 'He's being a dick.' I started to climb onto my camel. I saw Tom stumbling towards us. He wasn't trying to be subtle about hiding the whisky. Andy noticed this, and as he got nearer, he seized it from him.

'Hey! Give it back.'

'No,' said Andy quietly.

Tom stood still, standing up straighter as he broadened his chest. 'Give it to me now.'

'Piss off.'

'Oi—' It all happened quickly. Tom tried to lunge at him and fell off-balance. Instead of letting him fall, Andy grabbed him by the shirt and swiped at him, punching him square on the jaw. Tom landed on the ground with a thud and a sharp yell.

He pressed his hand on his jaw and spat some blood on the sand, which quickly dried up into what looked like black treacle. 'Fucking cunt.'

Andy had turned around already and had stormed back to his camel, where I watched him slide the bottle into his bag.

I watched speechlessly but then realised I wasn't the only one. Rashi was watching.

He'd seen the bottle. Rashi was quiet. His usual happy face now had a frown on it. He wouldn't look at us as he prompted the camels to get up. Was he going to tell Dai? I glanced over, but Andy had his back to me.

## 38

We resumed the trek. Tom had reluctantly scrambled to his feet and got onto his camel, muttering all sorts of swear words as he touched his face and spat continuously on the ground. We rode in silence, the only sound being the heavy thudding of the camels' hooves against the sand. I was glad my camel didn't seem to want company. They walked in a line, with enough space between us, which didn't encourage conversation.

I looked at Andy's back, sagging slightly in posture. A part of his turban had unravelled and was blowing in the breeze. It was hard to believe that Andy, the corporate perfectionist, had punched Tom in the face. Back home, he was usually so rational, if not passive. Now, he'd lost control. If I hadn't been hung up on what Tom had said, I would have almost felt even more attracted to him.

I didn't want to believe Tom, but I couldn't get rid of that smug look on his face. I couldn't get into a panic here in the middle of nowhere. Tom was being manipulative. His pride was dented, and he was lashing out at me. Fair enough.

And say it was true that Andy had taken the job. So what? It didn't mean he was still going to do it, especially after last night. Andy didn't want to lose me. Yeah, it wasn't exactly ideal that there was a Plan B in the back of his mind, but maybe it wasn't a bad thing. Maybe last night he'd realised that I was worth it. Just like I'd realised he was.

It must have been half an hour when Andy slowed his camel down, and I caught up with him. I glanced back at Tom. He was staring darkly at his phone. His jaw was red, and his lip was swelling up.

'He'll sober up,' muttered Andy. 'The sun'll make him sweat it out.' He stretched out his right hand, studying his swollen knuckles.

I looked at his hand. 'That was some punch.'

Andy shrugged. 'He's been asking for it.'

'Rashi saw the bottle,' I said quietly.

'Are you sure?'

I nodded.

Andy grimaced. 'He might not say anything. But if he tells Dai, they might cut the trek short. Or charge us a fine.' He sighed. 'Fuck's sake. Why the hell was he drinking? What an asshole—'

'No! No!' cried Dai.

I turned around. Dai was yelling at Tom. Tom was pulling on the camel's reins, and the camel was jerking back and groaning. Dai grabbed our reins and thrust them at Rashi.

He ran over to Tom. 'No! No!' he repeated, flapping his arms. He wanted Tom to stop pulling, to leave the camel alone.

'I want it to go faster,' said Tom. 'This is boring me to death.'

Dai tried to get hold of the reins, but Tom pulled it away from him.

'I know what I'm doing,' he snapped.

The camel jerked and pushed. My camel started to shake in response. Andy's one grunted and tried to kick-start into a trot. Andy grabbed on to its neck while Rashi attempted to calm it down.

My heart was racing. These camels were enormous and each one had more strength than all of us together.

'Let's get off…' I started. I looked at Rashi. He was trying to control ours, but he kept on looking over anxiously at Dai.

There was another yell, and I turned back around.

'Shit…' I heard Andy swear, and I realised why. The reins were tied into the camel's nose. Tom had pulled on them so hard that the camel was bleeding, its blood dripping onto the sand.

Dai was talking to him in rapid Hindi, and Tom was drunkenly yelling back at him.

'Just leave my damn camel alone,' he snapped. 'I know how to ride them. This is not a stupid riding lesson—'

'The camel's bleeding!' yelled Andy. 'Just listen to him.'

'Fuck off.'

Dai kept on gesturing for him to get off the camel, but he wouldn't budge.

'Get off!' I yelled. 'He's telling you to get off. The camel is hurt.'

Tom was fuming. Jaw clenched, he finally jumped off the screeching camel, landing with a thud on the ground. As Dai tried to calm it down, Tom unhinged his backpack from the saddle.

'This is absolute shit. A fucking kid's trip. Can't believe we paid for this.' He grabbed his backpack and pulled it over his shoulders.

'Hey, what are you doing?' said Andy. 'Just calm down for a minute.'

He gave a cold laugh. 'I'm leaving.'

He marched off, back up the trail made by the camel hooves. There was nothing around except for infinite sand dunes. Tom's shoes sunk into the sand with each step as he trailed down the dune, his yellow backpack swaying back and forth.

Rashi yelled after him. Dai was too busy tending to the camel. Rashi handed me the reins and ran over to Dai, speaking to him in rapid, urgent tones. Dai looked up and saw Tom walking away. He yelled over at us, pointing madly at Tom, presumably asking us to call him back.

'Tom!' yelled Andy. 'Oi, get back here!'

I was silent, watching in disbelief as the yellow backpack grew smaller in the distance. Surely he was going to turn back. What on earth was he thinking?

'Tom!' shouted Andy. 'What the fuck is he doing?'

'Boy! Boy!' yelled Dai after him, now leaving the injured camel to Rashi. He ran over to us and gestured to Tom's figure. 'Boy!'

Andy continued to yell, and Dai roared and whistled and made any noise to make Tom turn back.

'Fuck's sake, I'll go get him,' said Andy, checking over the side to see if he could get off. He started to lift himself off the camel, but Dai gripped him with his hand. 'No! No!'

We looked at each other in total incredulity. There was nothing around us. Vast emptiness. Sand dunes. The nearest hamlet of a village we'd seen was a two-day trek away.

Dai and Rashi parked our camels, and we got off. Dai tended to the injured camel's nose. They spoke to each other in loud, angry voices.

Andy looked furious. 'He's fucked. He's such an asshole. Why the fuck would he do that? There's nothing around us…he's going to…he's fucked.'

I kept on glancing at the figure in the distance. The yellow backpack was still in view. Why wouldn't the guides go after him? Anger and panic swelled within me. Andy kept on swearing, casting back looks.

'We have to do something,' I said.

'He's not our responsibility,' he finally said.

'Yeah, but—'

'He's not though, Antonia, is he? He's really a stranger we met in a hostel in Nepal.'

I looked at him, exasperated. 'Tom!' I yelled, my voice booming and going nowhere.

'Don't waste your time,' Andy said quietly. He crossed his arms over his chest. 'He's a full-grown adult. It's not our job to save his arse.'

My heart was beating fast. I looked away, wondering how long we'd have to hang around in the desert before finding shade. I didn't want to look at Tom's fading figure anymore.

Rashi and Dai continued to talk. I noticed Dai had a phone out. It was an old, black thing with a long antenna that looked like a walkie-talkie. Rashi was trying to help him get it to connect.

I turned around to look back at Tom.

The vast, golden sand dune appeared untouched.

Tom had disappeared.

## 39

I knew I should be worried, but I was too furious to care. Dai was speaking to us. He was looking grave, and Rashi was looking at the floor.

'Boy…' he started, looking for the words. He gestured to the water bottle. 'Boy. He drinks?'

I looked at Andy.

'You mean water?' I asked. 'If he's got water? I don't know.'

'No. No. Rashi says boy drinks. He drinks. Makes Gods very angry.'

'He's asking if Tom had alcohol,' muttered Andy. 'Rashi told him.'

'He drinks?' asked Dai again.

Andy was quiet. I looked from Andy to Dai. Why wasn't Andy saying anything? What difference did it make?

'Yes,' I said, 'he drank alcohol.'

Andy shot me a glare.

Dai raised his hands to his face and covered it. He gave a low groan.

To my horror, I saw that when he removed his hands, he was crying. Rashi was standing very still, his eyes fixed to the ground.

Andy was silent.

It took some time to get Dai to talk again. We learnt by his mourning how much the Gods in the desert meant to him and his ancestors. We'd insulted them by just bringing alcohol, and now that Tom was drunk, we'd betrayed the Gods' trust. I felt even guiltier about last night's escapade.

The sounds of his cries shook us. It felt like years of his hard work had been thrown away. We were so uncomfortable and ashamed in his grief, we couldn't even look at each other. I could have lied. I knew that's what Andy wished I'd done.

But somehow I felt like the Gods were watching us, too.

~~~

Dai managed to get hold of the trek manager with his satellite phone. They planned to send jeeps in, first to send out a search party for Tom, then to pick us up the next morning and drive us back into the city.

The jeeps would take some time to come in and locate us. We rode the camels a few more hours to some flat ground where we set up camp, all of us in stony silence. Rashi wouldn't look at me as he helped me off the saddle.

I kept on apologising, but Dai seemed not to hear us. He went on his business, meticulously unsaddling the camels, roasting rotis, cooking *dahl* and setting up camp. He didn't say a word to Rashi or us, and he didn't eat or drink a thing.

Andy wasn't saying much either. I couldn't tell if he was just furious or worried. As we sat around our campfire, I broke the silence.

'Do you think they'll find him?'

Andy stared numbly into the flames. 'I don't know.' He scratched his arm. The lack of any further reassurance made my hands clammy.

I stared into the crackling flames until my eyes stung.

~~~

I hardly slept that night. As furious as I was, I was anxious to know if they'd found him. I was too nervous of Dai to ask him the next morning.

As we sipped our chai, the silent landscape around us was interrupted by the roar of engines. The jeep had arrived. In it was the English-speaking tour manager, with two other Indians.

He jumped out and came over to us while Rashi and Dai loaded our jeep in silence.

He didn't greet us, and I noticed he didn't acknowledge Dai or Rashi either. He immediately took out his pad and pen.

'What happened?' he asked us both.

I looked at Andy, who was looking slightly startled.

'Tell me what happened,' he said louder, looking from Andy to me.

'Hang on. Did you find him?' I asked.

He ignored me and scribbled something down.

As Andy began the account, I felt anger starting to build up again.

To my surprise, he went soft on Tom. He said Tom had wanted to control his own camel and had injured it.

'And there was alcohol?'

Andy fell silent but looked at me.

'Yes,' I said. There was no point in lying about it. Rashi and Dai would have told him.

'Rashi found it in your bag. We have it,' said the manager.

Andy glanced at his pad. 'Yeah, he drank some. He didn't remember he was breaking the rules until afterwards.'

The manager kept on scribbling. He shot us a look. 'We take you back now to police station.'

'What? Why?' asked Andy.

'To make it official.'

'Make what official?'

'You testify.'

I stared at him. 'But—'

'Antonia, don't.'

I closed my mouth. Seriously?

'You come to police station now.'

## 40

It took us seven hours in a cramped jeep to get back to Jaisalmer. We arrived in the city early evening and were ushered straight to the station. We were given two white plastic chairs to sit on in front of two stern-looking officers, answering question after question, giving them the same story. They wrote notes, occasionally repeating a question.

We thought we were wrapping up when the manager stepped forward and started speaking to the policeman in Hindi. They talked in a low voice, looking over at us.

The air in the room seemed to change. Andy didn't look at me, his own hands folded on his lap, and was watching the men, his lips pressed together, a frown forming on his brow.

'You need to pay a fine,' said an officer, finally switching to English. He started to look through his papers. 'Seventy-thousand rupees.'

I made the conversion in my head. That was over eight hundred pounds.

Andy had made it too. 'Absolutely not,' he said, in the tone he saved for work calls.

The officer pointed at the Indian papers, all scrawled in Hindi. 'This is the fine. The misconduct of your friend.'

'Tom isn't our friend. This was his fault and he'll have to pay for it.'

'The police have not found him.'

'What?'

I felt light-headed. Where the hell was he? What if something had happened to him? What if he was dehydrated? How had they taken this long to find him—

'He's not our responsibility,' Andy's words interrupted my thoughts.

'We don't make the rules.'

'Yes you fucking do,' said Andy, finally snapping out of his collected manner.

'Okay. Your friend is not here. We take it down to thirty-five-thousand rupees.' That was four hundred pounds. Two hundred each. 'Last chance.'

'And what if we don't pay?'

'Then you stay here at the station until we find your friend.'

'For fuck's sake,' said Andy.

But they'd got to him. He wouldn't look at me while the officers and the manager pretended to finalise some forms. We each gave our part.

As soon as we left the station, I grabbed Andy's arm. 'They haven't found him, what if—'

'We don't know that. They might have. They're not going to tell us if they have, are they? They just wanted money.'

'How are you so sure? He might still be in the desert. He could die there.'

Andy shook his head, marching down the streets.

'Where are you going?'

'The hostel,' he snapped. 'All his stuff's there. We'll be able to tell if he's back.'

~~~

As soon as we arrived at the hostel, the assistant called the manager, and we heard him running down the stairs.

'Your friend,' he said breathlessly, 'your friend came here.'

I looked at Andy, astonished and relieved. 'How did he—'

'He came here last night, and woke up other guests. He drink too much. He took bags and left. He not pay. You need to pay!'

I sighed. Andy looked ready to punch a wall.

It wasn't too much more, about fifteen pounds. We settled the bill in silence underneath the manager's glaring eyes.

He pocketed the rupees and gestured at our bags. 'You cannot stay here.'

It was past 10 p.m. now. We were exhausted, starving and desperate for some water.

'Let's just go find somewhere else,' I said.

Andy looked defeated. His eyes were red with exhaustion.

'Come on,' I grabbed his hand. 'Let's get some sleep. We'll sort everything out tomorrow.'

~~~

After futile attempts to find a last-minute hostel availability, we'd settled for a room in a guesthouse. There was only a single bed free, so we slept stiffly and uneasily, pressed together at awkward angles.

It was past midday when Tom wrote back.

*Hey. What's up?*

*I lost it.*

'Just calm down,' said Andy, 'you'll scare him off, and we need to meet him—'

'Calm down?'

Andy started to type back, but I grabbed the phone from him.

*Where are you?*

He came back to me shortly.

*Jaisalmer. The Fort Hostel.*

I quickly typed back.

*We'll meet you there in half an hour.*

~~~

My heart was pounding as we walked to his hostel. I was furious. He hadn't even apologised. I went over his text in my head. *What's up?* Seriously? After the fine, the police station, the worrying and ruining the camel trek, that was all he came up with?

Andy, on the other hand, was calmer. He was trying to see the meet-up as a business encounter.

'We just need to get the money from him and leave. Don't get all emotional on him. He's not worth it, and we'll only drag it out.'

'I don't know if I can help myself.' I was so determined to lay my hands on Tom, I almost got run over by a rickshaw.

Andy pulled me back and let a crowd of people walk past. 'Just let me do the talking.'

~~~

We arrived first. Tom was nowhere to be seen. We sat on the hostel steps in the shade, and at half past, we saw him descending slowly down the stairs and sauntering towards us.

His face was severely sunburnt, and his jaw was a brilliant purple. He must have just come out of the shower, his hair was still wet and his face was damp.

'Sorry, I was taking a nap,' he said. His usual smile had shrivelled into a smirk. I wondered if his bruise was bothering his mouth. It must have been killing him that he couldn't hide it.

I could hear Andy muttering to himself, and he stormed in front of us as we looked for the nearest cafe. I tried to keep up with Andy, and Tom walked at his own pace, well behind us. As we crossed a road I looked over my shoulder, but Tom looked past me.

We reached a shack selling lassis and coffee, with a few plastic chairs and tables strewn beneath a canopy. We ordered three coffees, although only Andy touched his.

'How was the rest of the trek?' Tom asked. I noticed his swollen lip now had a blister on it. It looked white, pussy and sore.

Before we could say anything, Tom raised his jaw at Andy. 'You look fucking proud of yourself, don't you?' he said.

Andy half laughed and crossed his arms over his chest, shaking his head.

I didn't want to witness another fistfight. 'How did you get back?' I asked quickly.

The smirk reappeared on Tom's face, but he didn't look at me. 'Easy. Walked back the same route and ran into another trekking group. It's not exactly an original experience, is it? They called up a jeep.' He lifted his coffee but didn't sip it. 'Don't tell me you guys were worried.'

I clenched my jaw.

Andy pushed his empty cup away and it rattled against the saucer. 'We had to pay quite a bit of money for you.'

Tom gave a small snort and stirred some sugar into his coffee. 'Why?' he asked, almost as an afterthought.

Andy began to explain. He told him about the jeeps coming to pick us up to take us to the police station. How we paid full price for his fine and the hostel. I couldn't believe how calm Andy sounded. The whole time, Tom fixated on him. I wondered if he was trying to prove that he wasn't scared of him, or if he was blatantly trying to snide me by completely ignoring me.

'Look, there's no need to drag this out further,' said Andy. 'We'll settle this now.'

Tom laughed. It was a silent, empty laugh. He took out his wallet and started counting out rupees. 'Hostel,' he counted notes. He placed them down in a small bundle on the table in front of Andy. He put his wallet back in his pocket and pushed his untouched coffee away.

Andy looked at the money but didn't pick it up. 'You're missing the fine.'

Tom raised an eyebrow. 'Not my problem you were scammed.' He stood up from the table.

'You're kidding, right?' I asked.

He ignored me again and looked at Andy instead, whose nostrils were flaring but who was focusing on breathing.

'I paid my part.'

Andy was quiet and I wondered what kind of meditation was going on in his head. He reached over and took a sip of my coffee. 'How much can I pay for you to fuck off?'

Tom's lips were so tightly pursed, they almost disappeared were it not for the swollen wound. He stood up and reached for his phone, which he stuffed clumsily into the front pocket of his jeans.

'Where are you going?' I tried to reach for his arm, but he abruptly pulled away, snapping my grip.

For the first time, he looked at me, and I could see disgust forming in his eyes as he made a gesture to wipe his arm. 'Don't you fucking touch me.'

I sat back, my hand shaking.

He left the table, stuffing his wallet into his other pocket. He moved through the cafe, and we watched him squeeze past benches and chairs until he was out on the street, crossing the road.

And then he was gone.

## 41

Tom was really gone.

It was back to Andy and me. We hovered in cafes around the desert fort for a couple of days. I was focused on my guidebooks, researching where to go next and trying hard not to think about what had just happened. I wanted to go somewhere as remote and picturesque as possible. I wanted a distraction, but I also wanted to raise two fingers up to Tom and prove we would do something just as adventurous without him.

'I think we should go to Kashmir,' I said to Andy one evening.

He sipped on his beer. I leant forward to show him the guidebook and pictures that I had found on my phone. I knew nothing about Kashmir, except what I'd seen in a documentary starring Levison Wood. It was a military-controlled zone, but it looked beautiful; lush valleys, expansive lakes, cold nights and calmness. I explained that it used to be a war zone between Pakistan and India, and tensions were still high. The army patrolled the streets, and conflicts occasionally broke out with little to no warning. It was also right on the border with Pakistan, and we'd have to keep to the boundaries laid out by soldiers.

To my surprise, Andy didn't argue or voice much of an opinion. His only concern was the cold weather, but he decided to buy another jumper in the market before we left. I wondered if he was trying to please me after the night we'd had in the desert. Or maybe he was still a bit stunned at what had happened with Tom and—like me—wanted a distraction.

The journey to Kashmir took us a few days on different trains and buses. It was 1,700 kilometres away from Jaisalmer. That was more than the length of the UK; or a drive from Paris to Budapest. Or it would have been—on decent buses on relatively well-maintained roads.

These buses would have been rendered illegal anywhere other than India. The seats were plastic with no cushions, litter covered the floors, and sleeping during a sixteen-hour journey was nigh impossible.

The driver would either stop every ten minutes to smoke or take a piss, or he wouldn't stop at all for a seven-hour stint. People smoked on board, changed their babies' nappies and ate hot curries.

It was our longest journey yet; a day-long train to Ajmer and then a day and night bus to Srinagar, the largest city of Kashmir. The bus crawled along in a u-bend, up past Agra and the Taj Mahal, around Delhi, through Rishikesh and Jammu. At each city stop, masses of people would jump off, and whole new populations would board. The skin colour changed from fairer to darker, and as we moved further away from the tourist hotspot, we were stared at more and more.

For the first few hours, I slept. I was tired. My knee wasn't fully recovered. While a few weeks ago, I would have been aware of every culture difference, I now barely registered the concoction of smells coming from spices and people. I leant my head against my backpack and watched as we left the arid region of Rajasthan behind.

I woke in the early evening to a landscape of forests and rivers, the bus considerably colder. There was a woman next to me, and Andy was fast asleep on my other side. I wrapped my pashmina around me.

As my senses became more alert, thoughts drifted into my head. I couldn't quite believe the way Tom had left us. Things had changed so quickly, and he'd turned on me so suddenly. I wondered where he was now. Maybe he was in Sri Lanka already, in a hostel, chatting up a new girl. The thought made me uneasy. Then again, perhaps he was wandering aimlessly down the streets of India as lonely as could be. That didn't make me feel any better.

Part of me thought Tom was a drunken asshole who'd stepped way out of line. But another part of me felt guilty. I felt like I'd led him on and had encouraged a connection. I felt like we'd formed a friendship that was almost something more. I missed him. But I couldn't entertain that thought. I had to stop looking at my phone. I had to accept that he wasn't going to answer any of my messages. It was platonic. It had always been strictly platonic. Surely that had been obvious. I had to stop thinking of him. He really was just some guy we'd met in a hostel, who we'd probably never meet again.

~~~

As we got closer to Kashmir, the bus was stopped by soldiers. We had to step out and show our papers and passports. The closer we got to Srinagar, the more of a military presence there was. We could see big army trucks, some occupied, others abandoned.

A couple of times, Andy pointed out a soldier standing alone at a viewpoint, patrolling. It was an eerie feeling, to be in a place where blood had been shed not long ago and tensions were ongoing.

However, the journey also brought us closer to the mountains. I couldn't quite imagine how we'd been in Jaisalmer a few days ago, smothered by heat and sand dunes. Now we drove past the vast, snow-capped range of the Pir-Panjal and the Greater Himalayas. The dirt roads gradually turned into icy tracks. It was cold, and the frigid air filled the van. Neither of us were equipped for it. We'd left our battered Annapurna gear in Nepal, thinking we were done with winter. I lay my jumper over my lap, tucking my hands underneath my thighs, watching the world turn white around me.

In the early evening, we entered the city of Srinagar. Dal Lake was in the town centre, dotted with houseboats and rowing boats. People were shutting down what seemed to be a market, with crates of fruit and vegetables lining the streets. Men walked around in long robes, which looked like nighties, and woollen scarves wrapped around their faces. I saw no women. I wrapped my scarf tightly around my own head, not wanting to attract attention.

This time we were ushered into a homestay and welcomed. The host was excited to see unfamiliar faces. He explained in rustic English that they rarely had foreigners here because of the war. It was mostly Indians from Delhi coming on holiday. He didn't look or talk to me but spoke energetically to Andy, referring to me as if I wasn't present.

'You can take your wife around the market tomorrow. She might like the Kashmiri pashminas.'

I stared at him in fascination. This whole concept of not speaking to women seemed medieval.

We were escorted into our freezing cold room, which boasted a small balcony that looked out onto the partially frozen lake. The call to prayer dragged the noise inwards to the mosques, and we were left to look out at the tranquil city.

The lake was still, reflecting the houses and streetlamps around it. It was silent except for the gentle creaking of the houseboats. When the sunset and the skies reddened, the whole lake seemed to be on fire.

That night, I tossed and turned, my feet still frozen in their woolly socks. I must have drifted off, for when I woke, I realised my hands were tangled in Andy's. I felt the weight of his arms around me, my back lined up against his chest, my thighs in his lap, his foot touching mine. I stirred, and his hands tightened. His breathing was loud and steady in my ear. My hair had been pushed back to not tickle his nose.

I tried to remember the last time I hadn't shared a room with him. As far as I could remember, we'd been sharing a room—if not a bed—for almost five years. I knew his habits as well as one could. I knew he'd start twitching in a few minutes because he always did when he got too warm spooning me. I knew his snoring was louder and wheezier because he had a cold. I knew he hadn't brushed his teeth, and tomorrow we'd bicker over his morning breath while he'd try to get rid of his morning glory.

Since Tom had mentioned the job in London, I couldn't stop thinking about it. I wanted to ask Andy or swipe his phone and look for myself, but I was terrified of the answer. If he'd taken it, it would mean he'd lied to me. It would mean he had a whole backup plan that he hadn't shared with me. Why hadn't he told me yet? What was he waiting for? How long was he going to drag this out for?

Maybe he'd really decided not to go. Just like I'd decided not to go with Tom. The camel trek had been our second chance, a chance to save us. Maybe I just had to trust him.

## 42

Those few days in Kashmir slowly unfolded into a week. For the first time in a while, we were alone again. No Tom. No mixed dorms or Lonely Planet listed hostels. Just a low buzz from the locals.

We were trying to get used to being with each other again. Things felt calmer. I didn't see any backpackers here, and it made me think of the ones we'd met on the way so far; the Israelis, the expert hikers on the Annapurna Trail and Tom. They'd each formed part of our travel tapestry. We talked about them—updates we'd seen on social media, wondering where they were now.

We laughed about our disastrous attempts at hitchhiking that first day in Kutaisi, where we tried going the complete opposite direction, drinking vodka in the Svan house and how grim the Armenian hostel had been. We talked about how much we missed real coffee, fish and chips, a freshly poured pint at a pub, all things meat-based and wearing a clean shirt. Things slowly started falling back into place with us. It might have been many factors; we were in a new region, we didn't have friends to distract us—and we were finally sharing a bedroom with no one else.

Sex fell back into place. After what felt like months of excuses, I was sleeping with him again, slightly clumsily and more forceful, but we were trying.

We were trying to support each other. I went with Andy on a day-long hike that was mostly uphill to see an ancient temple, making sure to keep up with him and not complain about it being too steep. He came with me to visit a heritage hotel known for its British colonial-style architecture. There was hardly anyone there, and we explored the manicured lawns and fountains before climbing up the marble staircase. The hallway was decorated with heavy Persian carpets and ancient Sikh paintings, leading into what could have been any American hotel bar.

Having been in countries where finding a beer was a mission and frowned upon, seeing an entire bar stocked full of wine and spirits made my eyes pop. We let ourselves be indulged by a dozen waiters who served us cocktails at a fraction of European prices, each more vibrant than the last.

I surprised myself at how quickly I wanted to leave Kashmir. I'd seen it for a week, and I already felt like I'd ticked it off my list. I remembered when I first arrived in Georgia, and the first hike we did. I could have stayed in the Caucasus for months. I wondered if my energy was waning.

Maybe we could spend a week in the south of India before going back. We could quickly visit Goa. Andy might like that. We could stay in a nicer hotel there by the beach, where there were bars and restaurants. There would be hot showers, fresh linen and probably consistent wi-fi. From there, we could go on right to the very south, and explore Pondicherry.

Occasionally I thought about our next plans. I'd started to make up my mind about going back to the UK. I just didn't want to be the first to bring it up. I knew that as soon as I did, we'd be packing our bags and boarding our flight. I wondered how much more Andy was keen to travel. I didn't want to push him over the edge. I'd look across at him, ready to talk, and he'd meet my eye and smile, and instead I'd swallow back my worries. They were just my usual anxieties, after all. I didn't need to plan it all out now. We were in such a good space. Maybe he'd bring it up of his own accord. I didn't want to ruin what was finally going so well.

## 43

It was Andy's thirty-first birthday. I set my alarm to go off early and woke up a minute before it. I wanted to make it as festive as possible, even with our few resources. He was still snoring as I snuck out over his clothes which were in a heap on the floor.

Thick cold fog rolled over the city, but I managed to find a stall selling *parathas* (Indian flatbread), chai, fresh grapes, berries and *jalebis* (Indian sweets). I bought as many as I could carry. The seller helped me fit it all into a discarded shoebox, and I hurried back with it.

To my disappointment, Andy was awake when I got in. His hair was still wet from the shower and he was getting dressed.

'Where have you been?' he asked. He grinned as he saw the box full of treats, and I kissed him hard on the lips.

'Happy birthday.'

He took the box from me. 'Thank you.' I thought he would examine the treats but he set them aside on the table and pulled on his socks.

'Hey, do you mind if we have a chat?' he asked.

My smile disappeared. Andy finished buttoning up his shirt and pushed his backpack on his other side to make space for me next to him. I sat down slowly.

He ran a hand over his face. 'Look, I've been thinking of how to tell you this and…' He clenched his fist and tapped it on the windowsill. 'Remember the London job?' He inhaled.

I nodded. I knew where this was going. I'd thought of all case-scenarios. I was in control.

'I'm taking it.'

So it was true. I stared at him. 'Yeah,' I sighed, 'I know.'

'What…How?'

I grimaced. 'Tom told me.' I swallowed. 'I guess I didn't want to believe him.'

'I'm sorry. I was going to tell you. I just didn't want you to freak out and think I was ruining the trip. After that chat we had in Armenia, I wanted to find the right time.'

'Fair enough.'

'When I turned down the offer in Armenia, they offered to postpone the start date instead and I said yes. I figured that would buy us some time and I thought maybe I could convince you.' He fiddled with the straps of his backpack, tugging on the drawstrings. 'I know this is your dream, but this job is mine.'

'I get it. Honestly, I do. And I think you've made the right decision.'

'You do?'

'Yes, of course it is, Andy. You've worked your ass off for this.' I started to laugh. 'I know it doesn't seem like it, but I'm so proud of you.'

'Thank you.' His words fell short, and he pressed his lips together. He sat back, further away from me.

I glanced at his hands and realised he'd wrapped the backpack string tightly around his thumb. 'Andy, I'm okay with it, honestly. You've done this whole trip with me, and I'm really grateful.'

He ran a finger over the taut strings on his thumb, looking at the bed.

'When does the job start?'

He cleared his throat. 'Next month.'

'Well, that's plenty of time.' I looked down at my hands as I started thinking out loud. 'We should probably get train tickets to Delhi and then fly from there back to Edinburgh. We'll just need to collect all of our boxes from your parents and probably try to find a flat in London in the meantime.'

There was an uncomfortable silence.

I looked back up. Andy's nostrils were slightly flared, and I realised his face was pale.

I sat back. 'What's wrong?'

He ran a hand over his face. 'Antonia, I'm going to London on my own.'

I felt a ringing in my ears. 'What?'

'I think we should break up.'

I stared at him.

'What? But...but we're engaged,' I said, the words felt slow as I dragged them dumbly out of my mouth. 'We're...we're getting married.'

He sniffed and wiped his eyes. I wanted to comfort him, but I gripped my hands instead and stared at my engagement ring.

He swallowed. 'I'm sorry.'

I could feel my eyes stinging. The diamonds on my ring had blurred into a ball of fog. 'I don't get it. What about all the stuff you said the other night in the desert? You said you didn't want to lose me. Was that all bullshit?'

Andy sniffed again. 'No. I meant it. This is breaking me. But I still think it's the right decision. I don't think we're right for each other anymore.' He might have touched me or moved, but my senses were numb.

I heard his voice turn up and down in volume like it was surround sound. 'We've always been so different. When I met you, I loved your fire, your wildness, and maybe part of me thought I could contain you. But by doing that, I think I put out your fire.' He wiped his face. 'We're both too ambitious in our own dreams. I think we need to live those out, even though it means losing each other.'

'But I love you,' I heard myself say. It came out robotically. A tear splashed onto my hand, and the diamond became clearer. I wanted to take it off.

'Yeah,' he said hoarsely. 'I love you too. I can't see that ever changing.'

We sat in silence. I was speechless, motionless, urging myself to not exist. I wanted to disappear. I could hear Andy's occasional sniff.

I managed to stand up. I forced my legs to walk towards the door.

'Where are you going?' he asked.

'I need some air.'

'Antonia—'

I turned back and met his eye, feeling my face crumpling as I did. 'Fuck you too.'

~~~

The fog had swollen, and the skies were a menacing dark grey. I climbed up some stairs at the back of the hotel, which led to a rooftop. I sat on the edge of the building and stared out into nothingness. I could just make out some lake boats by their flickering lights in the distance.

My body shook, and my heart raced. I felt cold and empty inside. How could anyone do this to someone they loved? They didn't. The only explanation was that he didn't love me anymore. I wasn't enough for him—I wasn't worth fighting for. He was leaving me in India and going to London. He was leaving me. He was following his dreams—and I wasn't part of them.

I must have stayed there for hours. I refused to give in to panic. Instead, I glared into the distance, bathing in the numbness of denial.

A shadow interrupted my thoughts. The dim streetlamps ahead defined its hazy outline. It was Andy, looking for me. He followed the length of the hotel front, then wandered back again before staying still and hovering back and forth. I watched as his shadow faltered and heard footsteps go back inside.

I made no effort to follow.

## 44

I thought breakups were meant to be clean. There might be a drawn-out hug and tears, but the actual moment of one person leaving happened fast.

Andy and I took a week.

I decided to take the train back to Delhi with him, where he would then take his flight to London. Delhi gave me a better platform to choose where I'd go from there.

The train took fifteen hours. Sitting in the middle berth with Andy—and an audience of twenty—was less than ideal.

We were exhausted but couldn't sleep. Every time one of us nodded off, the jolt of the train, an elbow or a trolley woke us up. Then we'd look at each other, our eyes puffy with fatigue.

Andy fired questions and gave many instructions.

'Are you sure you don't want to fly back to the UK with me? You could fly back to Edinburgh. I'd rather you did that than stay alone here in India.'

'Would you like me to call your parents and explain everything?'

'I'll transfer you the money once I get the refund for the wedding bits. Should take a few months.'

'Don't worry about the flat deposit, I'll send that back to you.'

I struggled to come up with answers. There was too much rage, hurt and love in me to form actual sentences.

It was 4 a.m. when the train finally crawled into Delhi. The dark sky was already packing every crevice with smog. We trudged out, our backpacks like second skins. I felt like I was sleep-walking.

Despite the ungodly hour of the morning, the station was packed with locals travelling to and fro. This was Delhi, after all, one of the densest city populations in the world. As we trudged out of the station, the crowds increased in size. Now there were sellers, rickshaw drivers, touts by the hundreds, beggars of every shape and size, rats, dogs and cows. Kathmandu seemed like a beach holiday compared to this.

Andy charged forward, ready to find a rickshaw to take us to a decently priced hostel. He spotted a fervent youth, who cracked a grin when he realised he'd picked him. I watched as he haggled the price with him, two pounds down to thirty pence.

I climbed into the rickshaw. Andy tried to help me by picking up my bag, but I pulled it back.

'I've got it.' My voice was cool and steady. It had been like that since leaving Kashmir—as if all the warmth had been sucked out of it.

We spent the next couple of days in Delhi, where we mumbled niceties to each other, trying painfully hard not to talk about what would happen to each of us. During the days, we roamed the dusty streets. They were packed with humanity, rickshaws and shops. Walking was good. There was too much noise pollution to hear each other and too much stimulation to even think.

One evening, during a silent meal of korma curry, Andy spoke to me.

'What are you thinking about doing, then?' he asked quietly, picking on his naan.

I stared at him. He was the one who'd left me in this predicament. Why did he deserve to know what my next plan was? I had no idea what I'd do. I hadn't spared a moment to think about it. I was too scared to give anything too much pondering.

I looked up at Andy in silence. He was looking at me with his warm, brown eyes. I knew he wasn't asking out of malice. I knew he—rightly so—felt shit for triggering this. But I couldn't communicate that to him. I was still too shocked. Too furious.

# 45

It was departure day. For what felt like the millionth time, I watched Andy prepare his backpack. We talked little, our eyes puffy and faces pale from our last night together. We'd lain on the bed back to back, wordlessly, no sleep coming. As the hours trickled past, our backs grew warmer and somehow limbs became entangled. My denial took the form of anger and his resignation was shaped by sadness, and sex seemed to numb us both, until sleep overtook us just as the sun crept in.

'Is it okay if I keep the waterproof bags?' I asked.

He nodded. 'Yeah. Take anything you want. It's all yours.'

I watched as he tightened his straps. I looked down at my engagement ring. I wriggled it off my finger. There was a tan line and a mark from where it had sat for the last two years or so. I held it in my hand and then walked up to him.

He looked up and saw my palm. 'No. It's yours. Keep it. Please.'

'What am I meant to do with it?'

He shook his head repeatedly. 'Whatever you want. It's yours. I want you to have it.'

I slowly closed my grip on the ring, feeling the diamond rub against my skin.

~~~

We continued to exchange small talk as we walked down into the streets. I was exhausted, too tired to say much more, and he was silent as we dodged rickshaws, cattle and people. I followed Andy's steps meticulously from behind, as I had done for the last year.

Finally, we found a space next to a shop to stop.

'Let's get you a rickshaw—'

'Antonia…' He turned to look at me. His eyes were red again, his face wet. His huge green bag started to fall off him, landing with a thud on the ground as he stopped to lean against a wall.

I walked back to him and slid my hand into his. I sucked every wave of energy I had to keep it together. I couldn't allow myself to feel. I tried hard to look anywhere except at Andy's damp face, but gave up. He was wiping his face with his palms.

'Andy, look at me, come on.'

He reluctantly met my eyes. 'I love you.' He had his hand over his mouth. His words sounded muffled. 'I love you so much. I don't think this is right, I don't know…'

Every part of me wanted to scream at him for leaving me, for choosing his promotion over us. But I didn't have a fight left in me.

'Come on. You're going to miss your flight.'

'What happens after that? What are you going to do?' He looked intensely, imploringly, for an answer.

'I'll figure it out.'

'What if—'

'Andy, come on,' I hoisted his backpack. It was heavier than mine, and I winced as I lifted it up.

He wiped his face again and pushed himself upright, taking the backpack from me. I waved my hand out for an approaching rickshaw.

I forced a smile. 'Good luck negotiating the price.' He gave a step forwards and wrapped his arms around me. I breathed him in.

'I'm so sorry things didn't work out.'

'Me too.'

Andy pressed his lips against my forehead. 'You're the strongest person I've ever met.'

I needed him to leave now. He had to go. I couldn't hold my stamina for much longer.

I squeezed his hand one more time. 'Take care of yourself.'

'Bye, Antonia.'

I let go of his hand as he climbed into the rickshaw and looked back at me. I gave a small, mechanical wave. The engine sputtered and started, and in moments, he was gone. My best friend, my world, my everything, disappeared into the waves of dust.

I lowered my hand. I felt empty inside. As the rickshaw sped away, I lost myself in the swarm of people and the rising clouds of dust. I was jolted back into my reality, the streets of Delhi. Was this actually happening? I didn't understand. Why was Andy leaving me? We loved each other. Why couldn't we figure this out? Why weren't we fighting for our relationship? What happened to us?

I sobbed loudly and tearlessly into my hands, finding no answers.

---

I slept for the whole day in a muggy, hot hostel room. I heard backpackers coming and going—friends, couples, siblings. At night I wandered in a daze onto the hostel terrace, drinking beer, a lot of it.

I watched other backpackers exclaim in delight, fresh from Western lands, as they embarked on their new journey around India. Occasionally one of them would speak to me, but I was short and cutting. I sat in the corner, watching the happy couples the most, the ones who'd just arrived in Delhi and had months of travel ahead of them. They would walk hand in hand, take selfies, kiss mid-sentence, and I watched them cynically.

My heart was heavy, raw, shocked. I'd still not cried with tears, and I wondered if I would. I smoked the last of Andy's hash, feeling numb. For days I stayed in the hostel, every morning dragging myself to the reception where I would ask to book another night. I'd lie in the dark room until it was empty of travellers and then sit on the terrace, staring at the Delhi traffic beneath me.

I hadn't spoken to my parents in about a month. Our contact had fizzled over the months as they learnt to trust that I was being looked after by Andy and that we were being sensible. I wondered what they'd think if they knew I was all alone. I'd failed. This whole trip, a journey of a lifetime, whatever it was, had not been worth it.

---

It might have been a week before I finally tackled what I was dreading. I dug my dead phone out of the bottom of my bag and charged it up. I switched it on and saw several missed calls from my parents.

I dialled for my dad.

'Antonia, are you all right?' he answered immediately. 'Andy called us.'

Just hearing his voice made me sob. I couldn't speak, and he waited on the phone until I could.

I swallowed. 'I'm sorry. It didn't work out.' I tried to explain how he'd gone back to London, how the trip had driven us apart.

'I don't know what to do. I shouldn't have done this. You were right. I fucked up. I think…I think I need to come home.'

He was silent, and for a moment I thought he'd hung up. And then he spoke.

'I'm very sorry about Andy. We loved him, and we know how much he loved you. But it sounds like you were moving in different directions, and it wasn't right for either of you to compromise at your age. He was right to let you go. Your spirit is too big to be contained.'

I wiped my face.

'Are you safe?'

'Yes,' I sniffed. 'I'm in a hostel in Delhi.'

'Listen, pup. Don't come home, because you'll regret it. You've made it this far, and I think you're strong enough to keep going on your own. You're not someone who gives up.'

'I don't know if I can do this without Andy,' I cried. 'I don't know how to do this alone.'

'Yes you do. I've spent your whole life teaching you how to. Remember the stories. Remember all the challenges that your great-great grandfather faced.'

Through my tears, I rolled my eyes. 'Those aren't real stories.'

'Aren't they?'

## 46

The slanted wooden panels beneath the top bunk were the only things keeping me sane. I followed their patterns during nights of insomnia and followed them now as I lay on top of my sleeping bag. It had been over a week, and I was still here, stuck in the same dorm room. I was trying to figure out my next plan, but it was hard when my mind felt so hazy.

I kept looking at my finger. I'd slid the ring back on right after he'd left. I didn't know what else to do with it. My hand felt empty without it.

It was sometime in the afternoon. I only knew that because I'd watched all the backpackers take their stuff after breakfast. And that was hours and hours ago. I was the only one in the dorm room again. The faulty fan spat out humid, recycled air and would moan and hiss every twenty-three cycles.

Numbness. Hopelessness. Everything I had was slipping through my hands like water. My family, my career, our flat, my money and now…now my fiancé. The only thing that had been consistent in my uprooted lifestyle. Gone.

God, how it hurt.

Every time my mind drifted, I tried bringing it back to the wooden panels, following each one. It was something about mindfulness that Tom had told me in Nepal, about bringing your thoughts back to the present.

It wasn't really helping. I was consumed by toxic thoughts of Andy moving on. How could we have wasted so much time?

The idea of him being with someone else one day made me nauseous. The thought of him forgetting me made me want to crawl up into a ball. I needed to punish myself for not fighting for him harder. I knew I'd given him a hard time. What if I'd gone with him after Armenia? This was all on me. I'd caused this break-up.

I turned against myself. I felt useless, naïve and, worst of all, weak. I needed to do something. But I didn't want to stay in India. I needed a purpose. My chest started to tighten again.

'Focus,' I whispered to myself, trying to control my breaths.

I looked back at the panels. The paint had long since chipped off them and they were a rusty brown, most of them cracked. It wouldn't take many more backpackers for the whole thing to collapse. The fifth panel always caught my eye. The right side of it had been carved away, probably with someone's blunt penknife. Whoever it had been had mediocre sketching skills at best. It might have been some sort of animal or a rendition of Shiva, but to me it looked like Dobby from *Harry Potter*: an oversized head with pointy ears balanced on a stick neck that rose out of a fat body.

It was the sort of thing Tom would have drawn. Stupid, fucking Tom. We'd probably all be somewhere like Mumbai by now if he hadn't lost it in the desert.

But something had caught my attention. The Annapurna. Tom. The conversation we had on the rooftop. When he was talking about his depression. He'd mention something about walking. Spain. France. Yes, that was it: the Camino Santiago Compostela.

Maybe I could do it.

I could walk. I wasn't very good at it, and I hated hills. I was slow, I trudged rather than walked, and I moaned about it a lot. But maybe I was strong enough. It was a matter of walking, no matter how long it took me. This time there'd be no boys hurrying me. I could walk at my own pace.

And it was in Europe. I realised I yearned to be back in a modern, Western country. A land of showers, tampons, toilet seats and where cattle were fenced. The Spanish countryside would be a piece of cake compared to what we'd done so far. No rogue water buffaloes, for one. Plus, I spoke the language.

My mind raced. I needed to buy a plane ticket. But that was it, really. I had my walking boots and hiking gear. I was as fit as I'd ever been. Heck, I'd been walking for months.

I sat up, wondering if the receptionist would know where I could find wi-fi. I was hesitant to leave the room, mostly because I hadn't spoken to anyone in over a week.

I cleared my throat as my bare feet hit the ground. My muddy boots lay untouched below the bed, still dignified underneath a thick crust of dirt. They'd been through the Svaneti Mountains, the Armenian highways, partly deactivated minefields, the Annapurna Trail, Kashmir and a desert.

They were more than prepared for Europe.

~~~

I took the long train out of Delhi to the airport. It weaved in and out of the city. From the platform, I could see beggars—children and men—roaming the tracks. I turned back when I heard running footsteps and yells, and saw some policemen shouting and chasing the beggars away. They rounded some up, while most ran away, across the rails and over the fence to slums behind the station.

As I climbed onto the train and shifted in my seat against the window, I saw that one child was hiding. The police hadn't seen him, and he was lying low, under black bin bags, only his large brown eyes visible. He waited, looking around, and when he thought it was safe, crawled along the track.

He must have been about nine years old, only skin and bone. Lanky, dirty hair stuck to his face and neck. He tied the bin bags together, holding them over his shoulder, as he silently reached for litter, placing each one in his pocket. First, it was milk cartons, then it was water bottles, then it was chai paper cups and some stale biriyani.

He looked up and caught my eye. His whole body froze, and his wide eyes haunted mine.

I was transfixed.

As the train creaked into movement, I continued to hold my gaze. I didn't want to break it. Breaking it would mean that I was truly leaving India and that my travels in Asia were ending. The train picked up speed, and I forced myself forward. I felt a staggering rush of relief. I was leaving—I was going to Spain. I was going back to a more familiar world. I rolled my neck back, taking in breaths. Gone was Tom, the loneliest person I'd ever met. Gone was Andy, the man I thought I would marry. Neither of them knew where I was going.

But it didn't matter now.

I was free.

# PART 4

# SPAIN

## 47

As I walked out of Madrid Airport into the dark, wintry night of Spain, the first thing I noticed was the silence. It felt as if my ears were still blocked from the plane. Then came the clean smell of snow and icy air. As I wandered into the car park, not a single person shouted or walked up to me. I had to knock on a taxi window. I felt relieved to be speaking in Spanish—my native language—and be understood. The driver half-listened to my address before he reluctantly agreed to put his newspaper away and drove me to my pre-booked hotel.

We drove down the streets into central Madrid, where I stared out of the window. The roads were empty. Well, mostly. A woman in a fur coat walked her pug. Two teenagers stood outside a tapas joint smoking as a group of businessmen left a bar.

'It's so quiet tonight,' I said to the driver.

He frowned. 'It's just the usual for a Thursday.'

~~~

As the taxi dropped me off, I glanced at my backpack on the concrete kerb. Where it had once looked so majestic and powerful, it now looked tatty and destroyed. It was down to seven kilograms. After the Annapurna, I'd ditched the heavy winter clothes, sleeping mat and inflatable pillow. I'd also gotten rid of my jeans, trainers and almost all my toiletries. I was left with half a toothbrush and a stick of deodorant.

I picked it up and checked into a room. Oh, but how lovely this private room was, all for me. There was a double bed, with crisp white linen. My battered, tanned feet sunk into the velvety carpet. A welcoming bottle of red wine waited temptingly. There was a hot—hot!—shower at full pressure and fluffy white towels. There were miniature bottles of shampoo and conditioner. Next to the toilet was a small tray of tampons. I hadn't seen those in so long. And there was wi-fi and a television with Netflix and movies.

I sat down in the shower and let the hot water drench every pore of my body, until my skin felt like playdough. I wrapped myself in a soft cotton bathrobe and put my hair up in a towel. I poured myself a large glass of wine as I switched on the screen. I let myself forget about everything for a while and indulged in forgotten comforts.

~~~

Over the next couple of days, I planned out my Camino route. I decided on the iconic trail, the French Way, which would start in France, take me through to Spain and finally end in the northwest of Spain in Santiago de Compostela. It was a journey of 780 kilometres, which would take around a month to complete. I felt relieved as I studied the variety of terrain. It would start with the French mountains in the Pyrenees, go through more arid flatlands in the mid-north of Spain and finally end in the lush, wet region of Galicia. There would be a stage of the walk where for five days I'd be walking on a flat plain. The altitude of the highest point, just over midway, was 1,504 metres. I'd done five times this height now, so I knew I would be able to face it. Overall, I was simply delighted that, unlike my past hikes, this wouldn't be entirely uphill.

I would be referred to as a pilgrim, the official term for anyone on this hike. I learnt that I would be sleeping in *albergues* on the way, the official hostels for pilgrims, usually a basic dorm room. *Hosteleros*—the people who ran them—also provided a warm meal for a minimum price. The route passed through a few bigger towns—Pamplona, Burgos and León—where I'd be able to stock up on hiking gear if needed. There were also plenty of cafes and shops on the way should I need food and snacks.

I came across an official article from the Camino website stating that the worst month to begin was March. They were advising against pilgrims joining the route until the 'Beast from the East' storm had stopped battering Europe. It was now early March. Snow covered the pavements of Madrid, and I hadn't even considered how it would be affecting the north of Spain. I refused to give it much thought. I had flown all this way. I was ready to go.

~~~

After a nine-hour bus journey over the Spanish border, I arrived in the small French town of Saint-Jean-Pied-de-Port. There were cobbled streets and cottages overlooking miles of frosted green fields. A stone bridge was built over the river that flowed through the town centre.

After buying a cheap set of walking poles and a scarf at the souvenir shop, I hovered alone in the main square, hoping to gain confidence to speak to another pilgrim. Icy cold winds froze my cheeks and I looked around, struggling to find anyone who resembled a hiker or backpacker. The restaurants were mostly empty, if not shut for the season. Maybe I should have considered the March weather warning a bit more. I walked down to the only pub that was open, wondering if it was too early to grab a beer.

Two young men who I'd seen on the bus waved me over. I looked behind me to make sure they weren't gesturing to someone else, but they called me over again.

I beamed, relieved to see two other pilgrims, even though they reminded me of the Israeli hikers we'd come across on our first hike in Georgia. This time, their fitness didn't seem threatening. One of them was Polish, Lucas, with clipped short hair, a cross hanging from a pendant around his neck. The other was from Denmark, Erik. He had shaggy blonde hair, looked about twenty-two and had the energy levels of a Labrador. Luckily, they decided I was good enough company for dinner and invited me to join them.

I fretted briefly about my appearance. I was wearing thin harem pants with elephants that I'd bought in Pokhara, a grey T-shirt, that had once been white, and my broken and soiled hiking boots which looked like I'd taken them out of a bin.

My self-consciousness vanished when plates of sizzling cuts of meat and hot chips arrived alongside fresh pints of golden beer. After so many months of vegetarian curries, my mouth watered at the sight. I ate hungrily, feeling the steak and chips burn the top of my mouth with not a care in the world.

Lucas was ex-army. I could see it in his demeanour, a stiff and rigid posture, determined to walk the whole way to Santiago in three weeks. He hardly spoke at the table, but as we stood up to leave, he raised his voice.

'Have you heard of the three laws of the Camino?'

I shook my head.

He continued. 'Number one, always be honest. Number two, choose a luxury or bad habit to give up. Number three, cry once—it has to be real.'

We at once started speaking about rule number two. Erik wanted to give up Facebook. I thought about it for a while. I felt like I'd already given a lot up during the last year. Our trip hadn't exactly been a platter of indulgences. I'd slept on the ground, peed in the bush or squat toilets, struggled to find wi-fi and ate for fuel rather than survival. I loved my coffee though, even though it was mostly now in the form of Nescafé sachets, and they weren't too readily available. I'd been looking forward to enjoying a consistent *café con leche* in Spain, especially in the mornings.

What was another couple of months? I sighed. 'Fine, I'll give up coffee.'

I thought about the laws as I walked back to the *albergue*. As we crossed over the bridge, Lucas walked past me and said something so softly, I only realised what it was when he left.

'Make sure you walk alone.'

## 48

Alone I began. Today was meant to be a twenty-seven-kilometre walk. It was raining, and the drops were icy. A waymarker showing a yellow shell against a blue background indicated the path.

I tightened the straps of my bag and buckled it around me. It felt part of me now, just like my boots that had moulded around my feet. I couldn't quite believe I'd started off with over double the weight back in Georgia. I was down to the absolute essentials now: two T-shirts, two pairs of socks and underwear, a pair of leggings, a jumper and some waterproofs. I had a journal, a kindle, a sleeping bag, a water bottle and a toothbrush. I used my phone only to occasionally access an offline map.

I put my waterproofs and bag on like a suit. I adjusted every strap, tightening it all around my rain gear. Zips had to be done, straps adjusted, buttons up.

Fifteen minutes later, the rain stopped. I stopped halfway up a hill, uncomfortable and sweaty inside my rain gear. Mechanically, I reversed the process and took everything off. I rolled up my sleeves and re-adjusted the bag straps before getting back up.

I felt a raindrop on my face. Then another, and another. I sighed and started the process again. Erik and Lucas had also spoken about the Beast from the East shaking Europe. It was meant to be the worst winter that Spain had had in a decade and the snow was shutting parts of the routes down. Maybe that explained why there seemed to be almost no other pilgrims around. I'd expected crowds of people, fighting over bunk beds, racing to get a place in the *albergues*. So far, I'd only met two. And they were nowhere to be seen.

~~~

I followed the cobbled street that led me out of the French village and soon turned into a dirt track, winding up the French countryside. The rain was like white noise. There was silence all around me. I could see a couple of sheep dotting the meadows, but there was no other living being in sight. All around me were green fields and forests, and the medieval village of Saint-Jean and the cobbled streets looking like a hazy, tranquil watercolour painting.

I felt at ease walking. The past year had made my calf muscles and shoulders strong. The only thing aching was my right knee, where the wound from the water buffalo still hadn't completely healed. I'd removed the lump of fabric bandages and replaced it with a thick band-aid. I could feel the scar stretch uncomfortably beneath it as it rubbed against my leggings.

I tried to keep my mind off it and focus on the challenge ahead, but the burning sensation of the scar peeling forced me to think about my last journey. It was strange to be walking alone. I was a lone red traffic light, my backpack bobbing up and down on its own. For so long, I'd been used to following Andy's backpack or the back of Tom's head. It almost felt like they'd be around the corner waiting for me, complaining I was too slow. But there was no one to comment on my pace. It felt lonely, but I felt liberated.

I wondered where they were now. Andy had sent me a barrage of text messages, asking where I was, if I was safe, if I needed anything. I hadn't responded to any. I felt slightly guilty, not telling him I was in Europe. I wondered if he was in London yet. His family and our mutual friends probably already knew we'd broken up. He might be out at the pub with them all, telling them everything. Then again, knowing how respectful Andy was, he'd probably only told his own family and was now keeping his head down in London.

It hurt thinking about Andy, my chest clenched each time. I tried thinking about Tom instead. Had he made it to Sri Lanka? But my thoughts felt like a television channel that was frozen on Andy. Had he found a flat? Was he missing me? I tried to distract myself, but my mind replayed the scene in Kashmir.

*'I don't think we're right for each other anymore.'*

Andy's voice echoed in my head. A hard lump formed in my throat and I swallowed it down. Was his job worth ending our relationship for? Was he having second thoughts? I wondered if he was thinking of me as much as I was thinking of him. I needed to stop my thoughts from wandering. Whenever they did, I felt heavier and I moved slower. Right now, I had a hill in front of me to climb, and I could afford no distractions.

~~~

As the morning went on, the countryside trails seemed to be leading me to higher mountains. This must have been the beginning of the Pyrenees and I was excited to see them, despite the snow getting deeper beneath me.

A huge notice over a waymarker made me stop. It was written in French with an English translation underneath:

ATTENTION PILGRIMS:
PATH CLOSED DUE TO WEATHER.
PLEASE FOLLOW HIGHWAYS.

Brilliant. I was going to have to save my Pyrenees adventure for some other time. I turned around and followed a makeshift dirt trail which eventually led onto the highway.

I was getting hungry and the roads didn't exactly scream quaint cafes. Instead, I filled myself up with water and energy sachets.

I walked on.

## 49

I'd been walking for a few kilometres in a forest, when I heard some fast footsteps behind me. I turned and saw another pilgrim. He was short and bald. His limbs seemed to be going in all sort of directions while a panama hat bounced over his head. I slowed down as he caught up with me.

'Hello. *Buen Camino*. I'm Max,' he said quickly.

I introduced myself. 'Where are you from?' I asked.

'Austria.' This was his third Camino, he informed me. Without drawing breath, he spoke about reaching Santiago de Compostela.

'It's a huge anti-climax, you'll see. As soon as you get there, you'll be disappointed.'

Before I could answer, he continued talking about his backpack's technicalities and how it only weighed five kilograms. He explained he only carried essentials: two sets of clothing, a toothbrush and the world's tiniest sleeping bag.

'I don't carry books or journals,' he said.

I wondered what he did at nights. I depended on those.

He'd come out of a recent divorce. Not his fault, obviously, but a fate that was written in the stars. He'd met his soulmate at a concert. Inconvenient for his wife and children, of course, but what could be done?

Before I could find a response, he went on to talk about his profession.

'I'm a Guru,' he strolled alongside me, 'a Human Designer.'

'What does that mean?'

He frowned, shrugged, then took a long look at me and shook his head. 'It's very complicated to explain, of course. I can tell you who you really are. I don't think you'd understand. It's only people who are…well, I just don't think you'd appreciate it.'

'Right, never mind then—'

'When's your birthday?'

'Uh, twenty-first of April.'

'I need the time of your birthdate. Approximate.'

I actually knew the answer to this. '4.30 a.m.'

'Birthplace?'

'Santiago, Chile.'

In the middle of the forest, he grabbed his phone and waited for the signal to come through. He typed in my details on an app and then stared at his screen. His eyes widened a few times as he scrolled down.

He eyed me again, tutting. 'You're not meant to be on this walk.'

He shook his head zealously. 'See these graphs here.' He waved the infographics in front of me. It looked like a complex equation. 'You're one of two per cent of the population. Interesting. Very interesting. You have a unique relationship to nature and earth…' His voice trailed off. He was reminded of his point and gesticulated wildly at his phone. 'This means you're not brave enough. You're not cut out for this. This walk isn't a good idea for you.'

'I, er—'

'As for me, I'm in the top twenty per cent of the population. I'm ambitious, a do-er. I have a lot of success ahead of me. It's in my nature.' He grinned, his eyes bright. 'But don't feel bad about yours. You're designed that way. It's not your fault. Just remember that when you fail, it's best to accept it.'

'Er, okay—'

'It's been nice talking to you, but you're too slow for my pace. Maybe I'll see you tonight. *Buen Camino!*'

I watched him trot off, his minuscule backpack firmly tied to his back. Not wanting to risk running into him again, I sat down on a rock and opened my bag to take a drink of water.

What a pile of rubbish, I said, half-laughing to myself. Two per cent of the population based on my star sign that was put into some iPhone 6 app? How on earth did he make money out of that? I sipped on my water and felt a familiar clench in my stomach. What if he had a point? Maybe I wasn't cut out for this. It had only been twelve kilometres. There was another fifteen kilometres to go until we reached the next town, and my shoulders were already aching.

*Not brave enough.* It was another way of saying 'weak'. I'd wondered that myself. I wondered if Andy thought I was weak. Even Tom had joked that I'd been a coward after not following him up the goat trail. But there'd been a burning doubt I'd been carrying since starting this walk, and it was flaming up: would I have ever travelled on my own if Andy had decided not to come in the first place? I thought back to the evening where I'd pitched the travel idea to Andy before any of this and he'd agreed to come with me. Had I manipulated Andy into coming with me, knowing that he'd give in to coming if I gave him an ultimatum? It had been a risk, and it had worked.

I thought back to the Caucus Trail, hardly being able to keep up with Andy, feeling like a complete failure. I remembered feeling devastated when Andy had threatened to leave me in Armenia, terrified at being left alone. I thought about the Annapurna, when I doubted I'd ever reach the Thorong La Pass, almost quitting on the morning of the summit.

The 'hardlys' and 'almosts' had not stopped me from walking and despite the near-failures, I was still here, still going, and now on my own. I might not have been a natural athlete, and no matter how much experience I had, my shoulders and feet still hurt, but I had plenty of power in my head. I wanted to keep going, even if it meant going painstakingly slow. There was no one to catch up with this time, I could take as long as I needed.

Come on. It was day one. The self-proclaimed guru could fuck off.

~~~

I must have taken a more prolonged break than I intended. When I summited the first hill, sweating and spluttering, I saw no sign of people either in front or behind me. Good. I didn't need any more Human Designers in my life.

I wiped the sweat off my forehead and continued down the track, following the occasional waymarker. On and on, I trudged. I had no way to calculate how long I had left. I assumed I'd walked a kilometre every twenty-five minutes or so. The temperature dropped, and the sun looked paler with every minute it went down. I passed a broken road sign on my way and glanced at it, realising it was in Spanish.

I had left France behind.

When I saw the steeple of Roncesvalles, I cheered loudly to myself. As I descended towards the village, I expected to see houses, restaurants, and perhaps some grocery shops to restock on snacks. To my dismay, I only saw a large, Gothic-looking church. As I grew closer, I saw a cloister and a house alongside it.

It was almost dark now. I was probably in the wrong place. Maybe it was a bit further. I walked nearer. The door was open. Fantastic. I could ask someone in there.

I walked in, and a grumpy wrinkled woman looked up.

'Sorry, do you know—'

'*Pasaporte.*'

'Do you know where I can stay—'

'This is the only *albergue* that is open. Two euro for a bed. No towel or blanket.'

'Oh. Okay. Yes, please.' I handed her my passport and my pilgrim credentials.

## 50

That night a priest called us to mass, and in the icy winds, I walked to the even frostier church. I was last there, and sat down on a hard, cold pew. I counted five others, all men. I waved at Erik, but no Lucas or Max. They must have walked on to the next village. The priest spoke about the journey we were about to begin and how hundreds of pilgrims had done this before us, staying in this very same place for centuries.

He explained that they normally filled out their cloisters and houses with bunk beds and pilgrims, but there had been so few pilgrims this winter that they had shut it all down. We would be sleeping in a storage room at the back of the church where a few bunk beds had been crammed in.

He called on our nationalities—probably having glanced through the registry—Belgian, Italian, Danish, German and Chilean. We all had different places we called home, different languages and various afflictions to carry.

We were encouraged to sit alone with our thoughts. I felt safe here. I bowed forward. I was so tired, I held my face up with my hands. I wasn't sure how long ago it had been since I'd been to church, but still, I tried to pray.

*Dear Jesus, it's me, Antonia.*

*I know we've not spoken in a while. Andy broke up our engagement, and I think it was my fault. No. I know it was my fault.*

I swallowed a few times, blinking fast.

*I feel like Andy was trying to tell me to fight for him, and I was too busy focusing on myself. I left it all until too late. And now I'm wondering if I should go back to London and apologise, and make it all work again.*

*I came to walk this Camino, but maybe I shouldn't be here at all. I'm really just here because, well, it feels like there's nowhere else to go. I guess I'm just asking you to let me know if I'm doing the right thing.*

I must have been lost in thought, for when I looked up, only the priest remained. He was smiling warmly at me and walked me back to the *albergue*, where the few pilgrims were sitting down to eat.

~~~

There was something special about meeting people I would have never had the chance to speak to in real life. As I ate Spanish tortilla, I chatted to a Methodist priest from Milan and a German veteran.

Erik was there, sitting across from me, on his third glass of wine. He clarified that he had just turned twenty-one and had planned to do the Camino during his first year at university. He'd spent months researching and planning it, yet now something else had occupied his mind.

'Ten days before I flew over, I met this girl,' he said. 'She's stunning, and things got quite serious between us.'

I forced a smile.

'Anyway, she said she'd meet me at the airport when I get back, the sooner, the better. She says she misses me! So I'm going to do this as fast as I can. I'll book flights the day I arrive in Santiago. I just really want to see her, you know?'

My smile waned as I thought of my eventual airport arrival and not having Andy there to greet me.

I spoke to the others around me. There was an Italian, Mateo, who walked the Camino annually as a ritual to express gratitude. He told us he met his wife on the Camino some years ago. Shortly after, she died, and he walked it again, only to meet his second wife.

As the wine was poured and a course of steaming fish and potatoes came through, the conversations got louder. I was guarded.

I felt lonely and shy, wondering if the decision to do this walk had been a mistake. I pushed my fish around on my plate, too tired to eat, listening to others talking about why they'd decided to walk.

'Well, what about you? What made you want to walk all these miles?'

I swallowed some *vino tinto*. So far, I'd heard people with real reasons: divorce, career change or a family death. I was still jetlagged, my time schedule still dictated by Delhi. Still sunburned from the Jaisalmer sun. My knee ached and burnt from the unhealed stitches in Udaipur. I felt detached from the body that was sipping on wine on the hard bench surrounded by kind faces. My mind was hovering above them, trying wildly and unsuccessfully to process the strange journey of events that had led to this dinner tonight. There seemed to be an enormous lack of connection between mind and body which mostly made me feel numb.

I put my glass back on the table.

'I'm trying to get over someone.'

~~~

The first night was a shock to the system. I was shuffled into the storeroom—three bunk beds, hard mattresses, one toilet. We each took the first space we found, and there was no divider between myself and the man—I think the German one—lying beside me. Despite the excruciating twenty-seven-kilometre walk, I was wide awake. All I could hear were a rumble of snores, coughs and the rustle of sleeping bags.

I didn't look at the stranger next to me, feeling uncomfortable and stiff. What if I knocked them with my hand while they slept? I lay flat on my back, trying not to move. I looked at the high ceilings, feeling the cold breeze coming through the cracks. I heard the stranger starting to snore. There was no way I was going to sleep. I breathed out. I felt lonely. My cheeks felt damp, making my pillow cold. All I could think about was Andy.

## 51

The higher I walked, the colder the wind and the fresher the air. The views reminded me of Scotland with the low, menacing clouds and a glaring sun, projecting a startling light. There were white fields below me, snow-covered houses, stone-built churches and the occasional dark figure of a pilgrim moving in the distance.

I walked through the towns of Pamplona, Puente la Reina, Estella and Logroño. The Beast of the East was hitting Europe hard. I didn't need to look at the headlines to see how much snow had fallen; I was walking through it.

The hail bit my face, and I was always wet. At nights I peeled my clothes off and stuffed them as far into the radiator as I could, but a night in a damp room didn't entirely dry them. In the mornings, I had to shiver back into them in the darkness of dawn.

I'd been walking for more than twenty kilometres every day. My record so far had been thirty-two kilometres, which had left my feet swollen, tense and my body beat.

Although I hadn't hiked long-distance since a couple of months ago in Nepal, I knew my back and shoulders would need some time to get used to the backpack—no matter the weight. I knew I could avoid blisters by wearing two pairs of socks. I'd stuck plasters on my shoulders and collarbones to avoid sores forming between the backpack straps rubbing against my skin. I could manage a full day of walking fuelled by a cereal bar and a cup of tea, knowing I would recover with a warm meal in an *albergue* at night. I knew my legs would cramp up at night, and I'd feel like I'd been run over by a bus every morning, so I stretched and massaged my legs day and night. The creaks of my joints and the stress on the soles of my feet were just reminders that I was pushing myself and that I could do this.

I chose to avoid other hikers and walk alone because I wanted time to think and didn't feel like talking. I realised that the more I pushed myself, the more I concentrated on my steps and breathing. Walking was the one thing I could control.

On my tenth day of walking, I woke to ominous weather. Heavy rain had poured down at night and was not giving way. It flowed relentlessly in heavy torrents. The trail was an ocean of mud. My walking poles became stuck in the mire each time I pressed down. Every step was a gamble where I hoped I wouldn't fall flat on my face.

Drenched socks and no shelter, only kilometres of mud ahead, I had no choice but to keep going.

As I looked back to see how much distance I had covered, I realised another pilgrim was not far behind.

It was a young boy who looked about eighteen. I recognised his face from the past *albergues*. I'd heard that he was painfully shy.

We waved politely at each other but kept on walking.

When he was close enough, I stopped. I pretended to be fixing something on my bag, but in truth, I didn't want to walk with someone who would annoy me.

He reached me and stopped.

'Hey,' I said, trying to avoid eye contact. 'Horrible weather, isn't it?'

He nodded, not saying a word. I realised he wasn't moving, either. Was he waiting for me? I didn't want to ask.

I was getting wetter by the second. I decided to stop pretending and continued walking. To my irritation, he kept his pace, walking just a few metres behind me again.

Admitting defeat, I slowed down and tried to speak to him. 'How's it going?'

He shrugged and mumbled a word but stared fixedly ahead. Maybe he didn't speak English. I gave him a chance to say something, but nothing came out. I didn't have the energy to make someone talk, so I judged him rude and kept walking.

For six hours, we walked in silence. I walked fast and then slow, but he seemed to follow my pace. The rain was loud. It was difficult to see ahead and impossible to stop in the unyielding rain. There were enough distractions to keep us focused. I kept on thinking how grateful I was that the track was flat. I'd been on enough trails now to know that my greatest enemy was a steep uphill.

With no town or highway in sight and the evening fast approaching, the boy finally spoke.

'I need to stop.'

I looked back at him, having almost forgotten he was there. Guess he spoke English after all. He looked defeated. He was struggling to walk, his lips shivered and his brows were scrunched into knots.

I looked at the exposed fields around us, not a tree or shelter in sight. My face was drenched. 'We don't have a choice.'

The boy pushed his poles into the mud and started to lower himself onto the ground.

I recognised his frustration. This had been me not too long ago, trying to make it through the Annapurna and the Caucasus. I knew how exhausted he was, no longer caring about his pride. I recognised that the fact that he'd asked a stranger for reassurance was really a desperate plea for help.

'Hey, hey, come on, it's not too much further,' I said quickly.

'How much longer?' he asked.

I had no map or battery life. We were just following the road, and neither of us had seen the iconic yellow arrow in hours. As I told him this, his exhaustion reduced him to tears.

I fumbled for my phone and pretended to study the dead screen. 'Hang on. It's only twenty more minutes. We're almost there.'

I saw the lines fade from his forehead and his eyes focus back on the road.

'Okay,' he nodded. He stole a glance at me. 'Do you... Maybe... Do you have some water?'

I noticed his face turn scarlet as he asked me. I wondered how long he'd been gathering the courage for that. I handed him some, and he drank it down in gulps. I watched as he cleaned the bottle considerately, before and after. I put it back in my bag.

'What's your name?' I asked.

'Oscar.'

He didn't ask me for mine.

'Where are you from?' I tried again.

'Germany,' he said quietly.

He had a slight stutter, and I had to focus on his words to understand him correctly.

'Where in Germany?'

'Middle of nowhere. Near Holland. It doesn't matter.' I glanced at him, taken aback by his abruptness. I realised he was still focusing on the path, avoiding eye contact, tapping his walking stick mechanically on the ground. Despite his words, there was a childish and harmless manner to him.

I prodded him a bit more, realising that the more he spoke, the quicker the time would go by. I asked him what it was like growing up there.

'I like it there. I was home-schooled by Mother and helped Father on the farms.'

He didn't look at me and mumbled his words as if he wasn't used to talking.

'So, are you going back to work there?' I asked, trying to think of questions.

A small frown formed on his face. 'Father wants me to go to college. I don't really want to go.'

'How come?'

He tapped his stick harder. 'I am not good with people.'

I was amused by his honesty.

'So how come you're walking the Camino?' I asked.

'Father thought it was a good idea. We started together. He's gone home now.' He gave a soft sigh. 'He said he wants me to do it alone.'

We didn't quite reach a town in twenty minutes, but the chatting did make us forget about distance, and for the next hour, the trudge was substantially more manageable.

At long last, I saw some lights glittering in the distance. Despite the continuous rain, I pointed out the pinnacles of the church encased by a hazy mist. We practically ran towards the cobbled street town with white houses and bright coloured painted doors. On a red door, a large sign read:

ALBERGUE & PILGRIM MEALS: VACANCIES

'We're here, we made it!'

Oscar offered a tiny smile, which I gladly returned.

We walked into the hostel, looking like drowned rats. There was a crackling fire that warmed the whole room. Other pilgrims were already huddled around the grate, and they greeted and cheered us on as we came in.

'Shall we join them?' I asked Oscar.

He hesitated, and I could see his cheeks turning red as the others called us to the fire.

'Hey man, well done! You made it,' said one of the boys.

I watched as he walked towards the group, his face lighting up with pride when a pilgrim patted him on the back and others high-fived him. I wondered if his father had left him on purpose to encourage precisely this.

## 52

I drifted into the dining room, where I saw Erik sitting at a table by himself enjoying a beer.

He grinned, 'I wondered if you'd made it.'

I plonked down next to him, ordering a beer and a much-needed prosciutto sandwich.

'Whoa.' Erik was looking at my boots in horror. 'Have you been walking all this time in those? They're broken in a million pieces.'

'Are they?' I had a hard look at them. He was right. They were the only shoes I'd worn for the last year. They used to be a light grey. They were now a dark brown, the brand and laces wholly caked in mud. The soles had been broken since the descent from Annapurna. I hadn't paid too much attention to them in India, since the weather had been mostly dry. But now in the rain, my socks were always wet, and I kept changing them by hanging a pair on the back of my backpack, hoping in vain that the weak sun would dry them.

~~~

Early evening, I took a bus to Burgos, the closest city with a Decathlon. The rain hadn't stopped, and I needed new boots.

The salesman stared as I put my new boots on. 'Honestly, I have no idea how you've survived this far with those,' he said. 'They're practically fossils. All broken inside and out. Here, give them to me, and I'll bin them.'

I hesitated. 'No. I'll do that myself.'

~~~

I held on to my boots on the bus back until I finally reached the *albergue*. The *hostelero* took one look at them and started shaking his head and wagging his finger. 'No, no, no,' he spat in quick Spanish, 'you can't leave those here. They're completely wrecked.'

'I know,' I mumbled quickly. 'I'm going to throw them out.'

I dropped my bag off and wandered back outside, holding the wet boots by the laces. They're just boots, I kept telling myself. They're gritty, disgusting, smelly boots.

And so they were. But they were also boots that carried soil of past hikes—the Caucasus, the Himalayas, and the Indian desert.

I remembered buying them. My indecisiveness had driven Andy insane. I'd finally gone to the shop for the eighth time to try the first pair on again. Even though he knew them now by heart, he pretended to scrutinise them and watched me walk around the whole shop before agreeing with anything I said.

'I'm getting the Salomon ones. They have a better grip.'

'Definitely. Great idea. You'll need the grip for the hikes.'

'No. No. Sorry, I'm getting the Merrells ones. They're way lighter.'

'Yeah, that makes sense. You don't want to be carrying heavy ones.'

'No, okay, it's the Salomon ones. Just go. Take my card. Buy them. Don't let me change my mind.'

'Great choice. Grip is much better than weight.'

He pretended not to hear me when I changed my mind again. He'd made me wear them for two weeks in Edinburgh, walking around the city centre. Somehow when I was walking around the Meadows or trailing around Marchmont, I'd never really pictured what kind of treks they'd endure.

I never thought that I'd actually wear them every day for ten months and that the sole would unstitch and the laces would become hard as metal. I never really thought of them at all during the trip because they'd been warm, comfortable boots that had fitted just right. It was only now that I was letting them go that I recognised how much I'd taken them for granted. I'd realised how much I'd miss them.

But they were just boots.

## 53

I gradually entered what was rumoured to be the bleakest part of the Camino: *La Meseta*. Known as the Spanish table, the terrain was as flat as could be, dull and featureless. There was one big stretch of trail, with identical windmills left and right and blurs of fields. Had it not been winter, I might have been entertained by the changing colours of the fields, perhaps tracing wheat, cabbage or vineyards. But the presence of the Beast from the East meant anything that might be hinting at fertility was hidden by firm layers of frost and snow. It reminded me briefly of the tundra trail we took on the Annapurna, that had led us to the goat tracks. At least I didn't have to keep up with two male egos here.

People with time constraints—keen to get to Santiago de Compostela as soon as possible—chose to skip it by taking a bus to the next region. Others preferred to take advantage of the flatness and walked an insane amount of distance to get it over with. I could virtually see my endpoint at the beginning of the walk, yet it would take me 220 kilometres to reach it.

If I'd known I wouldn't speak to anyone for days coming up, I would have made more of an effort with the elder pilgrim at the cafe. I might have waited for Mateo, whose figure I vaguely recognised in the distance.

For five days, I walked alone. I was grateful for my new boots. I could move faster, my toes didn't feel like wet worms and my feet felt warm in socks that were no longer damp. I didn't have to stop anymore to change socks or tug stones or thorns out of my ankles and in between my toes.

There were no distractions in the form of a hill, rivers or even the constant noise of traffic. The tundra-looking fields stretched as far as the eye could see. The only sign of life was the occasional breeze that sent ripples through the grass like waves.

It was like walking on a treadmill, without any music or people watching. The highways were bare, except for the occasional car screeching past.

For hours, I focused on the watery sun ahead of me, still too cold to provide warmth, and the breeze from the cool mountains reminding me that it was still winter. Every couple of hours, I would see a waymarker telling me I was heading in the right direction, telling me that despite not seeing another soul, people had passed here before me.

I walked on. The vastness of the Spanish countryside opened up in front of me. Blankets of fields, void of anything moving—except for rows of cultivated crops—waited patiently for the spring. I was nearing the end of *La Meseta* as I could now see snow-capped mountains which loomed in the background and endless tracks of red, loose dirt that swirled into clouds of dust with each one of my thuds. I ceased to hear them and walked.

I realised how content I was in this solitary experience. Ahead and behind, the only sound accompanying me was the rustling breeze. I broke into a smile. I was alone.

I started singing, first feebly with mumbles to replace lyrics to songs I didn't know, slowly transitioning into a loud roar of a song. I went through all of *Les Misérables*, enacting Jean Valjean, Eponine and Cosette. I tried to work through the emotional plot, questioning if Javert was the real tragedy of it all, tearing up as I belted out his last song before he fell off the bridge to his death. It took me hours to patch it all together, and when I finally finished, my voice was hoarse.

By the look of the dangling sun, it was only mid-afternoon. So far, I'd not seen a single village. Now would be a convenient time to own a guidebook or a map, to see how far I had to go. Yet with my dead phone, I couldn't even tell the time.

There was only the dark green fields against the red tracks reminding me of home, a place I'd not been back to for years.

How funny that Chile would create such a pull on me when I hadn't identified with it in so long. Thoughts of my childhood came flooding through as the endless track seemed to move instead of me.

I could remember the smell of sweat on horses as their saddles were removed; green dew stains on my knees as I rolled down sour fig hills; sticking my hands into puddles of mud and lathering my arms and legs and imitating the squawking birds from the trees. I thought back to crawling on the garden walls and picking oranges and eggfruit, swing chains creaking as I jumped through the air and running into the freezing foamy water of the Pacific.

Homesickness was the sleeping beast I never wanted to poke. I'd woken it before, back in the dreary winters of Scotland, and had wrestled with my decision to leave Chile, wondering if I'd made a huge mistake. It had been Andy who'd given me a new focus, who'd made me realise that my dreams of living abroad and exploring the world were worth fighting for. He'd helped me figure out that there was purpose in building a new home together.

Only he wasn't here anymore.

Memories of home were coming back to me now in full force, and this time I didn't want to ignore them. But as I walked, I realised the memories were not malicious and triggering, but calming.

Maybe moving back to Chile wouldn't be a bad idea. I'd given life abroad a good shot, and I'd had my fair share of adventures. Perhaps it was time to go back after all. It would be easy to find a job and settle down. It would be familiar and safe. The thought of it made me feel warm.

I thought of the noisy household I'd grown up in, ice crackling in wine glasses, the sound of little bodies jumping into water, the smell of barbecued chicken drumsticks and the constant soft hum of the boiling kettle. I could hear the loud Spanish chatter that often got mistaken for sounds of fighting, but were really sounds of excitement, and dogs barking in anticipation of cars and people arriving for a late Sunday lunch.

I recognised that despite not fitting in, I still had a deep love for the home that had raised me. A home that had provided me with little sanctuaries to read my books and write my journals and given me the safety and encouragement to conclude my chapter there and start a new one.

I remembered moving to Edinburgh for the first time and meeting my new flatmates from all over the world. In a dinky, freezing flat within a hybrid of cultures and cheap wine, I'd had an ecstatic feeling of finally belonging somewhere.

It was late afternoon. The insides of my feet ached, but there was still no town in sight. My stomach gave a familiar twist of discomfort. I hadn't eaten since breakfast, thinking there would have been a cafe or a shop on the way. The sun was going down, and I could see the trail winding through the hills. I wondered if I'd taken the wrong turn. I hadn't seen a waymarker since lunchtime.

Each step was now a struggle. It pulled on the back of my knees, thighs and toes. I kept stopping to stretch. My bag dug in to my shoulders. I adjusted it as tight as I could to my body. I would rather have the tight straps cause blisters than carry extra weight.

I started to sing *Les Misérables* again, my voice feeble and tired.

I tried to revert back to the memories of Chile, but my mind only wanted to listen to the painful jolt of my muscles. I shuffled along, no longer bothering to lift my feet, as the sun slowly edged its way down.

It was dark when I saw a scattering of lights emerge from a small village. My body screamed in pain and relief.

As I drew closer, I realised with dread that the streets looked rundown and partially abandoned. I could see lights coming from the only open bar and hear a loud television.

I pushed the door open. The place looked like an untidy living room with white broken lights flashing continuously. A few men were drinking what seemed to be the local moonshine. None of them said a word but eyed me sceptically.

I wished I could walk out, but it seemed to be my only chance. I walked up to the bar. The man serving had a red face and deep pockmarks on his nose.

'Do you have a room?'

I could hear muttering in the back. He gave a low whistle, then shook his head. 'It's another two kilometres on.' He waved ahead. 'It's uphill. Should take you thirty minutes.' He grimaced at me. 'Are you on your own?'

I didn't like the way the men were looking at me.

'No,' I mumbled, 'my boyfriend's outside.'

I staggered out of the bar, increasing my pace. I walked the last two kilometres in tears, the exhaustion too much to bear. I knew there was no point in crying. There was no one around to offer sympathy, but still, the wetness on my face gave me an odd sense of release.

Then I saw an inn—as if drawn out of thin air.

It was a scene out of *Don Quixote*. Stonewalls and a thatched roof, with a tiny wooden bridge over a stream. Next to the inn was a watermill, trickling and turning. In the moonlight, I could just about make out fields behind it, a complete nature-haven.

It took everything I had not to crawl into the reception room.

A woman wearing fluffy slippers and an apron greeted me in quick Spanish. 'Now that's a late arrival.' She fussed over me and helped my bag off my back. 'You're in good Spanish time for dinner.'

I glanced at the clock behind her. It was 10 p.m.

'Soup, lamb and potatoes?' she asked. 'You're the only one here, so there's plenty.'

She started to lay the table as her husband offered me a glass of wine. I collapsed into a chair. It tasted like sweet nectar.

'Did you start in Castrojeriz?' he asked.

I frowned and shook my head. 'No, near Hornillos.'

'Hornillos?' he gasped. 'You must be a strong walker then.' He looked at me up and down with incredulity.

I shook my head, feeling my legs trembling beneath me. He studied the map on his phone.

'Hornillos,' he insisted again. 'You began there?'

'Yes…' But I was starting to doubt myself, fatigue catching up. I was pretty sure I'd started there. Hadn't I?

'*Cariño*, you walked forty-six kilometres today. You must have missed the turn to the last village. You did two days in one!'

My mind was foggy with tiredness. The next thing I knew, I was being ushered to my room. Expecting rows of hard bunk beds, my eyes widened when I saw a room with a large, double bed, an en-suite bathroom, curtains and a dressing table. The bed had a light pink duvet, soft white blankets and the fluffiest pillows I'd ever seen.

'Since you're the only pilgrim tonight, you can sleep in my granddaughter's room.'

I wanted to make full use of the bedroom, wash my hair in a hot shower, do my laundry and stretches at peace, but as soon as I inhaled dinner, I collapsed onto the bed.

Ten hours later, I was still wearing my raincoat.

## 54

There was a slight advantage of having done two days in one. As I continued the walk, I started recognising pilgrims I hadn't seen in a while. I wandered around a village one evening, looking for an *albergue*, when I heard my name and was blinded by shouts and hugs. I caught up with Erik and Mateo. They pulled up a chair and poured me wine. A plate appeared out of nowhere as Mateo served food from his plate into mine. I felt like I belonged. We sat there chatting for hours about our trials and tribulations, our blisters, the bunk beds, the progress. It was bliss.

While I relished seeing familiar faces, strangers who now felt like good friends, I still opted to walk alone. I'd pretend to be fiddling with my bag or ordered another tea and let them pass me. They weren't persistent. In fact, most of them seemed to want to walk alone too.

It came as a shock when I reached the next town only to see a full hostel, each bunk occupied by a new face and fresh smiles. Of course. The closer we got to Santiago, and the better the weather, the more pilgrims. People would take a week or two off to do sections of it. My patience was tested; peaceful nights were now interrupted by an orchestra of snores, there were queues for the showers and plenty of chatter comparing distances and fresh blisters.

That night, a Spanish man of about sixty slept in the bed next to me. I recognised him from earlier that day. He walked with a gait and trudged his way through the tracks and was even slower than me. He snored loudly and relentlessly all night. No earplugs or headphones brought peace to the inconsistent racket that he produced.

The next morning, he gave me a loud and cheerful greeting. I glared at him in return.

Despite the lack of sleep, I walked through the region of Castille and León, waking up with the cool breeze.

I sighed in despair when I realised he was in the same dorm—again. He waved at me in familiarity as I walked in, but I ignored him as I quickly slipped out of the room to shower. He tried to talk to me that evening out in the common room, asking about my walk, but I pretended to be busy writing my diary.

A while later, when I walked into the dorm, I could hear his thunderous snores, and I tossed and turned, furious.

~~~

The next day, I rose early and walked fast, trying to take few breaks in between, determined to get a few *albergues* ahead of the snoring man. I needed to sleep. As I arrived at the next town, I was horrified to see his face. He'd done the same as me.

'Is there another room?' I begged the *hostelero*.

The man shook his head. 'You can pay for a hotel if this isn't good enough.'

I jadedly signed in and repeatedly ignored the Spaniard's cheerful greeting. The dorm was full—more new faces.

To escape the hustle and bustle that evening, I decided to skip the early dinner and go to mass. Despite it being a historically religious walk, I realised that hardly any pilgrims were of faith. While I wasn't a strict Catholic, I did enjoy the occasional mass and silent prayer. Catholic mass was one of the few things that was consistent no matter where I was in the world, and it made me feel closer to home.

As I slipped into the stone church, I was handed a small piece of paper with a prayer and stood at the very back. I counted five of us.

One of them was the sixty-year-old snoring man. I saw he was fidgeting and rocking back and forth as he held the prayer in his hand.

There were no hymns and no communion, just a priest who spoke about the importance of pilgrimage, then came down from the altar and sat in one of the pews, bringing us closer to him.

'Would anyone like to share his or her reasons for walking the Camino?'

A New Yorker raised his hand. He spoke about a career change. He'd been a banker and was now quitting his job to work on his farm. He wanted some time to think.

A Frenchman spoke about having done a stage of the Camino for the last six years. It was the one time a year he got to escape work, his wife and three sons. It was time to himself that he cherished.

I was too shy to speak, as was a solemn Korean boy next to me, who was struggling to keep up with the language.

I thought we were wrapping up when the snoring man started to talk. His voice came out crackly and breathless.

'I've walked since France,' he started coughing and then swallowed. 'I take it very slowly. I've got a bad leg. I was told not to walk because of it. But I have to. I take lots of aspirins.' He looked down, at the pews, past us, and the priest. His hands shook violently.

'I have to walk. My leg will keep up. My...my only daughter... she...well...she...she killed herself. I...I don't know why.'

There was a rustling of paper. I couldn't look at him and looked at his hands instead.

His prayer was torn down the middle.

~~~

That night, dinner was served for the late eaters. The dining room buzzed as groups congregated at different tables, mostly men in their mid-forties on their second bottle of wine.

I poured myself a glass, and as I was about to sit down with the younger crowd, I saw my snoring man sitting alone next to the door.

He was fumbling through his pasta, his hands still shaking, making a mess of himself. Bolognese sauce stained his T-shirt, and he kept dabbing at it with a napkin. He dipped the napkin in the glass of water and almost spilt it as he did.

I asked him if I could join him. He didn't look half as cheerful as he had those other days, and I felt awkward as we sat together, eating in silence.

'*Me llamo Antonia*,' I finally said.

He seemed not to hear me as he fought his way through his food. But then the crackly voice came through.

'*Me llamo Pepe.*'

~~~

That night I let Pepe snore as loud as he needed and, somehow, I slept well.

## 55

It was now April, which meant the sun was scorching during the day.

It was not even 10 a.m., and already thirty degrees. I bathed myself in sunblock. As I rubbed it on, I could feel small, leathery patches on my shoulders and could see all the freckles that had been formed by exposure. I'd hardly passed mirrors, except for small grubby ones in communal bathrooms flecked with shaving cream, but I noticed I was firming up. As I washed in the shower, I felt muscles rippling in my arms. My calves were rock hard, and my collar bones looked more protruding.

How ironic that I was finally toned when I was least prepared to show it off. I'd not worn make-up in months, and I was mostly covered in sweat or dirt streaks. I had a smattering of freckles across my nose and had acquired crow's feet that made me look weathered. In an attempt to tame my messy curls, I wore a red cap.

~~~

I could manage longer distances now, but there were new conditions to deal with. There was a lot of walking on highways and roads with no sidewalk. I had to stop each time a car came past and make myself seen.

There were fewer stops for food, so I continually focused on collecting supplies and water while keeping a manageable weight.

And then there was a problem I'd not had to deal with at all until now; dogs roamed the streets, in packs and alone.

One morning the trail had become so crowded, I decided to take an alternative route. The path took me through to a small countryside hamlet where I stopped for a break on a stone bridge that overlooked a watermill. To my right was a grand manor painted in a light shade of pink with overgrown ivy dangling down one of its walls. I envied the homeowners. I sat with my back against the bridge and updated my journal. I embraced the solitude and the sound of the water and was grateful to not have a herd of pilgrims pass.

I heard some light footsteps behind me and noticed a girl with a large blue backpack coming down the trail. I was surprised to see another person off the beaten track. As she came closer, I noticed she was on her own.

She stopped near me and leant her backpack against the edge of the bridge. There was a small Canadian flag pinned on to her bag. She seemed to be in her late thirties. 'Hello,' she said, 'I'm Eva.'

I introduced myself, and we chatted about the trail.

'Where did you start?' I asked.

'Saint-Jean. Kind of wish I was still there. It was a lot quieter. It's getting hectic now.'

I noticed she had coffee-coloured eyes. Her curly dark hair was wrapped in a purple bandana. She had enviable long eyelashes and round cheeks that looked like she was always laughing.

'I know. I also began in France. There was less of a snoring competition back there.'

Eva grinned. 'Tell me about it. I think I'm going to make up my own trail instead of following the guidebook. Might try staying in different towns and leaving a bit later.'

We shared our irritation with enthusiasm and laughter. It felt good to be laughing with another girl. She didn't take her backpack off. Maybe she thought it was better to give each other some space. I pretended to be fixing something on to my bag and let her go on ahead. I wondered what route she was going to take. I wished I had asked her more about it.

~~~

After my morning break, I continued to walk past the bridge and the fairy-tale manor, when I noticed a farmhouse. As I approached it, I heard barking. I looked up ahead. Two vicious German shepherds were loosely chained to a post, metres from the trail.

I could see them from afar, and as soon as they saw me, they started snarling and growling, moving onto the trail. I backed away. Their chains must have been three metres long. They rattled against the flimsy wooden poles. Terrified, I knew I wouldn't be able to walk past them. I backed enough away until they couldn't see me, and the barking ceased.

I sat down on the trail. I wished I'd gone ahead with Eva. How on earth had she walked past them? I looked behind me but could only see the eucalyptus forest I'd just come through. I could see trees for miles behind me and country tracks up ahead. I looked to see if I could circle around the dogs. I tried to snake my way around the trees, but the branches kept scratching me, and my backpack kept getting stuck. There was no path in sight.

I decided to wait to see if another pilgrim would come by. Half an hour passed, then an hour, then another half hour. Nothing. The sun was now high, and I was almost two hours off schedule.

I didn't know what to do.

There were two options—walk past the dogs and get attacked, or walk a very long ten kilometres back to where I began.

What if they did attack me? It seemed ninety-nine per cent likely. All kinds of thoughts ran through my head. No one would know where to find my mangled body.

I tried to calm myself down. Eva had done it. She'd—hopefully—survived. So would I.

I grabbed my poles tightly. If I got mauled to death, at least I'd die fighting.

My heart thumped against my ribcage as I slowly approached them. Their barks were vicious. They were out to kill. Their snarls were low, their eyes wild. I grasped my flimsy five-euro hiking poles as firmly as I could.

I squealed as I walked. Loud growling. Roaring barks. The sound of chains creaking. 'Oh, God, oh God, oh, God!'

I looked firmly ahead. I closed my eyes. Don't panic. Don't breathe. Don't look. More barking. More chains clanking.

I could only keep walking.

My feet moved. The barking continued, but it was softer now. I was further away from them. I didn't dare look back.

I walked and walked until I could hear no barks and then collapsed into a heap. My face was wet. My nose was running. I was shaking from head to foot, and I panted, trying to calm my heart rate.

~~~

It took a couple of hours to regain some confidence. I trembled at anything that moved: a gust of wind, a falling branch, an engine starting in the distance.

I was now about ten kilometres past the farmhouses and walking through a forest of gum trees, on a winding one-way track that seemed to be the only way out. How much longer would it take to arrive in more civilised territory?

There was no way I could do another day like this alone. Where was this damn *albergue* anyway? The sun was almost down. Surely it couldn't be that far away?

I was out of the forest now, walking through open fields and past a small stream. As the sun hinted at setting, I entered the outskirts of a town, with all the houses firmly shut.

I heard a bark. I thought I imagined it, but one bark became many and louder, and then I saw a gang of dogs trotting my way.

I felt my body falter and shake as I once again circled the pack, my poles sticking out like weapons, yelling loudly as I finally evaded them.

Sick with relief, I looked for the yellow arrows but realised I must have taken a wrong turn. I looked at the map up on my phone, which confirmed my mistake. I had to backtrack my steps, back to the dogs, and then take a right.

I couldn't do it. It was only another four kilometres, but I had mentally and physically given up. I threw my backpack on the ground and sat on the track.

'Dammit!' I hammered my fist on the ground and punched my backpack. How could I have survived camping in minefields and standing up to water buffaloes yet couldn't deal with a few stray dogs?

I pulled my jacket tighter over my chest. It was getting colder by the minute. I needed to move or do something. The sun was barely there, and I was at risk of getting lost and not finding any accommodation for tonight.

I was wondering whether to knock on a door and ask for help when I heard footsteps approaching. I jumped in fright, thinking it was the dogs, but I saw the same girl with the blue backpack coming towards me. Eva.

'Antonia?'

Relief seemed to instantly warm my body. 'Oh my God, it's so good to see someone.'

'It's about an hour to the *albergue*. Want to walk together?'

I grabbed my backpack and scrambled to my feet before she could change her mind.

~~~

'What a nightmare,' she shared my fear when I told her about the German shepherds. 'There was a farmer feeding them when I walked by, so they weren't too interested in me. Thank God!' She winced. 'I think I'd probably have walked all the way back otherwise.' She paused to wipe her face with a buff. 'I did stop to have a late lunch in the forest, and I was so tired, I thought I'd have a nap. I didn't think I'd actually fall asleep, but I woke up about an hour ago!'

We walked through a forest and started going uphill.

'You're going to have to distract me so that I can make it to the top,' she said.

I filled her in on the book I was reading, *The Shadow of The Wind*, and we made it to midway. I took a break to focus on walking while she told me about the upcoming Women's Football World Cup.

'So how come you decided to do the Camino?' I asked.

'I needed some time to reflect. I work from home as a nurse, and I've been doing that for the last fifteen years. I've never really taken a holiday.'

We walked side by side, our poles digging into the ground as we walked up the hill. 'I'm turning forty in a few months. I'm not married and don't have kids, and I guess I wanted to achieve a milestone to celebrate myself.'

We worked out that we'd only started a day apart and had even stayed at some of the larger dorms together.

'Did you ever meet the Guru?' I asked.

Her eyes widened. 'I did! I heard him trying to calculate some guy's life the night before he went back to Austria.'

'The Guru left?' I asked, stunned.

'Yup. He said the cold had worn him out.'

She too had met Erik and had heard the snoring man.

'Did you ever meet Leo?' she asked me. 'The Belgian?'

'No, who's that?'

'Oh my God…' She laughed as we reached a steep bit of the trail. 'He's writing a play. It's his third attempt. I spent thirty kilometres walking next to him…' she tried to catch her breath, but kept walking, '…as he recited…every…single…scene…'

We roared with laughter, holding our sides as we tried to catch our breath, our voices echoing through the forest below.

We continued to trudge up the hill, taking a few stops to sip water.

She offered me a handful of raisins, patting them into my hand. 'It's good energy. We need it for this last stretch.'

'Thank you.' I shoved them all into my mouth at once.

'What about you then? What's your Camino reason?'

I chewed on the raisins, thinking of what to say. I didn't feel ready to spell anything out. Why was I here? At the moment, it just felt like I was avoiding any sense of feeling, numbing my mind with as much walking as I could. It was easy to let my mind clutter during the day and let it be taken over by exhaustion at night.

The raisins congealed into a blob and I forced them down. I tried opening my mouth a few times and starting a sentence, but then I shook my head.

'I'm not ready to talk about it. Sorry.'

Eva nodded in acknowledgement, a warm smile on her face. 'Don't ever apologise for looking after yourself.' She pointed forward with her pole. 'Come on, we're almost at the top.'

~~~

At the summit, I dropped my poles on the ground along with my backpack and stretched out my arms. I smiled as I looked down at the view. We were just in time for the sunset. The landscape of trees, valleys and river against pink skies unfolded in front of me.

I noticed a sensation was building up inside me. It made my lungs feel full, my heart tingly, my cheeks stretch—as if my body would burst with energy. It made my mind feel clearer, momentarily freeing me of anxieties. It still hurt to think of Andy. I still felt lonely and scared of what was to come.

But I was almost halfway on the Camino Santiago de Compostela.

## 56

I thought I recognised Erik and Mateo walking some distance ahead of me, but I was too far back to catch up. I walked through small cobbled towns, past stone churches and medieval bridges. One morning I pushed on through the green fields. I hummed quietly to myself, enjoying the view of white windmills in the distance. My humming was suddenly interrupted by a loud mooing.

I looked up.

A massive beast of a cow stood in front of me, its tail swinging from side to side. It mooed again. My mind replayed the water buffalo all over again.

I froze.

My heart thumped. I felt my face drain and my hands shake as I started to back away.

'You all right?' asked a warm, thick voice. The accent reminded me of Andy, fleetingly distracting me.

Please don't be Scottish. Please don't be Scottish. Please don't be Scottish—

'It's just a wee cow.'

Definitely Scottish.

I turned around to face the footsteps and did a double-take.

The man with the accent was laughing as he quickened his pace towards me. His backpack swished from side to side, and he carried a large camera over his shoulder. He must have been in his early forties. Dark blonde curly hair framed twinkly blue eyes. There were deep wrinkles in the corner of his eyes which became more pronounced when he smiled. He wore a checked shirt and a kufiya scarf around his neck.

'Come, follow me,' he instructed. He gestured for me to stand back as he went in front of me.

I walked close to him, willing to break into a sprint if needed, as he skilfully spoke and shoved the cow to the side, smacking the cow's rear. The cow mooed once more, completely unfazed, as it moved out of the track.

It started grazing on a patch of grass.

'You'd think it was a lion by the look on your face,' he chuckled. 'Here, have some water and take a breather.' He passed me his water bottle. 'I'm Liam.'

'Antonia,' I said hoarsely. I took his water despite having my own.

We continued to walk together, introducing ourselves. I told him I'd been walking since France and had been in Delhi before that.

He was from Helensburgh, a PhD student in Anthropology at the University of Glasgow, writing a book about Hebridean culture.

'I must be mad trying to write about something that's dying out. Reckon it won't be a bestseller.'

I gave him a sympathetic grimace. 'At least you're using your creativity. I'd love to publish a book too. Just don't know what it would be about.'

'Oh yeah? You write?' He turned and grinned at me. It was a beautiful smile that lit up his face. It crinkled around his eyes, which looked right into me. 'I think we might have a lot in common then.'

We spoke about travelling and I briefly outlined the journey I'd just come from. He seemed fascinated.

'Walking through the Svaneti mountains.' He whistled. 'That doesn't sound easy. And here you are, scared of a bloody cow.'

I laughed. 'I was almost trampled by a water buffalo in India.'

'And you're telling me you don't have material for a book?'

I asked him about his travels. A few years back, he'd been to India, Africa and the Middle East. He'd interviewed local tribes, had even lived with them, taking photographs of their culture. I was immersed in his stories. I listened as he told me about living in the Karakoram mountains.

'It's stunning. Just breath-taking. Valleys and mountains for miles. You can see K2 in Pakistan. I went there to do some research on the original Silk Road. I was camping there, and one night my tent froze and ripped. I went to ask a family in a yurt for help, you know, if they could patch it up or something. Ended up staying with them for two weeks. Of course, neither of us understood what the other said, but I reckon we became firm friends.' He stopped briefly at a narrow section of the trail where some trees blocked the way. He held some branches back to let me through. 'Anyway, I don't want to bore you to death with my stories,' he said. 'We've still got another few hours, and I'd quite like the company.'

I smiled. I wouldn't have minded listening to them at all.

'So where's home for you?'

'Uhm, Edinburgh.'

'No, it's not. No offence, but you don't have the graceful Scottish accent.'

I laughed. 'Fair enough. I've lived in Edinburgh for years, but I'm originally from Chile.'

Liam stopped in his tracks. There was a spark in his eye. 'Were you planning on keeping that a secret?'

Chile was the top item on his bucket list. He'd spent the last year pitching an article on the Andes to *National Geographic*. 'I find the Andean culture fascinating. There's been some funding at the university for a project in Chile and Peru, and I'm hoping to be part of it.'

He fired questions over. What was it like? What about the people? What part of the Andes had I been to? Had I heard of the plane crash in the mountains in '72?

Before I knew it, we'd been walking for hours. It was the appearance of the town that evening that broke us from our rapport, connecting us back to reality.

'Hey,' I heard Eva's voice. She came up to me. 'Any more wild dogs?'

~~~

The evening was mild, and the sun was setting late, so after our showers and stretches, Eva and I grabbed some beers and took them outside to the patio of the *albergue*. There was already a buzz of pilgrims eating and drinking.

I saw Liam sitting at a table with a few other men. I could hear an Irish and an English accent. He waved over at me, and I smiled back, but sat down with Eva instead, watching the sunset and clinking our beers together.

A while later, Eva went up to the bar. She returned with a grin on her face. Instead of our usual beer, she handed me a generous serving of whisky.

'This is a treat,' I said, reaching for the glass.

She kept smiling.

'What?' I asked.

She laughed. 'I think you know what. Your new man just bought us these.'

## 57

I enjoyed being in the company of Eva and Liam and his friends. With the lousy weather clearing, I decided to relax my walking ritual of being on my own and spend time with them. One warm spring morning, we walked through a forest. Eva was some distance ahead with the Irishman, and Liam walked beside me.

He kept asking me about my travels in India. I told him about the train ride, the camel trek and my brief stint in Kashmir.

'You went all the way to Kashmir? I've been blabbing on about the Karakoram Highway as if you were an amateur. The least you could do was tell me you'd been there.'

I laughed. 'Well, I was hardly there, really. I spent a few days in Srinagar and just wandered around the city most of the time.'

'So you didn't go to Ladakh? Or Sonamarg?'

I shook my head. 'No. I thought about it, but then...there was a change of plans.'

'Well, you've got to tell me now. What happened?'

'Do you ever stop asking questions?'

'Wouldn't be a good student if I did.'

I rolled my eyes. 'Look, it's not that good of a story.'

Liam pretended to study his watch. 'Oh, check that out, I've got all the time in the world.'

I hesitated. The last couple of days had been so busy and intense that it had been a welcome break not to think about Andy. I wasn't sure if I was ready to talk about this with anyone, let alone some hot PhD student. I could battle my thoughts alone, but sharing them would make my predicament all too real.

My face grew warm. 'I was travelling with my fiancé. He accepted a job offer in London. I wanted to continue the trip, so we broke up in Kashmir.' The words tumbled out, sharp and bitter. I told him how the trip had been my dream and Andy had never quite been on board.

I increased my pace up the hill. I could hear Liam behind me. 'All right. You okay?'

I kept going. 'Yeah,' I panted. 'Look, can we just talk about something else?'

I could feel a bubble in my chest, threatening to swell, and I tried to breathe deeply to keep it down. I saw Liam's feet next to me and forced myself to look at him. To my surprise, he was trying to contain a laugh.

'What?' I snapped.

'So you had your heart broken—that sucks. But you're twenty-eight, and you've got your entire life ahead of you.'

I was silent.

'What's better than to be young and free? You've nothing tying you down. You can do anything you'd like. Why on earth would you ever give up your freedom for someone who isn't entirely right for you?'

~~~

After lunch, we stopped at a river. We could hear the thunderous roar of a waterfall, and we strayed off the path to follow. As we walked deeper into the forest, the noise became louder and louder. Thick branches slowly opened the way to a translucent rock pool, surrounded by greenery. Trees circled the grassy banks, protecting it like a private sanctuary. It felt like we were the first people to have ever taken this detour. It was barely warmer than fifteen degrees, but the others didn't stop to think as they stripped down and threw themselves into the freezing cold water.

'Come on in!' yelled Liam across the thunderous water.

Eva giggled as she got down to her sports bra and undies, and I gasped as I watched her wade in. She winced and screamed, but she plunged in, hair and all. 'It's not that bad!'

I stood on the bank, watching them splash around. I took my boots off, my feet throbbing and sweating in musty socks. I peeled them off too and perched on a rock before dipping my roasting feet into the water. I squealed in delight. Hesitantly, I started to take my leggings and then my shirt off. My skin must have looked patchy with the different shades of suntan on my arms and legs, and my stomach was as white as salt.

I felt a pang of sadness as I remembered doing just this in front of Andy that night in the desert. He'd tilted his head back with a half-smile and twinkly eyes. His small laugh was still vivid in my mind.

There was only one way to stop these thoughts. I jumped into the freezing water. I let the iciness envelop my body as I squeezed my eyes shut, sinking into the water, before I swam back up, gasping for fresh air.

'Brave girl,' laughed Liam, swimming over to me. He reached out his arms to pull me further into the river, and I grabbed onto his hands. Holding my breath, I went underwater and emerged, splashing him. We swam around, yelling across the rumble at each other and playing like children. He touched me with his foot, and I yelped. We swam underneath the waterfall, the water hard against our shoulders, joking and laughing until I no longer noticed the cold.

# 58

The lusher valleys had given way to urban sprawl as we followed the highways and train tracks which led us to the town of Astorga.

Unlike most towns on the route, which had one *albergue* and a handful of houses, this one had a supermarket, a pub and the seediest excuse for a disco I'd ever seen in my life, with a damaged 'OK KARAOKE' sign outside it.

That evening, after a few beers, we all decided to slip into the disco, where music was playing loudly. We wore our full hiking gear, including muddy boots. I let my enormous, curly hair loose.

Inside was buzzing with locals, singing to cringy sixties hits. The sound system kept breaking down, so I mostly heard off-pitch voices.

'Let's do it,' grinned Eva, eyes sparkling.

I felt self-conscious with Liam and other pilgrims watching, but I'd had too many beers to think of excuses. We picked 'You Can't Hurry Love' by The Supremes and shuffled onto the stage.

The faltering white neon lights shone upon us, making it virtually impossible to see the audience and curing us of stage fright.

We sang at the top of our lungs, wiggling about on stage, twirling each other around and roaring with laughter. We were delighted to get an encore from the crowd. We sang 'Ain't No Mountain High Enough' and I made a mental note to ask Eva about forming a girl band after completing the Camino. I felt on top of the world.

We bounced off the stage and wandered over to the bar, which looked more like someone's old kitchen.

We ordered some drinks, and I saw Liam walking towards me. I held a tequila shot in my hand.

The music was loud, and he bent forward to talk into my ear. 'Can I get an autograph?'

His warm breath tickled my cheek. I met his eyes, and my smile widened even more.

'Guess who's up next?' I challenged.

He took the tequila shot from me and downed it.

~~~

With the dark night enclosing the streets, I led Liam from the disco. The town was mostly asleep, shutters closed and tables and chairs folded up. A dog mooched outside a closed restaurant, sniffing through black bags.

'Where are we going?' asked Liam, stumbling across the road.

A bin truck honked, and we jumped back to the pavement, giggling.

I'd had too many beers and too many shots. His smile looked really, really lovely. I grabbed him by the hand, and he twirled me around the streets to the pounding music that was barely stifled by the walls.

We slipped away to the riverbank and lay down next to each other on the grass, looking out over the water. I turned to my side and started to stroke his arm.

He smiled as he looked down at my fingers. 'What are you doing?'

I shifted towards him and stroked his cheek before leaning in and kissing him on the lips.

Liam pulled back. 'Hold on lassie, I think those shots have gone to your head.' He stroked my hair.

I looked at his face, his dimple lines etched into his cheeks. Lines that were so much like Andy's.

'Kiss me.'

He moved closer, and I felt him wrapping his arms around me. I lay back into his chest, and he kissed me on the side of my head. 'You're a sweet girl.'

I moved out of his arms and leaned over him with a hand on either side of his head. My hair dangled in his face. I could only see glimpses of his eyes and lips through my brown strands.

I lowered my lips to his. Before I touched them, he turned his head to the side.

I stroked his jaw. 'What?'

'Nothing,' he muttered. 'Fuck it.'

Before I could ask any further, his lips had met mine, and his hand was running through my hair and down my back, pulling me closer. My head was ringing in reaction to brand new sensations. I was so used to Andy's touch and smell. Liam's jaw felt rougher, spikier, and I could feel it rubbing like sandpaper over my chin. His mouth was wider, his tongue wetter, and his kiss was urgent, messy and frenetic. I wanted this. I wanted to feel wanted. And I didn't need Andy intruding on us. I pushed thoughts of him away, grabbed onto Liam's chest and shoulders and felt his hand move over to my waist. He rolled me onto my back. I held onto his neck as I stared at the dark canvas of stars above us, hearing the sound of the current and the wind rustling the trees.

~~~

I must have drifted into a light sleep. As I opened my eyes, I noticed the skies had turned from a navy blue into a light grey. I could hear ducks in the distance. I felt something hard beneath me rise and fall and realised I was asleep on Liam's chest. His arm was on my navel. I could make out the fuzz of dark hairs and his sport's watch. I shifted and felt him stir beneath me. A feeling of dread built in my chest.

'We should head back,' I said, starting to get up. 'We'll have to start walking soon.'

I felt his arms pull me back into his. 'Walk with me,' said Liam, his lips in my ear. 'Walk with me today and for the rest of it. We can reach Santiago in a couple of weeks and walk on to Finisterre.'

If I closed my eyes and just listened to his voice, I could pretend it was Andy. I just had to ignore the smell of cigarettes and unfamiliar aftershave. 'What about your studies?'

'I'll delay my flight.' He tucked my hair behind my ear. 'Didn't you say you wanted to go to Muxía? We can go there too.'

'You can't just change your flight.'

He budged next to me, and I felt him fidgeting. He grabbed his phone out of his pocket. 'Watch me,' he said, typing in his flight details.

'No, wait, don't.' I pushed his hand away. 'Wait. Let me…let me think about this.'

I held Liam's hand, and he looked down at our grip. He withdrew his hand and pushed his hair out of his face before leaning his cheek against a clenched fist.

'You okay?' I asked.

Liam lowered his hands and gave me a small smile, nodding. I felt the cool breeze on my arms. I shivered. He pulled his jumper over me, drawing me closer to him. His eyes were on my face. In the brighter light, I noticed bags under his red eyes and patchy stubble on his jaw. His cheeks looked flushed and blotchy from the wine. He looked much older than yesterday.

'Let's go back to the hostel,' he said.

I got to my feet, feeling unstable, and he slowly followed. I started walking down the path. I didn't hear his footsteps and turned around. He was standing with a hand in his pocket, the other pushing his hair back.

I reached out a hand to him. 'Come on then, we'll catch a couple of hours sleep if we go now.'

He looked at my hand but made no motion to grab it. I looked up.

His smile slowly faded. 'Antonia, I'm married.'

I looked at him dumbly as my hand fell limp. 'What?' My headache suddenly felt sharp.

His eyes were fixated on the hand I'd just removed. 'It's complicated. We're not in love anymore.'

I said nothing. I now felt quite sober.

He started to walk towards me, trying to meet my eye and I stared at his chest instead.

'I met her in high school. Got married a couple of years later.'

I gave a disbelieving, silent laugh. 'What the hell are you doing then?'

He scrunched up his eyes and then opened them. 'We've got something going on here. I thought you felt it too.'

He was waiting for me to speak. What could I say? That there had been something about the moonlight that had made him look just like Andy? That his accent, which had sounded so familiar, had lured me into a false sense of security? I shrugged. I only felt guilt and nausea—like I'd cheated on Andy.

I let go of his jumper, which fell into a heap on the ground. He didn't move as I turned around and walked down the grassy path back into town.

~~~

When I woke up, I could feel the room spinning. I forced myself to leave the hostel and began to walk. It was already midday, and there was no other pilgrim in sight.

My head pounded in the heat, and I cursed my luck as the whole morning consisted of going up a hill. I'd forgotten to put sun cream on, and I could feel the harsh sun rays burning my skin. I tried sipping water, but the drinks from last night weren't sitting right in my stomach. This was totally, one hundred per cent, self-inflicted.

I walked and walked, taking aspirins like snacks, hoping the sweat meant the alcohol was leaving my body.

By mid-afternoon, I felt shattered. The sun was still blazing, but I was now walking through a shaded forest. I was drawn to a cluster of rocks bundled up under leafy trees.

Defeated, I lay down on the flat, cold surface of a rock, grateful for the breeze that tickled my face. I wished I could sit under a shower and feel my headache disappear. I had no Eva or Liam to distract me now, and no matter how far I walked, I realised I couldn't shake off my guilt.

Flashes from last night came back to me. I could remember thinking that his lips were so unfamiliar. They were rough and full and suffocating. His smell was different too—a combination of sharper aftershave and cheap red wine. The more he'd kissed me, the more I realised I didn't want him.

He wasn't Andy.

I looked up to the labyrinth of leaves above me. Where was Andy? Was he sitting at his new desk in London? Was he thinking about me right now too? I pictured him alone in an empty flat, sipping on a glass of red wine from a corked bottle that he'd picked up from the local independent wine shop, cooking up a curry on his own, tidying up as he went along and saving the second portion for his lunch tomorrow. I could see him eating it standing up as he turned on the news for background noise and scrolled through his phone. I wondered if he was looking at my social media, wondering why I'd gone quiet on it, imagining where I was.

'I should have come after you,' I said aloud.

I wiped my face with my hand and then lay it on my chest. I pressed my hand against my skin until I could feel my heart beating underneath. I wondered if clutching it hard enough would stop it from hurting.

## 59

I was getting closer to the region of Galicia. It was known as the bath of Spain, partial to rain and very green. Today was my birthday. I got up early and left the busy dorm room, getting a head start.

I walked through green fields, beside the riverbank, wondering if I'd find a cafe later where I could treat myself to some wine or cake. Maybe I'd run into Eva, Erik or Mateo and we could have a tiny celebration.

I stopped for lunch by the river, unpacking a sandwich and some fruit I'd bought from the hostel last night. I searched for my phone, tucked in the bottom of my bag.

There was a flurry of missed calls and messages from my family. And then, as I scrolled down, this:

*Happy birthday Antonia,*
*I didn't want you to think I wasn't thinking of you today.*
*Love Andy*

My hands trembled. I had tried so hard not to think about him. For so many weeks, I'd wanted to walk him off. Yet there he was, alive and well, behind his text. Why was my heart in my throat?

I had a sudden urge to speak to him.

Of course, I had to speak to him. This was all so ridiculous. I missed him so badly—I wanted to see him. Enough time had passed that we could talk things through. He wanted me to get in touch. He wanted to see me again.

I walked for another couple of hours, the thought of finding a stable wi-fi connection the only thing keeping me going.

I reached a village dotted with cafes, all equipped with wi-fi. I walked into the first one. To my surprise, I saw Eva again. She grinned and ran over.

'Hello again.' She hugged me.

I forced a smile.

'How are you? And where's Liam? You look a bit—'

'Fine. I don't think I'll be seeing him again.'

'Are you okay?'

'Yes.'

To my annoyance, she took her backpack off.

'Here, come sit down. Do you want something to drink? What happened that night after you left the disco?'

She sat down, but I remained standing. 'Nothing. We just talked for a while.'

I could feel her eyes on me. How could I leave and go to another cafe without seeming rude? I was desperate to call Andy.

'Are you sure you're all right? You look a bit, I don't know, flustered.'

'I'm fine,' I adjusted my backpack. 'Listen, I have to make a family call,' I lied. 'Catch up with you later?'

'Of course,' she said. 'Come, sit here.' She stood up from her chair and picked up her backpack. 'I'll see you soon.'

~~~

It took me a while to dial Andy's number. My hands kept shaking as I scrolled down to his name.

It rang once, then twice. I felt sick.

'Hello? Antonia? Are you all right?'

My insides turned to mush. I'd craved his voice for so long.

'Andy...' My voice was hoarse. 'Yeah, I'm all right,' I bit down on my nail, 'I just thought I'd call.'

'About time too. I've been trying you for weeks.' He was babbling, like the way he spoke when he first met people or was nervous.

'What was that?' I could hear a lot of traffic on his end. A car was hooting and an alarm blaring. His Scottish accent, one I'd spent months trying to understand, seemed undecipherable. I wondered if it had always sounded this thick.

'Antonia, where the hell are you?'

I swallowed. 'I'm walking the Camino.'

More noise in the background. 'Hang on, I'm trying to find a quiet spot.' Muffled sounds and footsteps. 'The Camino? So you're in Europe?'

'Yeah.'

Silence again, and then a dragged-out sigh. 'Bloody hell. Antonia, I've been so worried. I thought you were still in India.' He gave a small, short laugh. 'Look, it doesn't even matter. I just...I'm just glad you're all right.'

'Are you in London?'

'Yeah, yeah, I'm just outside my office. Sorry, that's why there's so much noise.'

'Are you...are you enjoying it?'

'It's...' He breathed in. 'To be honest, the first couple of weeks were shit. I was so worried about you. I spent most of my time in a hotel. I just felt...I don't know...shit.'

'Yeah.' I nodded, thinking back briefly to the hostel in Delhi. 'I know.'

He sniffed. 'Anyway, I found a flat in Fulham. I've met a couple of friends and colleagues now, so I've been out for drinks with them. It's great, but, you know...' he hesitated, '...I'm not used to being without you.'

I was silent—too scared to say anything in case I lost control.

'What's the Camino like? Can't believe you're doing that on your own.' His tone sounded a bit more upbeat. 'I thought you hated hiking.'

I let a smile escape. 'Yeah. It's easier to hike when I don't have to run to keep up with a fiancé.'

Andy laughed. 'Well, I hope you're having fun.'

'I think you'd really love this,' I said. 'You'd love all the old churches and towns. Some of them look straight out of the Middle Ages.' I told him more about the pilgrim meals, the *vino tinto* and the *albergues*.

'It does sound amazing. I, uh, I miss the time off. I'd do anything for a cold pint in the sun right now. London, well, you know, it's pissing down, and I can hardly hear myself think. The people here compared to Edinburgh, well, fuck…'

I started to laugh, and he caught on, and soon we were both giggling down the phone.

'It feels good to hear your voice. I've, uhm, I've missed you.'

I closed my eyes. 'Me too.'

There was silence.

I clutched my phone. 'What happens to us now?'

'What do you mean?'

'Are we, like, exes? Am I your ex-fiancée?' The word sounded horrible.

Andy sniffed. 'I don't know. It's weird to think of you in that way.'

I swallowed. 'Andy?'

'Yeah?'

'I…I still love you.'

There was a familiar sigh. 'Yeah, me too.'

I breathed out. 'Listen, this is stupid. Let me fly over to London when I finish this walk. We can figure things out. I'll need to pick up my things in Edinburgh, but I want to see you first.'

Andy was silent.

'Hello?' I said.

'Oh, Antonia.' His voice broke, and I could hear him breathe in a couple of times. 'I can't.'

'Why? All I need to do is book a flight.'

'No. I…' He stopped talking.

'What?'

'I've met someone.'

I hung up quickly after that.

As I put the phone down, my heart broke.

I went back on social media. I wanted to delete him, delete everything—I didn't want a single reminder of him coming up again. And that's when I saw it—raw, gut-wrenching and painful.

Someone had tagged a picture of him with a girl sitting on his lap. They were holding hands. She looked like a colleague. She wore mascara, a silk headband and high heels and was undeniably beautiful. Underneath was a caption #workbenefits

What the fuck?

I analysed the photo as much as I could to find any sign of me in him. But the woven leather bracelet I'd bought for him in Georgia had been replaced by an expensive silver watch. The pendant with the Tibetan engraving that we'd chosen together in Nepal had gone. He wore a silk burgundy tie instead. His shaggy beard had been completely shaved, and his dishevelled hair was now finely clipped. He even seemed to have lost his tan. He looked happy. Happier. Nausea settled in as I felt my insides grow cold. It had hardly been more than a month. Had they known each other before? Is that why he'd wanted to move to London?

Tears clouded my vision. Maybe he'd only told me he was seeing someone else to upset me. This photograph was there just to provoke me.

Why couldn't I stop crying?

'It doesn't matter,' I whispered to myself through gritted teeth. 'It doesn't matter anymore.'

I could feel the ground beneath me tremble. I wished it would open. I wished I could sink into it—

'Antonia?'

A voice interrupted my thoughts. I looked over. Eva was standing at the door. Had she heard everything? I didn't even care.

'I thought I'd wait a little longer.'

She walked up to me, but I turned around, trying to hide my face. 'Sorry.... It's just ...my birthday...Andy texted...he's met someone...I...'

I felt her touch my arm. 'You don't have to talk about it.'

My face crumpled but I managed a nod.

I felt her wrist holding my arm. 'Shall we walk together for a bit?'

~~~

For the next three hours, we walked in total silence, Eva a couple of metres ahead of me. We climbed a few hills, and for the first time in memory, I was appreciative of them. The climb allowed me to focus on my steps and my breathing, calming the panic and clutter inside me. Whenever we stopped for a break, Eva kept the chat light, discussing the route, the views and the deteriorating quality of our snacks. If she'd heard my entire call, she said nothing about it.

Villafranca was the last town we arrived to together. She was going to stay on for a few days and had arranged to assist in a vineyard.

We walked mostly in silence for five kilometres until we reached the crossroad where she would turn left, and I would turn right. We hugged goodbye.

'Thank you for sticking by me,' I said.

She smiled. '*Buen Camino*, Antonia. Look after yourself.'

## 60

The path went on, this time through lush fields and gentle hills. I reached a crossroad, with arrows pointing both left and right. It was early evening, and it was pouring with rain. I'd already walked all day and was looking to call it a night in the next hour.

I hit a left.

Before I knew it, the path had me going up a steep hill. I was hoping it would wind down soon, but in a couple of hours I realised I was too high up, and I knew I might as well keep going.

The higher I went, the colder it got. What was rain turned into hail and then snow. The view down the valleys was incredible. There was not a soul to be seen.

I continued to climb. The sun was starting to disappear, and I tried hard to play down my worries. Something would show up soon. There was no point in panicking.

I continued to walk, trying to avoid checking the time and keeping my focus on the trail ahead. With the sun now gone, it was freezing cold and dark. The rain hadn't stopped. I forced my feet to move for what must have been another half hour until, at long last, I saw tarmac. Relieved, I staggered down the smooth, hard surface which led me to a tiny village. I could make out a church steeple and a handful of stone houses amidst soaked cobbled streets.

I knocked on the only *albergue*, and after a few minutes of waiting, a man popped his head out. 'It's closed,' he said firmly, '*cerrado, cerrado.*'

I stuttered a shocked response. Where else could I stay? I was exhausted.

He shrugged and recommended flagging a taxi to take me to the next village. He didn't seem to have the time to care and quickly shut the door.

Defeated, I leant against the stone wall, the rain angrily hitting my face.

Then, a woman walking past saw me and stopped.

She asked if I was looking for accommodation, and before I could answer, she told me to follow her. She took me to the village church.

'Chilean missionaries are staying here—they'll be happy to host you.'

'Thank you.' I was surprised. I'd not seen a single Chilean on my travels.

Inside the church, there were six people from my hometown.

'*Hola, bienvenida!*'

All of them started talking to me at once, trying to warm me up and feed me at the same time. Five of them were recent graduates, missionaries, who'd flown over to Spain for a Catholic congregation. One of them was a young priest, quiet with a broad smile that never seemed to leave his face.

They didn't hesitate to share all their food with me and cooked up a feast of beans, potatoes and mince. There was warm bread and butter, and even some chocolate from home. I felt a rush of nostalgia as I spotted the familiar gold and red chocolate packaging that I hadn't seen in years. I hungrily ate the nutty chocolate. The syrupy taste was exactly as I remembered it.

Part of me was home.

~~~

My Chilean Spanish started off stiff as I racked my brain to find the right words. After an hour, I found myself talking animatedly about the Camino so far.

Maybe it was speaking in such a familiar tongue that I hadn't spoken in for so long, but as the hours went by and the candles burned down, I found myself talking about how I'd arrived in Spain, flying to Madrid from India. The sentences kept sliding off my tongue.

I found myself telling them about India too, the desert, the water buffalo, the Annapurna, Kathmandu, the Caucasus, Scotland… and Andy.

When I finished, I was flushed. My face felt warm, despite the church being near freezing inside. I realised how quiet the room had become. I wished I had a glass of wine instead of some herbal tea, but I took a cold sip out of my mug.

One of the girls in front of me spoke. 'So where are you going after the Camino?'

I stared at my mug. 'Back home. To Chile.'

She laughed. 'Not after that story, you won't. I think you're brave enough to do whatever you want to do.'

Brave. That word sounded good.

I wanted to feel it too.

~~~

The next morning as the Chileans packed me up with breakfast and snacks, the priest came over to me.

He stood at the door. 'Antonia, would you like to come with me to confession before you leave?'

He spoke with a Chilean accent, my accent, his face warm and non-judgemental. My heart beat fast as I followed him down to the church.

~~~

It was a small, intimate chapel. There were low ceilings and only a couple of pews on each side. The smaller space made me feel more at ease.

I sat next to him in the same pew. 'I don't really know what to say. I've not had a confession, well, in a long time.'

I thought briefly back to my Catholic school when we got shuffled into a room at age nine and had to confess all our lies to the priest. Mortifying.

'Why don't we have a conversation instead?' he said.

I was quiet, and he looked out on to the altar. The silence made me feel awkward, but I couldn't think of what to say to fill it.

'What are you carrying with you?' He smiled. 'I don't mean in your bag. I mean in your head.'

As I stared at the wooden cross, I blinked fast.

I breathed in. 'I was engaged. My relationship ended.' I felt splashes on my hand. 'And I think it was my fault. I didn't try hard enough to save it.'

He sat there, not saying a word.

'I had doubts. We wanted different things. But I really loved him. And I'm so worried that I've made a huge mistake.' I wiped my face. 'Sorry. I don't know why I'm so upset. It's just a break-up.'

'You are grieving.'

'I'm not. He's not dead.'

'If you've gone in different directions and won't ever be in touch again, what's the difference?'

I wiped my face, and he sat there, waiting for my breathing to settle.

'Believe it or not, it's a beautiful thing to grieve. Your sadness shows how much you loved him and how important the relationship was. I think you did try hard enough. Maybe you both did. But from what you said yesterday, I think you knew it was over.'

I sniffed. 'We were together for almost six years. I was going to marry him. I was…I was so in love with him.'

'Is it worth sacrificing all your happiness for the person you were six years ago? You might be a different person now, one with new dreams. And that's okay. I think sometimes it's hard to let go of an old version of ourselves. But we need to do that, to see how much we've grown.'

I closed my eyes. 'I don't remember who I was before him.'

'Then that's why you're walking the Camino,' he said. 'This walk strips you of conventions and luxuries. You carry basic essentials for survival. This brings out exactly who you are, your core self. Walking on your own is the beauty of it. You have no distractions and you can't hide from your thoughts. Slowly you will figure out which ones are necessary and which ones you can let go of.'

I wiped my face.

He continued. 'I think you're overwhelmed at being on your own for the first time in a long time and finding out who that is. I think she might turn out to be a rather great person.'

'I don't know if I can be on my own.'

'*Cariño*, you don't have a choice.'

'So what do I do when it's over?'

'Has there been a day on the walk where there was torrential rain or snow? Or a day where you simply did not want to keep going?'

I nodded.

'So maybe you stopped. Maybe you checked into an *albergue* earlier. Maybe you had a warm meal and a good night's sleep. What did you do the next day?'

'I don't know. I guess I kept walking.'

'Then that's what you do,' he said. 'You keep on walking through the pain. You keep on going. And soon enough, it will feel less painful.'

He kept looking at the altar. 'Antonia, you are very important. From what you said last night about your journey, I can feel your *joie de vivre*. I know God loves you, but I think he really likes you too.' His warm eyes twinkled. 'You didn't take the wrong route yesterday. You went the hard route, through that snowstorm, up that hill, and it led you all the way to a town where the *albergue* was closed. You could have taken a taxi. The man could have let you stay there. Yet you were still guided our way. To a church tucked away in the middle of the Spanish countryside, to six Chileans from your very own hometown. Are you telling me that spirituality doesn't come into that? Do you really not think God was on your side, rooting for you, that whole time?'

I swallowed. I'd never thought of it that way. God was someone to think highly of, someone to worship and show respect to, like a parent. I'd never really thought we were buddies. He had more important things to do than to cheer me on.

'I think it breaks His heart too, to see you grieving. But He knows it's for a reason. That reason might not be clear now, but it will be later. It might even be sooner than you think. You have to have faith in Him.'

I nodded.

'I want you to do one thing. When you're walking the Camino, there will come a time when you'll be alone, and it will feel right. And at that time, I want you to stop in your tracks. I want you to pray an "Our Father", and I want you to scream it from the top of your lungs, with every meaning you can extract out of it.'

I felt a small smile forming on my face. 'Okay.'

The priest slowly stood up, and he gestured to the exit, where my backpack was propped against the wall.

He walked me to the door. 'What are you going to do now?'

'Keep walking.'

## 61

I trailed through the region of Galicia on my own. I walked further into the intensely green and rugged landscape, encased by mist and dramatic skies. The views reminded me of Scotland, and I felt an intense desire to return.

Unlike when I had first begun in Saint-Jean, my mind felt clearer and sharper. I opened it up to thoughts and reflections, letting them sink in before letting them go.

It had taken me over 700 kilometres to accept that my relationship had been broken long before Kashmir. It was a hard, thorny truth to swallow. It hadn't been Andy's drive to get his promotion or my determination to be on the road. It hadn't been Tom's fault either. It had been damaged from the start, back in Edinburgh, during those exciting and excruciating years of our mid-twenties where we were trying to figure out what we wanted from life. Inevitably and naively, we'd tried to figure that out together, stubbornly denying the glaring incompatibilities that neither of us wanted to understand.

It took me some time to accept that I wanted to leave Andy even though I loved him. I realised that all the subsequent events from the moment we arrived in Georgia weren't a journey but a fight. A fight to keep the relationship from sinking, to keep Andy loving me, to keep myself loving him. When that ended in Kashmir, a new one began, a fight to detach myself from a person that was superglued to me. Days and weeks were spent scraping off residues, whole parts of me going with it.

There was one afternoon where I sat in a forest on the edge of a village. I turned on my phone in a fit of anger and started to delete the photos of him. One by one, I erased them, watching our history trickle into the trash folder until there were too many of them, and I gave up. How could I delete six years of memories, six years of being defined by someone, six years of living, breathing and sharing the same space with another being?

Then came the excruciating social media stalking. How could I grieve for him when his digital footprint was still moving? Instead of mourning the empty space in me, I gazed at photos on the screen of him smiling, laughing and living without me. Photos showed the man I was meant to marry, the man who made love to me over a thousand times, falling in love with someone else. I finally realised the dull power that came in the irreversible act of blocking him.

And then there was a bitter truth to accept, about six years being a waste of time. I struggled to understand what the point was and why the plug hadn't been pulled earlier. Why had we both kept trudging on? Maybe we'd been too scared to hurt each other's feelings and even more afraid of hurting ourselves.

I figured that I learnt what it was like to love and be loved and to have a best friend to take me through my twenties when the world seemed hostile, demanding and lonely. Andy had come with me on a trip of a lifetime, one which I wasn't sure I would have been brave enough to do on my own.

I slowly unpacked a new truth; that Andy's decision to leave me had not been selfish. I started to see his decision as his bravest and most magnanimous act of love: he'd let me go, knowing that I wouldn't have been able to free myself. He'd had the guts to do what I couldn't, even though he knew it would break both of our hearts. As I uncovered this new perception, my anger began to lift. I still felt the impact of his loss, but now I also felt grateful.

One morning, as I crossed one of the most beautiful stone bridges I had ever seen, I stopped by the banks and knelt by the damp soil. There, I slid off my engagement ring. It was a ring that had signified a meaningful and tumultuous relationship. A ring that deserved a poignant ending. A ring that is now buried somewhere in the western forests of Spain.

It took me a while to understand that I'd lost a part of myself in my relationship, pieces slowly chipping away, until I was a faded, shredded version of what I could be. I thought back to the beginning of the Camino when I'd started alone, and how insecure I had felt. Only now did I fully recognise that I'd been underwater and was taking gulps of fresh air.

I started to think back to versions of myself at age ten, sixteen and twenty. Most of all, I looked back at the little girl, who didn't speak the right language in a new country, who didn't fit in at home or at school. I realised that in not belonging there was freedom. She was tough, determined, full of dreams born from stories. She was brave enough to leave everything she knew and fly to Scotland on her own and make a new life for herself. That girl wouldn't have let a relationship consume her. She would have been brave enough to take control of her life and steer it in a new direction. It was that girl I strived for. In her memory and for her future, I walked, and walked and walked and walked.

As I moved on through the forests and fields, I could taste the end. I noticed a waymarker that indicated I had one hundred kilometres left to go. For the first time during the Camino, I was excited to reach Santiago de Compostela.

I was excited because I now knew what would come after—I was going back to Scotland.

Chile had my childhood. It would always have that. But Scotland was the country that had made me brave. I owed Scotland that much—to go back and show it what it had made of me.

## 62

I spent two quiet nights in almost empty *albergues* by the highway. I would walk until I was tired, finding the first available accommodation. One night I even stayed in a room by myself above a petrol station that I was almost sure was next to a brothel.

Fifty-two kilometres to go.

I started early, only hearing the light thud of my feet against the trail as the countryside undulated in front of me. I was feeling strong, excited and ready. My bag was no longer weighing me down. My calves were defined and sharp. I walked and walked and only sat down for a rest for the first time at around 3 p.m. I sat outside, eating a ham and cheese sandwich, when a yellow arrow caught my eye: twenty-seven kilometres to Santiago.

Twenty-seven. That was all that was left.

I must have already walked twenty-five kilometres. Oddly, my legs weren't tingling yet, and my shoulders weren't sore.

It was early afternoon and the sun was high. I knew I could push on a while more. Yes. That's what I'd do. I would walk as much as I could, perhaps another ten kilometres, and then leave the last little stretch for the next day.

I would reach Santiago tomorrow.

The trail took me onto the highway, where the tarmac seemed endless. The sun hardly budged, and my face radiated heat. The challenge was mental rather than physical. I walked carefully, with blaring lorries and cars speeding past me. The busyness excited me. All these people were on their way to Santiago too. The big city—the final city—awaited me. I wondered what Santiago would be like. Would the cathedral be enormous? Would it be swarming with pilgrims? It was the endpoint of so many walks around Europe.

It would be the end of my walk.

In a few days, I would wake up one morning, and instead of walking all day, I'd fly back to Scotland. The thought of it seemed surreal. Edinburgh seemed like a past life. I wondered what the Water of Leith trail was looking like in spring, and if the trees were in full bloom, transforming the commuter footpath into a forest walk.

I kept going. It must have been a few hours when I saw a dirt track leading back into the forest. The sun was weak, but it was still there.

I found another arrow between the tracks:

Seven kilometres to Santiago.

I stared at it. Had I come this far? I paused to look at the waymarker. I could feel my legs cramping up. I needed to keep moving. Seven kilometres. Just seven kilometres. I could do this. I could get to Santiago tonight.

I gritted my teeth and moved my legs. I felt them throbbing.

'Come on, come on.' My breath was shaky, and I was down to my last sips of water. I could feel my skin tingling with sunburn and dehydration.

Five kilometres.

I grinned widely to myself. The end was so near. I urged my feet on, each step now painful and hard against the hard concrete. This last push seemed more challenging than the Thorong La Pass, and the steep hills in Georgia. The difference was that instead of being frustrated, I was ecstatic. I had come this far on my own. I felt my smile warm up my insides. I thought briefly of Andy. Would he be proud of me if he saw me now? I noticed how quickly the thought disappeared. I didn't need him to be proud. I'd done this for myself. This would be my very own achievement.

I bit my lip with each stride. My left foot was acting up. How ironic. It was my last day, my final stretch, my last kilometres and only now could I feel a single blister developing on the sole of my foot.

Three kilometres.

I forced myself to stop. The blister was agony. The sun was down, but it wasn't yet dark, and the skies were a blend of light purple and grey. I took my shoe off. There it was—a swollen, bubbling blister. I realised the only reason it had formed was because my faithful sock had finally broken in two. There was a rip on the bottom, and my skin had been rubbing directly against the sole.

I took both boots off and tied them to my backpack. I stripped my socks off and took my flimsy Havaianas out of my bag. I started to laugh.

I was going to finish this thing in flip-flops.

## 63

The pinnacles of the cathedral glittered in the distance. As I grew closer, they disappeared, hidden by the buildings. My steps quickened, faster and faster.

I followed the streets into the heart of Santiago de Compostela. It must have been 9 or 10 p.m.—prime dinner time in Spain.

Streetlights lit the cobbled stones, which looked polished by the light rain that had fallen earlier. I walked down a narrow lane that boasted cafes and wine bars.

It was a city like any other. Souvenir shops were open late, selling postcards, caps and Camino shells in every shape and form. People sat outside restaurants, drinking *vino tinto* and eating tapas. I breathed in the smells of meat stews and roast potatoes, looking forward to my own hot meal. Bustling waiters glanced at me as I walked past, not overly interested in yet another pilgrim reaching the end of her journey. One of the waiters waved his napkin at me.

'Just five more minutes to the cathedral!'

I gave him a thumbs up.

A busker sat at the edge of a stone fountain strumming a beautiful Spanish-sounding tune. He met my eye and winked at me as he continued to play. I pretended that tune had been made for my arrival, and I heard the echoes of it following me down the alleyway.

I could hear laughter, cheers and happy chatter from the cathedral square.

And then I saw it, magnificent, tall and gold, with the looming cross.

I broke into a smile, and I sighed into my hands. I felt tears of joy streaming down my face. I realised I had been panicking about finishing, with no one there at the finish line to share this celebration with. But as my body shook with excitement and relief, I crossed my arms over my chest, hugging myself tightly.

I was here for myself. I'd made it, just as I was. I probably hadn't been fast or highly skilled or particularly brave. Perhaps I could have tried harder and done things differently, but then that wouldn't have led me here.

I was enough. I'd chased an adventure of a lifetime, faced my fears and had survived. I was stronger because of it.

And I was exactly where I needed to be.

# *Epilogue*

A week after arriving in Santiago de Compostela, I flew back to Edinburgh. As luck had it, the trees by the Water of Leith were in full bloom just as Edinburgh was experiencing the best weather it had had in years. I lay down by the riverbank in a T-shirt and shorts, by Dean Bridge, looking up past the overgrown vines at the cloudless sky. I knew I'd made the right decision to return.

It was difficult to pick up my boxes. We'd left them with Andy's parents and I had to meet them again, without Andy, mumbling formalities and saying my goodbyes again. I had to sort through them, knowing Andy had been there first. He'd left practically all of our shared possessions to me. There were boxes of stuff that had held promises of our future, patiently waiting for our return. Some he hadn't even opened. One was full of photographs of the two of us, from our last six years together. It felt like he'd left me to deal with all of our grief.

I rented out a room, moved in with new flatmates, found a job at the university and slowly made friends. I gave Edinburgh a fresh start. I kept up my walking, through the city, the countryside and the Highlands.

Tom was in touch a few times. From Sri Lanka, he'd moved back to Southeast Asia and settled for a job as a walking guide in Vietnam. We kept in touch, occasionally discussing books or sharing photos of our time together. Our conversations got more and more frequent until one morning, he told me he wanted to come to Edinburgh. That's when I realised how much I'd idealised him. In a time where I was blind, he was everything to me that Andy wasn't. When I told him my feelings weren't there, Tom cut all contact. I still worry about him, the loneliest person I'd ever met.

After the conversation with Andy on the Camino, we never spoke again.

Over time I heard through a mutual friend that he was thriving in London. He and his girlfriend had moved in together. I don't know if he ever thought about the life we might have had together. I wondered if he looked back at the memories of our travels. I liked to imagine that every once in a while, he'd think of the extraordinary times we had crossing the glacial waters in Georgia, or camping in a minefield in Armenia, reaching the top of Thorong La Pass or riding camels in the desert. I don't know if he held on to his turban, any of the photographs, his boots or backpack. I like to think that he did.

What I do know is that my own heart finally healed. It took plenty of walks, writing, good coffee and wine, but it happened.

I spent some time reflecting on my childhood and the stories my dad had told. I researched my great-great-grandfather and, it turned out, my dad had most of his history already. He'd been born in Scotland, and left home at seventeen. He'd been an early Edwardian Scottish traveller. He'd dedicated most of his life travelling through the Middle East, India and Africa. He'd kept diaries, sketches and photographs. He'd spent most of his time in Rajasthan, Cairo and Cape Town, before returning home to Edinburgh.

He was a family member I recognised myself in, even though he was generations and lifetimes away from me. Despite the distance in blood lines, it made me feel rooted to my family. It made my decision to stay in Scotland far easier. It was the country where all his stories had begun. It gave me the motivation to create my own new chapter.

As for my parents, they flew over to see me after I'd settled back in. Over wine and melted candlewax, it was me telling them extraordinary stories about desert escapades, Svaneti mountain bothies, losing my backpack in the Himalayas and exploring Kashmir. A few months later, Dad announced he would be flying to France to walk the Camino. A year later, Mum did the same. At age sixty, both my parents walked a dutiful 800 kilometres from France to Spain. I was so proud of them.

About a year after my return—as I came home from work—I noticed a man moving into the apartment below me. We chatted in the hallway. He was from Aberdeen and had moved to Edinburgh for a new job.

Despite my hesitations, I accepted the Scotsman's invitation for a drink. I thought—like previous dates—I'd leave feeling empty and down.

But he made me cry with laughter. For hours I wiped my eyes, and when I left him, I was still beaming.

The dates continued, and I started to feel again. I felt the butterflies—I felt the excitement. My heart raced when he kissed me for the first time. Moving in together was a natural and easy choice.

We spent weekends and holidays on Scottish country roads, getting to know the isles, lochs and glens. I realised I didn't need to fly thousands of kilometres east to get my travel fix. The mystical Scottish Highlands were even more majestic and breathtaking than any trail I'd followed before.

A couple of years later, over the sunset at Loch Awe, he asked me to marry him. There was no doubt in my mind when I said yes. There was no panic or anxiety when we thought about our future, only confidence and excitement. Six months after our wedding, we had our first son and, a year later, our second.

Ironically, we now live in London.

I felt the potential to fall in love again. I felt the strength in me to laugh, learn and love. And after everything, I felt hopeful.

I sometimes think back to that moment where I sat on a pew with a priest, where he hinted at this kind of life, telling me I'd be happy again, that I'd maybe even find love again, and I remember how impossible that had felt.

Be brave enough. Take those risks. You might fall flat on your face.

But maybe—just maybe—you'll soar.

# *Acknowledgments*

This book was as much of a mental journey as it was physical. The writing took place in various kitchens, bedrooms and coffee shops while I searched for a flat and a job after my travels. The editing of my first drafts took place during the evenings in the Edinburgh attic of the Skriva Writing School. Thank you Sophie Cooke, and my fellow writers, for giving me the encouragement to keep going and finish the book.

Thank you to Claire Wingfield, whose precious feedback and necessary questions turned my first drafts into something readable.

Thank you to Sparsile Books. The word 'sparsile' means 'a star, not belonging to any constellation' and I can't think of a more significant team to have worked with. To Lesley Affrossman, my publisher, thank you for recognising my journey, for championing women travellers and for investing your energy – even on Christmas Day – to make this into a book. Thank you to Alex Winpenny, Jim Campbell, Wendy Ross and Stephen Cashmore for all your work.

To my parents, thank you for letting me fly high, make mistakes and trusting me. You mean everything to me.

My family have always been sources of inspiration and friendship. Thank you for supporting me on my adventures. The benefits of having a family scattered all over the world means there is always someone awake for a call. Thank you for your patience, humour and for believing in me. I love you all madly.

As my book came closer to the finish line, life became chaotic. I got married during the height of Covid, moved countries and received two wonderful interruptions: H and J, born within eleven months of each other – somewhat of a record. My postnatal recovery mostly took place with a laptop on one knee and a baby on the other.

To my sons, you have taught me the most primal kind of love there is. I hope this will inspire you to go on your own adventure one day.

Thank you to Peter. You stood by me with a cup of tea every time I ripped up papers, sobbed in defeat, or ran around our flat with new ideas and a flurry of post-its. Thank you for recognising how important this was for me to finish – especially when I didn't.

Finally, thank you to all the readers who have got me this far! Your support means the world to me.